Lecture Notes in Computer Science 2236

Edited by G. Goos, J. Hartmanis, and J. van Leeuwen

Springer
Berlin
Heidelberg
New York
Barcelona
Hong Kong
London
Milan
Paris
Tokyo

Khalil Drira   Andrea Martelli   Thierry Villemur (Eds.)

Cooperative Environments for Distributed Systems Engineering

The Distributed Systems Environment Report

Springer

Series Editors

Gerhard Goos, Karlsruhe University, Germany
Juris Hartmanis, Cornell University, NY, USA
Jan van Leeuwen, Utrecht University, The Netherlands

Volume Editors

Khalil Drira
Thierry Villemur
Laboratoire d'Analyse et d'Architecture des Systèmes du CNRS
7 Avenue du Colonel Roche, 31077 Toulouse Cedex 4, France
E-mail: {drira,villemur}@laas.fr

Andrea Martelli
Alenia Spazio
Strada Antica di Collegno, 253, 10146 Turin, Italy
E-mail: amartell@to.alespazio.it

Cataloging-in-Publication Data applied for

Die Deutsche Bibliothek - CIP-Einheitsaufnahme

Cooperative environments for distributed systems engineering : the
distributed systems environment report / Khalil Drira ... (ed.). - Berlin ;
Heidelberg ; New York ; Barcelona ; Hong Kong ; London ; Milan ; Paris ;
Tokyo : Springer, 2001
    (Lecture notes in computer science ; Vol. 2236)
    ISBN 3-540-43083-0

CR Subject Classification (1998): D.2, C.2.4, H.5.3, K.6

ISSN 0302-9743
ISBN 3-540-43083-0 Springer-Verlag Berlin Heidelberg New York

Springer-Verlag Berlin Heidelberg New York
a member of BertelsmannSpringer Science+Business Media GmbH

http://www.springer.de

© Springer-Verlag Berlin Heidelberg 2001
Printed in Germany

Typesetting: Camera-ready by author, data conversion by PTP-Berlin, Stefan Sossna
Printed on acid-free paper   SPIN: 10845818   06/3142   5 4 3 2 1 0

Preface

The engineering life cycle for complex systems design and development, where partners are dispersed in different locations, requires the set-up of adequate and controlled processes involving many different disciplines.

The "design integration" and the final "system physical/functional integration and qualification" imply a high degree of cross-interaction among the partners. The in-place technical information systems supporting the life cycle activities are specialized with respect to the needs of each actor in the process chain and are highly heterogeneous between them.

To globally innovate in-place processes, specialists must be able to work as a unique team, in a virtual enterprise model. To this aim, it is necessary to make interoperable the different technical information systems and to define co-operative engineering processes, which take into account "distributed roles", "shared activities", and "distributed process controls".

In this frame an innovative study, aimed at addressing this process with the goal of identifying proper solutions – in terms of design, implementation, and deployment – has been carried out with the support of the European Community and the participation of major industrial companies and research centers.

The Distributed System Environment (DSE) European Project – contract IST-1999-10302 –, within which this study was carried out, started in January 2000 and will end in January 2002. It is managed by an international consortium whose members have strong involvement in space business: Alenia Spazio S.p.A. (co-ordinator of the project), EADS Launch Vehicles, and Industrieanlagen Betriebsgesellschaft (IABG). The other members of the DSE project belong to technology providers and research centers: Silogic, Società Italiana Avionica (SIA), University of Paris VI (LIP6), Laboratoire d'Analyse et d'Architecture des Systèmes du CNRS (LAAS – CNRS), and D3 Group.

The content of this book presents the information and the results that emerged during the user's requirement analysis and the state-of-the-art survey, which provided a clear picture and understanding of the major user's needs and current available technology. It provides analysis of different projects and practices and an overview of products and tools relevant to the fixed objectives.

September 2001

K. Drira
A. Martelli
T. Villemur

Table of Contents

Chapter 1. Introduction

K. Drira, A. Martelli, and T. Villemur

Chapter 2. Research and Development Projects

B. Baurens, P. Chilaev, V. Krivtsov, and V. Volochinov

Chapter 3. Relevant Existing Practices

D. Avino, R. Becchini, P. Chilaev, H. Follet, V. Krivtsov, A. Martelli,
and V. Volochinov

Chapter 4. Middleware

R. Becchini, P. Chilaev, V. Krivtsov, I. Viglietti, and V. Volochinov

Chapter 5. Product Data and Workflow Management

K. Drira, M. Molina, O. Nabuco, L.M. Rodriguez-Peralta, and T. Villemur

Chapter 6. Communications

B. Baurens, L. Costa, A. Dracinschi, S. Fdida, V. Roca, and R. Vida

Chapter 7. Groupware
B. Baurens

Appendix A1. Product Classification Summary

Appendix A2.

References

Author Index

Cooperative Environments for Distributed System Engineering

K. Drira[1], A. Martelli[2], and T. Villemur[1] (Eds.)

[1] Laboratoire d'Analyse et d'Architecture des Systèmes du CNRS, 7 Avenue du Colonel Roche, 31077 Toulouse Cedex 4, France
{drira, villemur}@laas.fr http://www.laas.fr
[2] Alenia Spazio, Strada Antica di Collegno, 253 - 10146 Torino, Italy
amartell@to.alespazio.it http://www.alespazio.it/

Summary

The Engineering Life Cycle for complex systems design and development, where partners are dispersed in different locations, requires the set-up of adequate and controlled processes involving many different disciplines.

The "design integration" and the final "system physical/functional integration and qualification" imply a high degree of cross-interaction among the partners. The in-place technical information systems supporting the life cycle activities are specialised with respect to the needs of each actor in the process chain and are highly heterogeneous between them.

To globally innovate in-place processes, involved specialists shall be able to work as a unique team, in a Virtual Enterprise model. To this aim, it is necessary to make interoperable the different Technical Information Systems and to define Co-operative Engineering Processes, which takes into account "distributed roles", "shared activities" and "distributed process controls".

In this frame an innovative study, aimed at addressing this process with the goal of identifying proper solutions - in terms of design, implementation and deployment - has been carried out with the support of the European Community and the participation of major industrial companies and research centres. The content of this book presents the information and the results that came out during the user's requirement analysis and the state of the art survey, which provided a clear picture and understanding of the major user's needs and current available technology. It provides analysis of different projects, practices and overview of products and tools relevant to the fixed objectives.

Keywords

Distributed Systems Engineering, Middleware, Product data, Workflow management, Groupware, Multicast Communications, Technologies, Supporting Tools and Products.

K. Drira, A. Martelli, T. Villemur (Eds.): Cooperative Environments, LNCS 2236, p. 1, 2001.
© Springer-Verlag Berlin Heidelberg 2001

Chapter 1. Introduction[1]

K. Drira, A. Martelli, and T. Villemur

1.1 Presentation

The Engineering Life Cycle for complex systems design and development requires the set-up of adequate and controlled processes involving many different disciplines. The industrial teams for these projects usually involve many levels in the procurement/supply chain, with system and product knowledge geographically distributed. In large International programmes the partners are dispersed in different locations: the co-operation among all involved actors and the integration of the different engineering artefacts produced by each partner generate high cost overheads on the projects and make quite complex the deployment of optimised engineering processes. A worldwide co-operation is increasingly required to make feasible initiatives such as the International Space Station or Large Commercial Satellites Networks. In this frame, industrial plants providing specialised expertise and production capabilities are required to put together their effort to design and develop the new systems. The "design integration" and the final "system physical/functional integration and qualification" imply a high degree of cross-interaction among the partners as well as the definition of appropriate engineering and management processes that recognise this complexity.

On the other hand, the in-place technical information systems supporting the life cycle activities are specialised with respect to the needs of each actor in the process chain. Considering the provided products, the engineering methodologies, the skills and involved engineering disciplines technicians as well as managers make use of highly heterogeneous systems in terms of platforms, software environments and applications.

To globally innovate in-place processes, involved specialists shall be able to work as a unique team, in a Virtual Enterprise model, in spite of geographical barriers and heterogeneity in used support environments and tools. To this aim, it is necessary to make interoperable the different Technical Information Systems and to define Co-operative Engineering Processes, which takes into account "distributed roles", "shared activities" and "distributed process controls". In each involved Industrial Plant, this new Process Model shall be dynamically adapted to the different customer-supplier networks required for different projects.

In this frame an innovative study, aimed at addressing this process with the goal of identifying proper solutions - in terms of design, implementation and deployment - has been carried out with the support of the European Community and the participation of major industrial companies and research centres. The content of this book presents the information and the results that came out during the user's requirement analysis and the state of the art survey, which provided a clear picture and understanding of the major user's needs and current available technology.

---

[1] Parts of the introduction are coming from [50]

K. Drira, A. Martelli, T. Villemur (Eds.): Cooperative Environments, LNCS 2236, pp. 3-6, 2001.
© Springer-Verlag Berlin Heidelberg 2001

1.2 Project Framework

The Distributed System Environment (DSE) project is a European research project co-funded by the European Commission - contract IST-1999-10302. It started in January 2000 and will end in January 2002.

The project is managed by an international consortium whose members are industrial companies with strong involvement in space business and acting as users of DSE, Alenia Spazio S.p.A. (co-ordinator of the project), EADS Launch Vehicles and Industrieanlagen Betriebsgesellshaft (IABG).

Technology providers and research centres are also members of the Consortium providing specific contribution to the definition and development of the DSE system: Silogic, Societa' Italiana Avionica (SIA), University of Paris VI (LIP6), Laboratoire d'Analyse et d'Architecture des Systèmes du CNRS (LAAS – CNRS) and D3 Group.

Project Goals

The DSE project is aimed at defining and building up a modular environment to support large-scale application of Collaborative Engineering Platforms within the European Industry. The system will be able to effectively support engineering activities carried out during the whole System Engineering Life Cycle. DSE will in particular put special emphasis on Design and Verification activities in large International projects involving a complex and multi-level customer-supplier network.

The main project objectives are focused on the improvement of the Collaborative Engineering Process by enabling:

- **Distributed System Design & Analysis Tasks,** requiring the distribution and collaborative evaluation of analysis and simulation results among Customer, Prime Contractor, Level 1 Contractors and Suppliers
- **Distributed Design Reviews,** involving different nodes, for the consolidation and the formal assessment of the systems design in a distributed Review Team.
- **Distributed Systems Verification Engineering Process,** allowing the evaluation of system test since the preparatory phases and up to the test results; connecting the main sites where the system has been designed, integrated and tested with specialised test facilities where specific tests are conducted.

As a specific objective the Project is aimed at building up an Environment for running LAN and WAN based distributed engineering processes, to the benefit of industrial and professional organisations. This environment will be based and developed on a multi-layer Architecture, with a generic and open infrastructure (for communications and groupware) and a users community specific layer, enabling data and application sharing among heterogeneous tools in use during the systems engineering life cycle.

The DSE implemented environment will at the end be validated against real space reference scenarios, measuring the benefits for different user profiles and supporting processes re-engineering to take full advantage of collaborative paradigms. Two sets of scenarios in particular will be used as a reference to build up and validate the DSE system: "Collaborative Design and Analysis" and "Distributed Verification"; both of them referring to actual space system process. In the first case, for instance, the

Automated Transfer Vehicle (ATV) Preliminary Design Review (PDR) will be taken as a reference and will be re-engineered simulating the customer, reviewers and contractors being part of the actual ATV PDR. In another case engineering sessions, simulating the approach of ATV up to its docking to the International Space Station (ISS), will be held and the relevant ATV, ISS and Control Centre simulators, running in different sites, will be interconnected by DSE.

In the Distributed Verification scenario, the adoption of Collaborative Platforms and Applications will be experienced for the monitoring and controlling of a real space system under test from remote locations. This will minimise the collocations and will allow experts form the System Integration Site to on-line support the preparation and execution of the tests in the specialised facility.

The use of the DSE system in real space, as well as non space, projects is expected to produce great benefits in terms of:

- **Shortening** the development cycle and costs by early involvement of different teams, from suppliers and sub-contractors to end-users, in a cross disciplinary
- **Taking advantage** of synergy/opinions of the various groups and different specialists
- **Early detecting** engineering bottlenecks in the design of new systems allowing the identification and implementation of technical as well as managerial solutions
- **Supporting** Rapid Prototyping as a support to concept design and system engineering
- **Sharing** design (pre-computed) and simulation (computed online) data, ensuring at the same time the industry/organisation property rights

Specific information on the project objectives, status, plan as well as Consortium members can be found in the DSE Project website at: http://cec.to.alespazio.it/DSE/.

1.3 Application Domains

Many business areas, where a system design life-cycle is required, are nowadays looking forward for an effective environment able to keep under control the engineering process: the requirement definition and specification, requirement traceability, architectural design, etc. The need of distributed resources and information shared among dispersed teams is increasing rapidly. This is true not only in space business, that was the main application domain chosen, but also in many other business sectors where different contents but similar processes are applied. In the automotive industry, for instance, the use of a collaborative engineering environment can help the industry to efficiently interact with the many suppliers as well as within its own departments with the aim of bringing products to market in a shorter time. The use of analysis tools facilitates the design process, allowing manufacturing engineers to make better decision faster. Similar considerations can further apply to Naval architecture, Marine engineering, aircraft design, etc.

Finally, different application fields where this State of Art can be applied, have been identified:

- Design, development and operations for large space Infrastructure and Commercial systems
- Architectures and operations of Engineering centres, training facilities, test facilities
- Software development and testing
- Remote staff management and technical co-ordination
- Customer/supplier chain strengthening
- Development of specific software products (e.g. middleware or groupware oriented products)
- Process modelling improvement

They complete the initial application domains, extending therefore the applicability of the tools listed.

1.4 Book Plan and Organization

Chapter 1 is the overall context where this study was realized.

Chapter 2 presents in a synthetic way the main precursor projects relevant to the Distributed System Engineering domain.

Chapter 3 presents the applicative support tools required for the cooperative scenarios. The requirements for the design and simulation are first described. Two lists of the main tools, associated with their characteristics are then given.

The underlying middleware technologies required as general glue between the different components are presented in Chapter 4. Two are emerging: the High Level Architecture (HLA) and the Common Object Request Broker Architecture (CORBA). The middleware support tools and environments are investigated.

Chapter 5 presents the Product Data Management, the Workflow technologies and the Session Management Models. They are all illustrated by a set of tools, environment and platforms, together with their detailed description.

Chapter 6 presents the basic concepts of multicast technology, required to efficiently transmit information between group of users. Multicast solutions are then reviewed and associated with the implementation protocols.

Chapter 7 investigates the groupware domain, composed of general collaborative tools to manage the high-level interactions and information sharing between groups of users in co-presence. The main standards for collaborative supports are presented, with a list of application tools, supports and equipments in relation with collaborative standards.

Chapter 2. Research and Development Projects

B. Baurens, P. Chilaev, V. Krivtsov, and V. Volochinov

2.1 Related Projects and Reusable Products

The following precursor European and European Space Agency projects highlighted in the table below are of interest for the distributed systems engineering synthesis in respect of taking advantage of accumulated experience and reusable results.

Table 1. Projects and their characteristics

Projects	Domain	Reusable Results and Remarks
Esprit IV EDISON	Distributed Simulation	HLA compliant middleware approach (on-going) and Middleware (reusable)
ACTS MULTICUBE	Distributed Simulation, Teletesting, Collaborative Engineering	Lessons Learnt in using the European ATM Network capabilities and services. Concepts Feasibility demonstrations.
Esprit ATV-DSD	Distributed Simulation	Feasibility Demonstration (achieved)
ACTS DIANE	Distributed systems engineering	Asynchronous Distributed Systems with Telemedicine and Teleengineering applications using IP over ATM
Esprit ADVANCE	Distributed Concurrent Systems	Common Basic Services (completed in 1996)
French RNRT@IRS	Internet-2	QoS Management mechanisms based on Ipv6 (on-going)
Esprit SEDRES	Systems Engineering	Prototypes software translators compliant with draft ISO STEP AP 233
Esprit MATES	Distributed Working Environment	Distributed Engineering Environment Concept
Esprit VEGA	Virtual Enterprise & GroupWare	GroupWare Design Concepts CORBA Access to Step models (COAST) infrastructure
Esprit CAVALCADE	CSCW & Virtual Reality	Co-design Approach and Tool-set concept
Esprit GLOBEMAN 21	Intelligent Manufacturing Systems	Virtual Enterprise Concepts and Approaches
Esprit FRONTIER	Multi-partner Collaborative Design Optimisation	Concept for multiple objectives system design optimisation
Esprit TRAWE	Distributed Systems	Distributed Data Base Applications

K. Drira, A. Martelli, T. Villemur (Eds.): Cooperative Environments, LNCS 2236, pp. 7-13, 2001.
© Springer-Verlag Berlin Heidelberg 2001

Esprit MASCOTTE	Distributed Systems	Middleware and Distributed Objects concept
Esprit ANIA	ATM Networking Applications	View on Industrial Applications
Esprit VEPRIM	Virtual Enterprise	Product Information Model concept
ACTS TEAM	Automotive oriented Collaborative Work	ATM-WAN and Euro-ISDN based feasibility demonstration
Esprit ADONNIS	Collaborative Design Distributed Simulation	Experiment Results and Feasibility assessments
RACE PAGEIN	Broadband Network Experiments	Collaborative Visualisation in a Multi-node network Topology feasibility demonstration
ESA ATV DIS-RVM	Distributed Simulation Collaborative Engineering	Experiments on Space Scenarios (Results and Perspectives)

The following paragraphs analyse the achieved results of important precursor projects in order to understand the relevant reusable technologies and common practices for distributed system engineering.

2.2 MULTICUBE

The ACTS MULTICUBE Project was concluded in 1998 and focused on CSCW industrial trials aimed at supporting understanding and experimentation of required communication technologies for multimedia traffic in a multi-point to multi-point network set-up. MULTICUBE involved Alenia as leader of the co-ordinated Aerospace and Automotive Industrial Trials, using the European ATM capabilities to build-up and operate the network connecting the participants, as well as the telecommunication partners provided technologies for IP multicasting and extended signaling.

MULTICUBE Results, in particular the matured awareness of CSCW and Networking technologies and their evolution, would be fully capitalised in DSE, ensuring minimisation of risks and a full considerations of lessons learnt in using Broadband Networking at European and International Level.

More detailed information is available in section 3.1.2.4

2.3 SEDRES

2.3.1 Practical Achieved Results

One of the achieved results of SEDRES was the production and verification of a set of tools interface for data exchanges across a series of tools for requirements specification and management and for system design. The set of data was organised according to the STEP AP233 data model (the definition of these data models are another result form SEDRES). It has to be noted that real software implementation of the tools interfaces allowing data exchanges was done for specific and well defined tools (Teamwork, StP, etc.). Physical data exchange was performed through STEP Part 21 files (standard for physical representation, ASCII text, of the actual data using a specified data model).

2.3.2 Practices and Lessons Learned

Use Scenarios for testing data models were performed and specific system engineering processes has been tuned.

Conclusions from the Use Scenarios were formulated and they face how tools should integrate within an overall design process, what practical issues need to be addressed in terms of mechanisms of performing transfer and finally, what additional functionality is required from the existing import and export interfaces. This leads to objectives for SEDRES2.

2.4 SEDRES 2

Purpose of this paragraph is to provide concepts and information about the ongoing project SEDRES 2. The major work packages in the SEDRES 2 project are:

- The definition of the extended scope of the data model, the determination of the methodology to be applied in, the scope of the validation Scenarios, and the evaluation objectives, which will qualify and quantify the competitiveness benefits.
- The production of the data exchange standard, which will rely on internal experience (implementation and validation) and will take into account the external view captured through the SEDRES network from the standard (AP233 etc), application (engineering sectors) and technology (tools / infrastructure vendor) axes.
- The development and integration of prototype tool interfaces and the evaluation environment that are required to perform the validation scenarios, and a minimal investigation of relevant systems engineering environment technologies. The development of the evaluation environment is required in the analysis of the effectiveness of the standard.
- The evaluation of the standard through the performance of Validation Scenarios. Each scenario is inspired by operational projects and is representative of part of the system engineering process involving actors working collaboratively and concurrently. The associated process is mapped onto the responsibilities of each partner and the functionality of the System Engineering tools in order to identify what are the key data exchanges taking place in the process. The project validation scenarios will consist of an aircraft related scenario and a space vehicle related scenario.
- The development of a business case for full SEDRES network which is responsible for the communication with the standardisation world, other application domains and the range of technologies supporting the standard. The SEDRES network initial operation will be started, with the development of a web site and liaison into external work, included other related Framework projects.
- The broadcasting and preparation for exploitation of the results of the project, to ensure a wide dissemination of the aims and results of the SEDRES 2 project across aerospace and other communities.

2.5 DIANE

DIANE (Design Implementation and operation of a distributed ANnotation Environment) application consists in a distributed multimedia annotation system (in other words, a multimedia news system) enabling to manipulate such data as sound (microphone recording), images, screen captures, mouse movements, pages and hyperlinks, texts, etc. It is designed for a distributed environment consisting of user terminals and annotation servers, which are used for storing and accessing to annotated documents. DIANE includes a data transport system allowing access to annotation servers both in real-time mode and in store and forward manner and which supports in particular both ATM and more conventional narrow band network technologies.

The project started in July 1996 and ended in September 1998. More detailed information is available on: http://www.silogic.fr/diane/Default2.htm

2.5.1 Practical Achieved Results

The work consisted in the design and implementation of an annotation system to:
- create multimedia annotations on any application output
- store and link them in shared spaces
- browse annotations and invoke their presentation

Investigate and define architecture relating
- scripting and presentation of multimedia documents
- stream synchronisation (graphical annotations, sound, mouse movements...), security management, transport system

The validation and administration of the annotation service has been achieved in three user trials:
- tele-medicine involving the Pathology Departments of the Hospital General in Manresa and the University Hospital of Vall d'Hebron in Barcelona (Spain). Pathologists were involved in assessing the use of DIANE in two main tasks:
  - consulting each other for a second opinion or diagnostic help with difficult cases
  - preparing and presenting teaching sessions on specific topics
- tele-training at European Center for Parallel Computing at Vienna (VCPC), an Austrian computing centre specialised in parallel programming techniques and tools. VCPC offers training and support to its customers in form of teaching units based on DIANE.
- tele-engineering at Pioneer France Maïs, multinationals company where the research activities are distributed all over the world. The immediate advantage of using DIANE has been perceived against traditional e-mail exchanges. Indeed, communicating their research result has proved easier and new type of additional information (such as voice comment) to enhance the dissemination of their result could be added.

2.5.2 Practices and Lessons Learned

2.5.2.1 Applicability

DIANE fills a lack for a tool that provides asynchronous distributed communication with instant authoring capabilities. It comes at the intersection of three technologies or horizontal markets: multimedia authoring tools, streaming, and groupware.

DIANE proved to bring new interesting solutions and achievements in all fields where users need to exchange extensive information, or where submission of plain text is not enough. This is specifically suitable for tele-working, collaborative work, tele-engineering, distant learning.

2.5.2.2 Technical Issues

The system has been mainly developed in Java, using among others the AWT for the Graphical User Interface, the Java Media API for the management of stream and time oriented medias, Java RMI for distribution of objects and general application protocol, secure socket layer (SSL) for security issues. Quality of service was provided through the use of ATM based networks.

2.5.2.3 Compatibility and Growth

Although available on many platforms (Unix, Windows 95/NT), DIANE is a proprietary solution, which makes it difficult to integrate completely into existing Information System architectures, and solutions. It is true that DIANE accepts as input many of the standard formats but once the DIANE documents are created they are only accessible through DIANE clients. This has required organisations to commit and trust to future developments of DIANE. It represented a substantial obstacle to incorporating DIANE into image or multimedia processing in organisations.

Further needs of extensions towards IP networks and Web-based technologies have been evoked for authoring and publishing.

2.6 EDISON

EDISON is a European research project co-funded by the European Commission in the frame of the Esprit Programme. It started in March 1998 and ended in September 2000.

The aim of the EDISON project is to specify, develop, experiment and exploit a generic and integrated architecture for Distributed Interactive Simulation Facilities (DISF), in order to support interaction and cooperative work between geographically distributed facilities for simulation modeling, processing and post-processing.

The EDISON infrastructure is a modular package which includes: a simulation framework providing the applications with common simulation services (scheduling, real-time kernel, etc.), a middleware containing the vital services necessary for distributed simulations (time management, intelligent distribution mechanisms, extrapolation and prediction mechanisms to hide network latencies and jitters, etc.), a communication framework, a supervisor and groupware functions.

2.6.1 Practical Achieved Results

The EDISON infrastructure is qualified through three pilot applications, each focusing on a different utilisation paradigm and a different phase in a system lifecycle. The "Hardware-In-the-Loop" pilot application consists in a system validation of the ATV-ISS space rendez-vous (the Automated Transfer Vehicle is a spacecraft which docks automatically to the International Space Station in order to refuel and re-supply it). The "Numerical Models" pilot application deals with the engineering analysis of vibroacoustic effects in manned space systems and car design. The "Man-In-the-Loop" pilot application, based on a mission rehearsal exercise, involves the space European Robotic Arm (ERA) and ATV teleoperations by ISS astronauts or ground operators.

2.6.2 Practices and Lessons Learned

The DISF approach can be used to solve simulation problems only attainable in the past either within long time frames or at the cost of expensive computer facilities. The use of geographically Distributed and Interactive Simulation Facilities is therefore of paramount interest to:
- reduce facilities overall costs (non-duplication of components, teams knowledge and skills),
- allow the interactive use of remote simulation resources, making the work more flexible and efficient,
- shorten the development cycle of new systems by anticipating detection of design, integration or operational problems,
- minimise travels and long collocation of experts.

The overall lessons learned regarding the use of Distributed Interactive Simulation (DIS) for space missions is mitigated: the DIS technology implemented through High Level Architecture/Run-Time Infrastructure (HLA/RTI) technology works fine, but the potential users need to be aware of some limitations. The advantages of a DISF approach based on HLA technology are as follows:
- HLA is near to become an IEEE standard (is nominated as 1516 Draft), and it is likely that it will be generally adopted by various communities all over the world
- HLA has been designed to promote interoperability and re-use of existing simulators. This principle is clearly a strong benefit.
- Being a standard, a vast number of tools and tool suites will be developed in order to help the users to create, analyse, record, replay, render, debug and test distributed federations.

However, the HLA has today some limitations:
- The current implementations of RTI (respecting the interface specification 1.3) do not offer a fully deterministic behaviour. This has implications regarding the stability of the RTI software itself, and could create inadequate delays in simulations.
- The tuning of the RTI is not a trivial task as there are many parameters upon which the performance depends.

- The implementation of a DIS exercise is not a trivial task; it requires the involvement of different people ranging from network experts, to system administrators, to HLA experts, to the end users.
- A minimum network access could be a very cheap solution, but depending on the application more expensive solution could be required. Especially, when DISF data exchanges between simulators are complemented with people to people interactions, which are requesting groupware tools.

Chapter 3. Relevant Existing Practices

D. Avino, R. Becchini, P. Chilaev, H. Follet, V. Krivtsov, A. Martelli,
and V. Volochinov

3.1 Collaborative Systems Design and Analysis

3.1.1 System Design Process for Aerospace Domain

3.1.1.1 Requirements and Design Definition

The requirements engineering specifies how the system should support the user's activities and provides a design strategy for how the system should be built.

The requirements engineering is composed of two important activities: the Requirement definition usually done by the Customer and the Requirements specification usually done by the Contractor.

The requirements definition contains the synthesis of the information gathered in earlier steps while the requirement specification should contain enough information to guarantee the success of the continued design process by specifying the information that is necessary to design a system that solves the situation of concern identified. It should specify in detail the functionality the system should provide.

The difficulty of correctly specifying and prioritising the requirements for complex systems involves long requirements definition phase requiring the users located in different sites to exchange information and to analyse the system data using traditional communication ways.

The design engineering is a process that starts from a need expressed through requirements. Actually most product design activities are performed in centralised ways, often with people seated side-by-side working on the projects. Communications are direct, and problems could be resolved quickly.

The space system projects involve and in future will involve companies distributed around the world. Members of the project teams may all work in different sites. This can cause significant problem. In this dynamic environment, people are frequently less able to talk face-to-face, or resolve problems over a table. The size of e-mail attachments is limited. Telephone conversations are inadequate for describing changes in the design and the meetings are required. Greater proportions of time are spent in travel, which is costly, time-consuming, and can be ineffective (given that much must be done in a short time). Remoteness makes it difficult for individuals to interactively examine or review documents, or describe their ideas graphically.

Thus there is an increasing need to improve methods to support remote collaboration.

The Distributed System Engineering (DSE) environment will allow the Customer and the Suppliers to work in collaborative and distributed way, decreasing a lot the time to complete the requirements definition phase. During the Requirement Phase the Customer and the Contractor can be connected to their project area and create or

K. Drira, A. Martelli, T. Villemur (Eds.): Cooperative Environments, LNCS 2236, pp. 15-39, 2001.
© Springer-Verlag Berlin Heidelberg 2001

modify the requirement definition document simply by clicking on the file icon displayed within the DSE environment. The engineer has access rights to the tool to modify the file that automatically is invoked and the file downloaded for viewing or modification. Once the modification has been completed, the changes can be accepted and the file checked into the repository to be available and viewed by others team, involved in the preparation of the requirements of the project.

The actual process to define and control the System Design for the Aerospace domain is very complex having to manage design changes, enable future design re-use, co-ordinate engineering teams located in different sites. The DSE will focus on improving team productivity, providing the infrastructure necessary to make the engineering teams efficient, even if they are dispersed over different sites, without changing the existing design environment. In this environment the different teams interact with each other, simultaneously access and operate on the applications built with the design tools, refer to global data repositories or archives, collectively create and manipulate documents and conduct a number of other activities via video-conferencing.

DSE Platforms will help the design process, providing users of different disciplines with a Shared Design Environment. The involved teams (dispersed in different geographic locations) can concurrently define the system, each assuming a different perspective depending on the provided discipline skills (e.g., System Engineering, Structural Engineering, Thermomechanics, Electrical/Electronics Engineering, Software Engineering, Control Engineering, etc.), or on the allocated responsibility level (Prime or Subsystem Contractor).

3.1.1.2 Preliminary Design Review

Program life cycle is divided in several phases. Results of each phase must be obtained before the beginning of the next one. For those reasons, a phase is generally closed by a "rendezvous" for verifying that phase objectives are achieved.

These "rendezvous" are called program reviews. These are critical assessment of documents, products, process or organisation. Project review goals are:

- To obtain independent view over program achievements,
- To bring difficulties and potential risks to light in order to reduce them,
- To assess the progress report,
- To put documents and products in a reference baseline corresponding to the end of the phase,
- To support management in deciding either to begin the next phase or not.

Preliminary Design Review (PDR) is one of these rendezvous at the end of the Definition phase (Figure 1).

The System PDR is the point at which the industrial consortium shall demonstrate that the system design has been established in compliance to agreed requirements and that the Subsystems definition has reached a definition level adequate to start the development phase.

Automated Transfer Vehicle (ATV) Preliminary Design Review is actually a representative example of what are the existing practices to execute a review where:

- customer, prime contractor and first level contractors are geographically distributed in Europe,
- the review baseline is made of several hundreds of documents,

- more than one hundred of persons are involved in the process,
- the process lasts 3 months.

The PDR is a process for which a number of Contractors have to submit to the Review Team a large set of documentation. Each reviewer submits Review Item Discrepancies (RIDs) which are examined during the collocated Review. For each RID, a decision is taken which actual implementation has to be tracked.

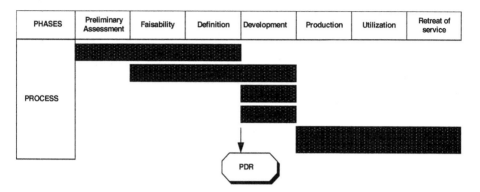

PHASES	Preliminary Assessment	Faisability	Definition	Development	Production	Utilization	Retreat of service
PROCESS							

Fig. 1. The System PDR

ATV PDR Review Baseline

The review baseline holds 200 documents which total size is up to 10000 pages. These documents are made of text and graphics; some of them are not totally under electronic media. They need a large variety of office and technical software (MS-Office or other, modelling or simulation software, mathematics software, etc.) to be visualised on computer.

A small part of it (less than 10 documents), including PDR main baseline requirements and some major documents is accessible on the ATV PDR Web-site for viewing and local printing.

ATV PDR Organization

The prime contractor supports the kick-off meeting by presenting for a day, at customer's facilities, the overall project technical status including development schedule and organization of the review baseline.

25 copies of the baseline are necessary. These copies are distributed to the review groups at customer's facilities where the review group meetings take place for Review Item Discrepancy (RID) generation (Figure 2). Each review group has an individual meeting room with the necessary facilities needed to support the groups work: fax, phones, copymachine and permanent secretarial support. The number of RID goes easily over 1000. RIDs follow serial and parallel circuits between actors.

Generation of the ATV PDR RIDs is allowed on the ATV PDR Web-site. This site is accessible by all registered ATV PDR reviewers/users.

Responses to RID by prime contractor are discussed with review groups representatives at prime contractor's facilities. All review group representatives shall be present at the same time to facilitate the coordination between groups.

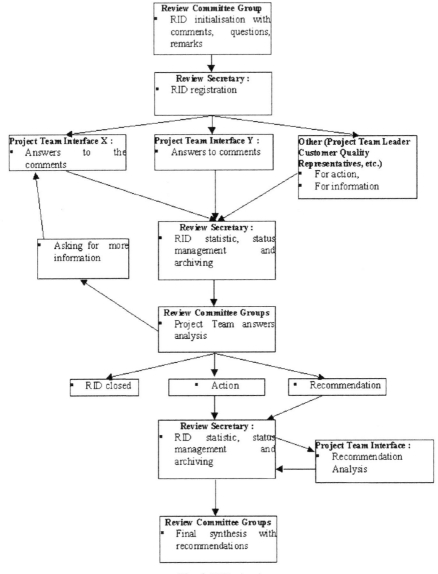

Fig. 2. RID circuit

An overall PDR secretariat assists the chairman and the review groups in terms of RID numbering system, RID log generation and general administration.

Actors involved in the PDR process are members of:

- The review board,
- The review committee,
- The project team.

The main steps of the review are (Figure 3):
- To prepare the review,
- To execute the review
- To process review results

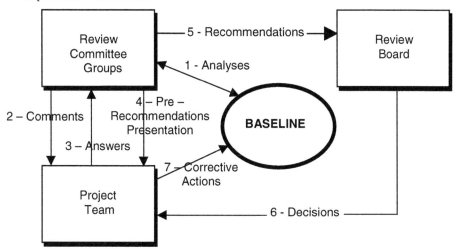

Fig. 3. Review process

To support these processes, the DSE shall provide an integrated set of capabilities shared over the network:
- Interactive access to, and control of, collaborative engineering operations and CSCW Tools
- Video-conferencing and White Board Support
- Distributed Multimedia Databases
- Transparent accesses to, and use of, the Collaboration Network.

3.1.1.3 Simulation Models
It is important to provide designers with means to compare design solution alternatives and support the decision making process. Simulation models are expected to support this task.

The ATV Simulation Models Engineering task includes three phases: the "Analysis" phase, Technical Specification review, Architecture Design.

During the "Analysis" phase the Contractor with the Customer support issues the Models specifications and the Interfaces specifications.

The activity will be conducted by the designated Subcontractor Engineering Staff Members, collocated at Customer site at successful conclusion of the Kick-off meeting, establishing the proper liaison with the Customer Engineering Team.

This activity will be completed after the Customer approval of the Technical Specification and Interface Requirements and generates constraints for the Start-up of the Design implementing the agreed requirements, minimising any risk for further development tasks.

A Technical Specification Review will be organised at the end of the previous phase.

The ATV Simulation models Architecture Design will be provided in an integrated team, under the Customer responsibility at the Customer premises.

Using the DSE environment these activities could be performed in a distributed way. The Contractor engineering Teams could work in collaborative and distributed way with the Customer for the requirement definition and the preparation of the relevant documentation as well as for the building of the Design. Each Engineer independently can design and simulate its specific component in two ways either using a local license of the tool or using a remote license and after the DSE allows the design teams to integrate these component models into a comprehensive model of the complete system.

Simulation Models will have reached a refinement level supporting the focused assessment of the system performance and operations aspects.

3.1.1.4 Collaborative Design of Spacecraft Control System
Objectives of the Spacecraft Control System Design Scenario
The scope of this analysis is to assess the benefits and possible limitation of implementing distributed engineering techniques in order to:
- Support engineering discussions and evaluations,
- Involve early in the design phase different specialists and teams, including suppliers and sub-contractors
- Take advantage of the synergy/opinions of the various groups involved in the design phase
- Shorten the subsystem development cycle and costs,
- Detect engineering bottlenecks as early as possible.

Description of the Space Control System Design Scenario
In that scope, modeling of the following engineering situation can provide a representative example of a typical Phase B work loop:

- Russian or US partners use an ISS simulator including a given model of the ISS Attitude and Orbit Control System (AOCS),
- Aérospatiale Matra Lanceurs uses an ATV simulator including a given model of Mission and Vehicle Management (MVM) and Guidance, Navigation and Control (GNC) functionality,
- Both engineering teams need to work together to define the best trade-offs and find an optimal solution in the following contingency mission scenario:
- For some reason when ATV is near from docking, it could happen that the ISS Control Moment Gyro (CMG) subsystem becomes unavailable. Such functionality failures have indeed happened several times onboard Russian "Mir" Space Station, mainly because of onboard computer malfunctions.
- Note, that the CMG subsystem is distributed onboard the ISS: some gyros will be installed on the Russian segment of the station, and some on the US segment.
- If CMG were switched-off, change of the AOCS mode would require engaging the reaction (jet) control system. Moreover, this change will not take place instantly.

With regard to this situation, the following issues and questions arise:
- Is there any problem in such a case?
- Does ATV stay safely in the approach corridor?
- How quickly should switching to jet thruster stabilisation mode take place onboard the ISS (an issue to be considered by the ISS AOCS engineering team)?
- When should ISS de-saturate its stabilisation wheels by switching to jet thrusters stabilisation mode?

"Simulation" of this engineering process leads to the following "Collaborative Design" scenario:

The above mentioned ATV and ISS simulators are interconnected and the consequences of a failure that leads to perturbations in the attitude stabilisation and angular motion of the ISS on the performance of the ATV GNC can be viewed immediately. This allows for much quicker and effective diagnoses and identification of possible way-outs due to interactive collaboration of remote groups of experts.

3.1.2 Products

3.1.2.1 DOORS

When requirement specifications are written, it is important that related requirements should be cross-referenced (traceability must be applied to any requirements definition of specification). The traceability between the requirements is provided using a standard DOORS tool.

DOORS (Dynamic Object-Oriented Requirements System) is a multi-platform, enterprise-wide requirements management tool designed to capture, link, trace, analyze and manage a wide range of information to ensure a project's compliance to specified requirements and standards. Through an intuitive user interface, DOORS can be accessed by hundreds of concurrent users on a network, maintaining vast numbers of objects (requirements and associated information) and links.

DOORS includes a complete on-line Change Proposal and Review System that lets users submit proposed changes to requirements. Inter-project linking allows projects to share requirements, designs and tests, and promotes traceability to corporate or other standards.

Distributed Data management (DDM) supports remote users who need temporary, remote access to all DOORS features. Working against a subset of the DOORS database off-line, remote users can incorporate their updates back into the master database.

DOORS even provides user-defined, multi-level traceability for unlimited relationships like requirements to test, requirements to design, design to code, requirements to tasks, and project plan to roles.

3.1.2.2 MATLAB

MATLAB is an integrated technical computing environment that combines numeric computation, advanced graphics and visualization, and a high-level programming language. It provides hundreds of function for data analysis and visualization; numeric and symbolic computation; engineering and scientific graphics; modelling, simulation, and prototyping; programming, application development, and GUI design.

MATLAB is used in a variety of application areas including signal and image processing, control system design, neural networks.

MATLAB is easily extensible allowing you to create your own applications. It enables you to solve many numerical problems in a fraction of the time that it would take to write a program in a language such as Fortran, C, or C++. You can also link to external software and data from MATLAB. MATLAB code, called M-files, and data files, called MAT-files, are platform independent, so sharing your ideas and designs across platforms is seamless.

3.1.2.3 Simulink

Simulink® is an interactive tool for modelling, simulating, and analyzing dynamic systems. Commonly used in control system design, Digital Signal Processor (DSP) design, communication system design, and other simulation applications, Simulink enables you to build graphical block diagrams, simulate dynamic systems, evaluate system performance, and refine your designs. Built on top of MATLAB®, Simulink offers immediate access to an extensive range of analysis and design tools. Through its seamless integration to Simulink, Stateflow® provides event-handling simulation and supervisory logic.

Traditional approaches to system design typically include building a prototype followed by extensive testing and revision. This method can be both time-consuming and expensive. As an effective and widely accepted alternative, simulation is now the preferred approach to engineering design. Simulink is a powerful simulation software tool that enables you to quickly build and test virtual prototypes so that you can explore design concepts at any level of detail with minimal effort. By using Simulink to iterate and refine designs before building the first prototype, engineers can benefit from a faster, more efficient design process.

3.1.2.4 ACTS MULTICUBE

ACTS MULTICUBE is a MULTIpoint to MULTIpoint broadband-switched network service for distributed MULTImedia applications. MULTICUBE wants to develop, test and validate an advanced ATM signalling broadband infrastructure supporting CSCW (Computer Supported Collaborative Work) tools involving real users. Real designers from consortium's user companies carry on their everyday activities using the selected CSCW tools on a high speed ATM WAN offering on-demand multipoint connections. Evaluation of performance and of perceived QoS are performed by real users in their working environment. Multipoint communications use IP multicast over ATM multicast in the interconnection of users' high-speed LANs through the European ATM network.

The project takes into account standards with the objective to assure the wider interoperability of services. At the network level the control and signalling for the ATM multipoint functionality take into account results obtained in European Community (EC) projects, while the multicast functionality at the IP level is based on products already commercially available. Signalling and control issues are closely related to International Telecommunications Union (ITU), European Telecom Standards Institute (ETSI) and European Institute for Research and Strategic Studies in Telecommunications (EURESCOM) guidelines. The application environment is based on the TCP/IP stack.

3.2 Collaborative Systems Verification

3.2.1 System Assembly, Integration, and Testing

A successful System Design Phase leads to well identified lower level components, as procurement or developmental items, and enable the start of the System Assembly, Integration and Testing (AIT) preparation, while subsystems are detailed designed and manufactured.

The System AIT Process again involves many disciplines and aims at first defining a framework for definition of the system verification requirements and of necessary facilities for the test campaigns. Usually, in large systems life cycles, tests are bottom-up performed (from lower levels up to system level), and within each level the configuration is incrementally assembled and tested, with missing components replaced by simulators. The access to specialised Test Facilities (TF) is also often required, to conduct environmental tests. For instance, in Space Industry, Thermal-Vacuum, Radiation, or Vibration Tests may require a large facility to accommodate for test a system representative model. Tests in these facilities require months for their preparation, conduction and evaluation, with many specialists from the system (or subsystems) teams collocated in the TF sites. This imposes that the system plans include sufficient time slots for the collocations and that, during their performance, the involved specialists shall not be involved in other demanding test activities.

The effective remote access to specialised TF and the collaborative conduction of Test Preparation, Execution, and Evaluation activities can enable an optimised AIT Process, in which the involved specialists will be able to co-operate on a multi-node test network. During Remotely controlled and Collaborative Tests, the Prime Contractor will also be able to concurrently proceed with other complex test activities, with benefits for the overall test campaigns duration and costs. This would also ensure an optimised utilisation of the Integration and Test Facilities.

The controlled Verification of the System also requires that the Verification Requirements at the beginning and that the Test Results at the end are properly managed and correlated. Verification databases are usually in place to support the process. In DSE, the Verification DB shall be distributed and shared over the Multi-node Test Network and made interoperable with any Multimedia Database provision. This will ensure that structured verification information as well as visual objects can be effectively shared among all "Collaborative members".

Furthermore, the Verification includes all Analyses, Inspections, and Review of Design methods complementing the Tests by demonstrating the system compliance to agreed requirements. Computer Aided Tools and Simulation (CAX) are also in the AIT Phase the primary support to achieve the verification objectives. Use of advanced visualization capabilities, as based on 3-D CAD geometrical representations and simulation capabilities providing the functional representation of the system. It will enable both Design and AIT Teams to validate the design (prior to commit for development) and the test procedures (prior to commit for the final test facilities configuration), thus minimising risks for late design changes or system tests delays. Additionally, such tools reduce the need for physical models of the systems, with evident benefits in terms of schedule and costs.

3.2.2 Thermal-Vacuum Space Simulation Test Scenario

3.2.2.1   Context of the Scenario

Before launching a spacecraft (SC) Satellite or Module, it has to undergo to a sequence of qualification or acceptance tests in order to minimize the risk of mission loss. These tests check the systems behavior on the following situations:

- under vibration and shock,
- under acoustic waves,
- under space conditions (vacuum with cold background and solar radiation),
- the compatibility of all electromagnetic components in the integrated system,
- the mass properties of the integrated spacecraft,
- the magnetic properties of the integrated spacecraft,
- the vibration modes patterns of the integrated system.

Because of the physical time scales that govern the heat flow processes, the thermal-vacuum test usually is the most effective and most time consuming among the tests. The thermal-vacuum test was therefore chosen as a DSE verification scenario because many possible DSE benefits will be proportional to the duration of the work. In what follows spacecraft simulation test (SST) always means the Thermal-Vacuum test step.

3.2.2.2   Objectives for the Space Test Scenario

The objective of the SST is to demonstrate the predicted stabilized and transient temperature distribution throughout the SC and to demonstrate the performance of the SC's thermal and electrical subsystems under simulated orbital conditions on stations (i.e. at the operational orbit in space).

The test cases include equinox, eclipse and winter solstice conditions for the thermal subsystem and qualification of the integrated SC as an operational system when subjected to an environment simulating the worst case hot and cold conditions expected in orbit.

The measured temperature behavior obtained from the SST is used to validate the theoretical thermal-mathematical model.

3.2.2.3   Chronology of Space Test Scenario

A typical SST time duration for a Scientific Satellite is 6 weeks, apportioned as follows:

- 2 weeks of preparation, in parallel, of test facility and test article (including test equipment installation in the chamber)
- 1 week of satellite functional testing, inside the open chamber, using the Engineering Ground Stations Equipment (EGSE) in the control room and the "long cables" connection to the satellite
- 2 calendar weeks of thermal testing, including thermal cycling, hot and cold soaks and reduced functional test of the spacecraft
- 1 week of satellite functional testing after environmental exposure (possibly reduced w.r.t. the initial) and removal from the test chamber

3.2.2.4   Description of the Space Test Scenario

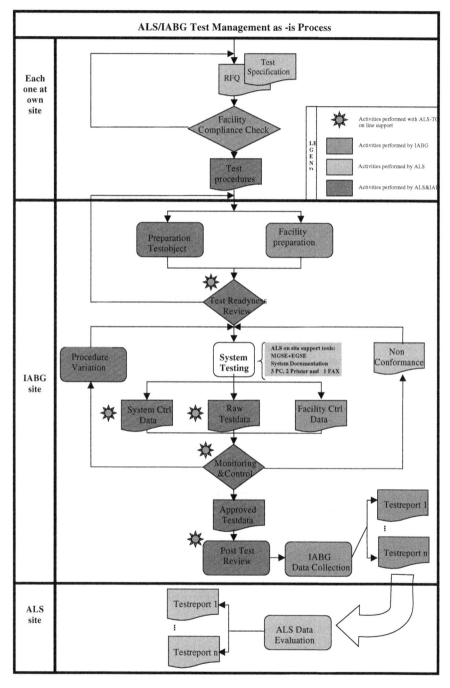

Fig. 4. Test management flow between ALS and IABG

Actual (as-is) Test management flow between Alenia Spazio (ALS) and Industrieanlagen Betriebsgesellschaft (IABG) is depicted in the Figure 4.

The SST could be also divided into 4 main phases:

Pretest Phase

The main contractor in the construction of the SC (ALS) contacts the test facility (IABG) and declares his intention to perform the SST for test object XYZ-SAT. He conveys his intended test specification (including test configuration, test cases, test equipment etc.), additional information on the SC (SC documentation, including 2D drawings of SC geometry and interfaces, etc.), the proposed schedule.

The test facility evaluates these information's checking whether it is able to meet the conditions and finds out possible improvements and/or extensions on its equipment which will become necessary in order to perform the SST. Suggestions to alter the originally intended test are exchanged among ALS and IABG. Critical items concerning locally given circumstances at the test facility are clarified by inspections of responsible ALS representatives.

The pretest phase ends with the approval of an agreed test procedure document.

Test Preparation Phase

ALS ships the SC together with the needed specialized tools, ground control and checkout equipment (1 week work for 5 people) to IABG. An ALS team sets the SC to the required test configuration supported by various subcontractor teams (if necessary). The Thermal support team and/or IABG specialists prepare SC for thermal measurements. This involves mounting of thermal-sensors at the defined locations on SC, fitting of test heaters to SC, fixing test thermal blankets to SC, fitting of special simulator equipment according to test procedure document.

IABG performs trials test runs of the thermal vacuum chamber. The test preparation phase ends with a general test readiness review.

Test Execution Phase

The actual testing proceeds through a number of simulation phases. The number of simulation phases is determined by the set of real physical conditions which the SC will meet in orbit and which have to be simulated during the test. The monitoring of the activities is made utilizing the checkout support equipment EGSE of the spacecraft and the chamber data acquisition system MEVA.

The EGSE is composed by a set of computer (Figure 5):

- CORE EGSE = which is the Server of the EGSE;
- The SCOE's = Special CheckOut Equipment which also could functionally substitute SC Equipment;
- And the FEE's = Front End Equipment;
  connected troughs a dedicated LAN.

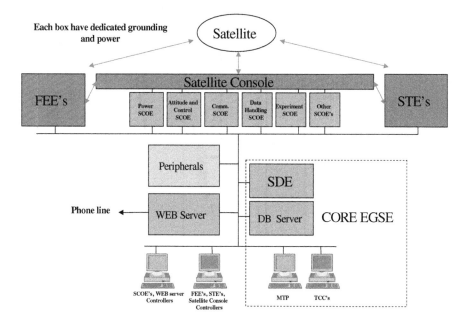

Fig. 5. An example of typical EGSE Architecture

IABG uses one computer console to monitor and control the vacuum chamber operation and a separate computer to control measurement collecting and recording activities.

The monitoring data are used to support the eventual trouble-shooting analysis, which is made also with the remote control of Specialist in TORINO (utilizing teleconferencing and FAX).

During the activities execution, if the case, eventual Non Conformance Reports (NCR) are recorded (info on NCRDB see in section 3.2.3.2) and disposition are taken in order to solve the problems and optimize the time spent on the facility.

These activities are always make in strict conjunction with the ALS Torino plant utilizing FAX or e-mail and teleconferences.

A meeting of the test review board closes each simulation phase. The test review board has the same participants as the Test Readiness Review.

The test execution phase ends with a post test review.

Post Test Phase

The SC is removed from the chamber. Test equipment's disconnected from SC (Figure 6). Test reports are generated by the Facility which will became part of the Test Report, which will be produced by ALS.

SC is shipped back to main contractor or directly to launch site.

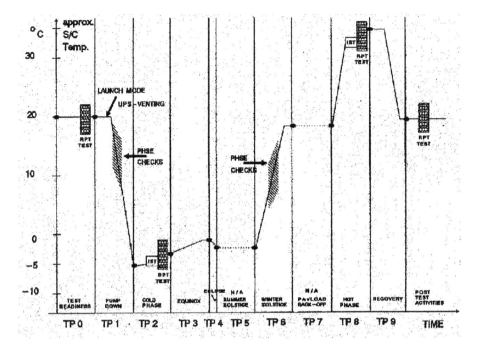

Fig. 6. Simulation phases in an example of an actual SST run

3.2.2.5 Control and Organizational Board

The Control and Organizational board is composed by:

- Test leader (ALS AIV manager or his delegate), all SC testing is directed by and under the responsibility of the test leader;
- SST conductor is responsible for the control and execution of all spacecraft SST test phases and all associated preparation and spacecraft handling activities (Mechanical Test Engineer from ALS)
- Test supervisor representing the customer organization (which owns and uses the spacecraft e.g. Space Agency), shall be informed on all progress of the test
- Test-facility leader represents the test-facility (IABG) against SST conductor and test leader

Normally this board meets (contacts each other) every working day.

3.2.2.6 The DSE Purposes

The Distributed System Environment (DSE) is intended to support re-engineering of the Verification Engineering Processes to enable distribution of the Systems Verification Engineering Process, since the preparatory phases and up to the evaluation of system test results. Connecting the main sites where the system is integrated and tested to specialised test facilities, where specific tests are conducted, will be in particular exploited.

3.2.3 Products

The products listed below are in use within the Systems Verification Engineering Process and are "generic" for this process. Besides there are few other products which are in use within the process as well but they are common to all DSE processes. These products are described in appropriate chapters of the survey: Exceed Web in section 4.2.12 and pcAnywhere in section 7.5.1.7

3.2.3.1 VIS/Mockup and VIS/View Data
This data are public domain data, which have been extracted from EAI WEB site: www.eai.com

General Description
Vis/Mockup and Vis/View are in use by ALS.

The entire Spacecraft (S/C) and its Support equipments 3D model inserted inside this "virtual environment" are utilized to support the Integration and Test Procedure preparation and Integration personnel training.

VisMockUp®
A powerful, real-time digital prototyping solution that provides interactive visualization and analysis of products so you can find and resolve manufacturing issues early in the development process (Figure 7). This solution combines advanced 2D and 3D visualization with robust analysis of large product assemblies.

VisMockUp incorporates a "best practice" approach to access, visualize and analyze complex product data - greatly improving productivity throughout the enterprise. With this EAI solution, you can dramatically reduce retooling costs, eliminate the need to produce costly physical prototypes, and improve your time-to-market for higher quality products.

One of the primary goals of any design team is to implement a "best practice" approach to detect product defects early in the design process. This enables release of error-free product data to manufacturing to strongly reduce or eliminate retooling costs. The overall need for costly physical prototypes is significantly reduced, and higher quality products can be brought to market in a shorter period of time.

VisMockUp is a powerful digital prototyping software product that combines advanced 3D visualization and 2D viewing with robust analysis features and collaboration tools. Using VisMockUp, designers can interrogate very large CAD assemblies for design problems early in the design cycle.

To improve the product assembly process, you can add an optional VisMockUp module: VisView® Enterprise-wide Product Data Visualization.

To succeed in today's competitive global economy, companies must treat their product data and process data as critical strategic assets. EAI's VisView® product line allows users to communicate product knowledge throughout the enterprise by delivering the right data to the right person at the right time.

Available Functionality
VisMockUp Sequence. Highlights:

- Dynamic interference checking - Detect interferences dynamically with powerful interference checking tools that allow users to quickly find and display interferences and collisions while viewing the product in operation
- Clearance matrix analysis - Perform complete analysis on large 3D product databases to locate and list problem areas, proximity calculations and more
- Cross sectioning - Dynamically section 3D digital mockups to find interference problems, perform measurements and save section images to share with team members
- Configuration management - Tailor product structure to a specific functional task
- Advanced 2D and 3D viewing - view easy to use 2D raster and vector formatted drawings, as well as documents and images; high-performance architecture permits viewing very large 3D CAD models and assemblies.
- Support for numerous 2D and 3D data formats and CAD packages

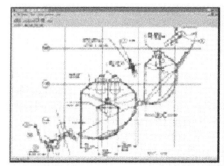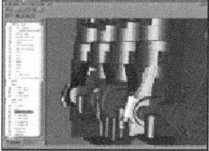

Fig. 7. The CAD assembly and the corresponding geometry in viewing windows

VisView
It enables users to easily interact with digital product data and view the latest drawings, 3D models, and documents from a single environment (Figure 8). Users can navigate to specific product information by clicking on a drawing, 3D model, product structure, or by entering a part number. VisView's object-oriented modular architecture allows companies to tailor the user interface and product structure to fit their business needs.

No longer is product data and information locked up in individual departments, but it can be shared throughout the enterprise using VisView to improve communication, expedite time to market and reduce overall costs. VisView Professional combines complete 2D viewing, measurement, annotation and comparison of 2D images and drawings with powerful 3D interactivity. You can quickly view and interact with large 3D digital product assemblies with VisView Professional.

Product databases are easily linked to VisView Professional, which means you can view product structures in context with the visual model. You can quickly select specific parts or entire assemblies of large 3D models from a product structure hierarchy.

VisView can display both the CAD assembly and the geometry, or visual representation of the model. The CAD assembly appears in one window and the corresponding geometry appears in the viewing window.

The high-performance rendering architecture of VisView allows users to view and interact with a single component or a large, production-quality digital product. Product understanding between departments and suppliers is improved by providing easy viewing and interaction with complete digital products.

VisView also integrates with product databases and leading Product Data Management (PDM) systems using VisNetwork PDM integrations.

VisView Professional's capabilities are extended with VisView Docs, VisView PMI View, VisView Configure and VisIssues Manager.

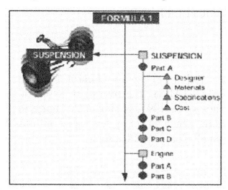

Fig. 8. Viewing product structures in context with the visual model

VisView Web Edition provides users with a web-enabled version of VisView. Additional features are:

- Advanced 3D viewing- high-performance architecture permits viewing of very large CAD models and assemblies
- 3D hierarchy display- Import and view actual product hierarchy from a CAD system, including part name, colors and hierarchy structure to easily find and display parts and assemblies
- 3D measurement- Perform 3D measurements on 3D product data with powerful measurement tools
- Compare revisions between 3D CAD models to analyze changes.
- 3D data support- Support for numerous CAD packages
- Advanced 2D viewing, 2D measurement, 2D annotation and drawing comparison
- Support for numerous 2D raster, vector and document formats

Type of Applications
Digital Mockup (DMU)

Learnability
Easy: 2 days Training

Platform
PC with WINDOWS NT
WS UNIX (HP or SGI)

Price
Server
    Basic SW (CATIA Converter + Vis/Mockup sequence + Vis/Network)
    around 16 KEURO
Client
    Vis/Mockup x WS UNIX around 11 KEURO
    Vis/View x WS UNIX around 2.5 KEURO
    Vis/View x PC NT around 1.8 KEURO

3.2.3.2 NCRDB
General Description
The Non Conformance Report & Lesson Learnt DataBase (NCRDB) has been
developed in Alenia Spazio (ALS). The overall structure of the Database, which is
operative in all ALS sites since 1997, is shown in Figure 9. The DB is based on a
Client-Server Architecture, which has been developed in Lotus Notes. The NCRDB is
accessible via LAN from all Company PC users.

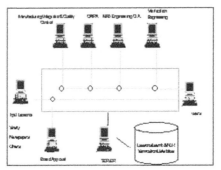

Fig. 9. NCRDB Client-Server Architecture

The Non Conformance Report & Lesson Learnt DataBase is a flexible tool to
control and manage in electronic way the lifecycle of following documents for any
technical program:

- Non Conformance Report,
- Disposition and Corrective Action,
- Preventive Action,
- Lesson Learnt,
- Assembly, Integration and Verification (AIV) Data.

The application supplies in output: processing's statistics, diagrams and reports.
    The workflow of each document is controlled through predefined document status;
every step of the workflow is managed by single user or Users groups who may play

one or more of the possible functional access rules (e.g. Originator, Authorizer, Material Review Board (MRB), etc.) allowed by the application.

The Non Conformance Report (NCR) workflow is fully configurable and strictly linked to Lotus Notes security features; no one can access the whole document or a part of it without the right permissions.

The application security is based on mechanisms of authentication based on public and private key (user name, password and ID file) while the access control list provides control at the DB file level.

During the NCR lifecycle it is possible to generate a specific Lessons related to the failure recorded in the NCR form. It is possible to generate and archive other Lesson Learnt originated from other event (e.g. newspaper, alert, etc.).

All the data are also accessible via the Corporate INTRANET using a standard WEB Browser.

Available Functionality
The tool provides the following functionalities:
- Capability to work in multi-user environment with a user friendly Man Machine Interface (MMI).
- Access through LAN and remote
- NCR Workflow Management from the NCR creation until the external closure.
- Preventive action Workflow management
- Creation and management of Lesson Learnt associated to NCR or others events.
- Preview and print of the reports , views and graphics
- Assembly, Integration and Verification (AIV) data management
- Statistic data management and report processing. Capability to generate reports and graphics by means of wizards
- Hypertext and keywords search
- Capability to store files attachment related to failure analysis
- User management: capability to create different users with different roles and security access level.
- Keywords Management: capability to create new keywords or application fields.
- A Discussion Forum DB is available on line to allow collection of DB utilisation, suggestions and questions.
- Integration with the e-mail
- Help on line
- Log

Learnability
Easy: 1-day training.

Platform
Lotus Domino Ver 4.6 (server and clients).
WIN NT 4.0 Service Pack 5.

3.2.3.3 AIVDB

This data are public domain data, which have been extracted from Space Software Italia (SSI) WEB site: http://www.ssi.it/frprogra.htm

General Description
The Assembly, Integration and Verification DataBase (AIVDB) is a flexible tool to control and manage the Assembly, Integration and Verification (AIV) activities for any technical program. AIVDB allows the multi-user access to work in parallel on the AIV activities on the same program or on different programs.

Available Functionality
- On-line help to facilitate the user operations. The on-line help can be easily customised
- Setting of Programs in terms of the associated:
    - Products
    - Verification Method (e.g. Review of Design, Test, Inspection, Analysis)
    - Verification Phase (e.g. Qualification, Acceptance)
- Creation and handling of the Verification Phase, the Configuration Items and the Configuration Item Tree of a user selected Program. A Configuration Item can be, for example, a Satellite itself, the Thermal Control Subsystem or any other subcomponents of a system of any complexity.
- Capability to trace the requirements in top-down and bottom-up way. AIVDB also prints the traceability results.
- Capability to identify and print the parentless and childless requirement within a Product Tree.
- Navigation among requirements. AIVDB allows the user to select a requirement and view the related parent(s) or child(s).
- Creation and handling of the AIV process selecting the Program, the Configuration Item and the Verification Phase.
- Customization of the AIV process according to the particular needs of the program. The AIVDB provided model allows the user to perform the AIV activities directly from the Requirement to be verified covering all the Verification methods, including the DEMONSTRATION Method used for the AIV process of DoD and NASA developed system.
- Creation and handling of the AIV Process Items. The AIV Process Items are the main part of the AIV process. Indeed, they are the relevant data of the documents to be used in the AIV activities. Examples of the Process Items are the Requirements, Test Procedures, Test Specification, Test Activity Sheet, Assembly Procedures and many others.
- Trace between different process Items. For example, it possible to trace from Requirements to Test Procedure, Review of Design, Inspection procedure and Analysis.
- Minimisation of the effort related to the insertion of the AIV process items by using the Import function. This function, based on the SGML (Standard Generalized Markup Language) technology, allows the automatic insertion of the data retrieving them directly by the documents. For example, a user that wants to

insert into the database the Requirements to be verified needs only to give the name of the file to the tool and click on the Import button. AIVDB will automatically read the AIV information from the file and store them into the DataBase.

- Grouping the requirements according to some common aspects in order to optimise the verification process of the requirements.
- Print or display the handled Process Items.
- Print of the Verification Control Document and the Verification Status Report
- Capability to create different users with different roles (e.g. Data Base Administrator (DBA), AIV responsible) and security access level.
- Back-up and Restore of all the AIV data directly from the tool.
- Inhibition to the Program resource access of unauthorised users via a role-oriented security mechanism.
- Capability to perform all the AIV Data Base Administrator (DBA) functions related to AIVDB directly from the tool. AIVDB prevents the use of DBA functions to unauthorised users via a role-driven mechanism.

Type of Applications
Data management and analysis software package.

Learnability
4 days training for people skilled in AIV discipline.

Maintainability and Support
ALS and SSI own the Source Code of AIVDB.

Impact of Utilization
Easy porting to other platforms due to the advanced development technology and to the standard ANSI C used as language to develop the products.

Platform
- Sun on SunOS 4.1.3
System Requirements:
- MOTIF
- ORACLE 7

Price
It is a European Space Agency (ESA) tool.

3.2.3.4   CATIA

General Description

CATIA is Computer Aided Design/Modelling/Engineering (CAD/CAM/CAE) software. This software gives you a broad range of integrated solutions that cover all aspects of:

- Driving enterprise competitiveness
- Task productivity
- Process improvement
- Product design and manufacture

Used in conjunction with products from ENOVIA Corporation, CATIA is the key engineering component to implement e-business solutions for the creation and simulation of your entire product life cycle from initial concept to product in service.

CATIA Version 5 is a completely re-engineered, next-generation product family providing newest object technologies, architecture, and standards (such as STEP, Java, CORBA and OLE). This places CATIA Version 5 at the beginning of a new technology curve that assures the future of the CATIA product line.

CATIA Version 5 Release 3:

- adds six new products
    - Sheetmetal Design 2
    - DMU Optimizer 2
    - Systems Routing 2
    - Plant Layout 2
    - Knowledge Expert 2
    - Generative Knowledge 2
- Enhances 30 previously announced products
- Expands interoperability with Version 4
- Withdraws support for Windows NT on DEC Alpha workstations

Available Functionality

- An infrastructure-based catalog of components enables companies to easily create and manage standard parts and assemblies.
- The native power of CATIA Version 5 for design in context has been reinforced. A label can be assigned to any existing geometry so that the geometry can be reused as a reference for design in context.
- The impacts of assembly dependencies can be analyzed through a graph.
- Concurrent engineering is enriched: any existing surface or wireframe element can be replaced by another element in a multiple part environment.

CATIA Platform 1 (CATIA P1) provides basic applications in a suite of feature-based solid modelling solutions that complies with Windows™ user interface guidelines. These solutions offer a familiar production environment for users who are already comfortable with native Windows applications. P1 solutions are an excellent vehicle for new CATIA customers who want to extend their design capabilities to embrace digital product definition and to position themselves for e-business.

CATIA Platform 2 (CATIA P2) provides an extended set of solutions based on a hybrid modelling technology. CATIA P2 solutions provide expanded digital product and process definition and review functions capable of operating on projects characterized by a high level of design complexity. An extended mechanical design solution addresses advanced design requirements involving multiple data representations, such as mechanical features and styled shapes. In addition, the capabilities of the CATIA — Knowledge Advisor 2 product allows users to capture corporate knowledge with rapidly iterative design alternatives and with significant error reduction. Other domain-specific solutions are and will continue to be delivered to address global digital enterprise requirements that span the mock-up, manufacturing, plant, and operations domains.

Type of Applications
CATIA is well-known CAD/CAM/CAE software. CATIA Version 5 is positioned as the leading process-oriented design system for manufacturing industries.

Maintainability and Support
IBM's Engineering Solutions worldwide services organization provides a robust portfolio of offerings to guide and assist you with the implementation of CATIA Version 5. These offerings are designed to provide the resources necessary for a smooth implementation of CATIA Version 5 in your current environment.
    Service offerings cover the following areas:
- Consultative services for CATIA Version 5 readiness in a CATIA Version 4 environment
- Installation planning for CATIA Version 5 in a compatible environment with CATIA Version 4
- Systems implementation of CATIA Version 5 in a mixed operating systems environment (UNIX and Windows) and/or multiple CATIA version environments (CATIA Version 5 and Version 4)
- Application best practices consulting for CATIA Version 5
- Consultative training assistance with planned CATIA Version 5 Computer Based Training
- Consulting on CATIA Administration for CATIA Version 5 in a multi-operating system and/or multi-version environment

For additional information on service offerings and how these professionals can assist with the implementation of CATIA Version 5 in your environment, contact your IBM representative or services organization or go to
http://www.ibm.com/solutions/engineering

Impact of Utilization
The CATIA Version 5 packaging model gives you an easy way to select the solution best suited to your user profiles and process requirements. At the heart of this model are:
- Platforms
- Solutions
- Configurations
- Products

CATIA provides the support of workstations locales.

Platform
- AIX
- HP
- IRIX
- Solaris
- NT Intel
- Windows 95/98
- LUM

3.2.3.5 DynaWorks
General Description
DynaWorks® is a software package for managing and analyzing dynamic environmental data, such as vibrations, shocks, acoustics and thermal measurements. These informations have been extracted from the http://www.dynaworks.com Web site.

DynaWorks® is composed of series of modules:
- Base module,
- Signal processing,
- Advanced signal processing,
- Geometrical display,
- Test specification,
- Real-time monitoring,
- Modal identification,
- Computer aided test management,
- Wavelet transform.

Available Functionality
- Comparison of measured and predicted environmental data
- Test management
- Real-time or off-line test analysis
- Derivation of test specifications

Type of Applications
DynaWorks® is a data management and analysis software package.

Future Evolutions
- Automated tests reports generated as Word or FrameMaker documents
- Improvements in displays

Reliability
DynaWorks® guarantees a high degree of security thanks to powerful tools that let you undo commands, recover after a software failure, save work sessions and define limits governing how.

Maintainability and Support

DynaWorks® operates on major workstations running UNIX with X Windows and the Motif graphical user interface and now on Windows NT 4.0.

The mouse-driven, windowing Graphical User Interface (in English and in French) is user-friendly and its multi-tasking, multi-windowing capabilities provide a high degree of flexibility for users working across a network.

Built-in on-line help makes learning easy.

DynaWorks® allows you to tailor your working environment, build your own functions, communicate with a variety of other software applications, and share data across different platforms.

Platform

Sun

- Sparc station, Sparc server and UltraSparc
- Solaris 2.5 or later

Hewlett Packard

- HP 9000 series 700 and 800, PA 8000 workstations and servers
- HP UX Version 10.20 or later

Silicon Graphics

- IRIX 6.2, 6.3, 6.4, 6.5

Windows NT

- Database development kit is available on Windows NT 4.0 and Windows 95

Chapter 4. Middleware

R. Becchini, P. Chilaev, V. Krivtsov, I. Viglietti, and V. Volochinov

4.1 Middleware Technologies

4.1.1 High Level Architecture (HLA)

The distributed simulation revolution started early in the 80's with the SIMNET (Simulation Network) program sponsored by the US DoD ARPA (Advanced Research Project Agency), and aimed at producing distributed systems [32]. The necessity to have those simulators interact has lead in the 90's to two trends: the ALSP (Aggregate Level Simulation Protocol) and the DIS (Distributed Interactive Simulation). ALSP was designed for high-level training (Company, Division, etc.), and non real-time simulators. On the other hand, the DIS standard (IEEE1278) was created for real-time simulations at a finer level of resolution (Vehicle level). This latter standard was based on broadcasting communication methods, and defined therefore around 30 PDU (Protocol Data Units).

In 1996 the DoD Modelling and Simulation Master Plan has investigated the development of a new plan comprising the HLA (High Level Architecture), the Conceptual Model of the Mission Space (CMMS), and the DS (Data Standardization). The HLA establishes a common high-level architecture to facilitate the interoperability of all types of models and simulations among themselves and with Command, Control, Communications, Computers and Intelligence (C4I) systems, as well as facilitating the reuse of components.

The high level architecture has been developed in order to meet the objective of the American Department of Defense Modelling and Simulation (M&S) master plan: to establish a common architecture to facilitate the interoperability of all types of models and simulations amongst themselves and with C4I systems, as well as to facilitate the reuse of M&S components. The HLA rational is based on the following premises:

- No single monolithic simulation can satisfy the needs of all users
- All uses of simulations and useful ways of combining them cannot be anticipated in advance
- Future technological capabilities and a variety of operating configuration must be accommodated.

As a consequence, the simulation developers need a composable approach to constructing simulation federations built from modular components with well-defined functionality and interfaces.

HLA comprises the three following components:

- 10 rules: a set of rules that must be followed to achieve proper interaction of simulations in a federation. They specify the responsibilities of federates (simulators) and of the Run-Time Infrastructure (RTI) in HLA federations (simulation exercises).

K. Drira, A. Martelli, T. Villemur (Eds.): Cooperative Environments, LNCS 2236, pp. 41-105, 2001.
© Springer-Verlag Berlin Heidelberg 2001

- Interface specifications: definition of the interface functions between the runtime infrastructures and the simulations subject to the HLA. It defines six service groups between the RTI and federates.
- Object Model Template (OMT): prescribes a common method for recording the information contained in the required HLA object Model for each federation and simulation.

The Architecture Management Group adopted version 1.3 of the specification documents in February 1998. Version 1.3 has been forwarded to the IEEE (P1516), and the process of making the HLA specifications IEEE standards is expected to be completed in year 2000.

Exhaustive documentation on HLA can be found at the following URL: http://hla.dmso.mil

The Federation Development and Execution Process (FEDEP) Model describes a high-level functional framework for the development and execution of HLA federations [31]. It specifies a set of recommended practices and guidelines for federation development and execution that federation developers can utilise. The FEDEP model is sufficiently general to be applicable to most HLA federations. The following chapters provide an overview of the FEDEP phases.

4.1.1.1 Objectives Development Phase

The purpose of Objectives Development is to:
- Generate and fully document the federation sponsor's problem statement.
- Specify a complete set of objectives to be addressed through instantiation and execution of the federation.

The outputs and content of this phase are very specific to a particular application domain. Applicable technologies and tools are not identified.

4.1.1.2 Scenario Development Phase

The purpose of Scenario Development is to develop a high-level specification of the federation scenario, which includes:
- Identification of the major entities that must be represented by the federation.
- Conceptual description of the capabilities, behaviour and relationships between these major entities over time.
- Specification of relevant environmental conditions.

As previously, the outputs and content of this phase are very specific to a particular application domain. Applicable technologies and tools are not identified and not planned for implementation yet [38].

4.1.1.3 Conceptual Analysis Phase

The purpose of Conceptual Analysis is to develop a conceptual view of the objects and interactions that must be supported by the federation to achieve the sponsor's study objectives.

Computer-aided software engineering tools can potentially be used to ensure consistency between the federation conceptual model, the Conceptual Model of Mission Space (CMMS), the federation scenario, and the federation objectives. However, these tools are not available yet. Furthermore, CMMS of the application domain are not developed to date.

The primary activity in this phase is to decompose the conceptual description of the federation scenario into explicit components expressed as objects and interactions. Another important element of the Conceptual Analysis phase is the characterisation of federation fidelity requirements. These requirements should be based on the high-level, coarse indications of required fidelity identified during the Objectives Development phase. During Conceptual Analysis, this information is transformed and extended into specific fidelity requirements at the object/interaction level. The physical representation of these requirements may be structured and formatted so as to be directly mapable to individual Simulation Object Models (SOMs) during Federation Design [31].

4.1.1.4 Federation Design Phase

The purpose of Federation Design is to establish the membership of the federation, and to develop the preparatory information required for supporting the development of HLA Federation Object Models (FOMs).

Computer-aided software engineering tools can potentially be used to map objects and attributes defined in conceptual model to existing FOMs and Modeling and Simulation Resource Repository (MSRR's) Data Dictionary. However, these tools are not available yet.

The activities to be performed during this phase are:

• Develop a mapping between the object and interaction classes specified in the federation conceptual model, and an appropriate set of object and interaction class names (and associated semantics) given in the MSRR's Data Dictionary.

• Assess the possibility of reusing existing FOMs that have been previously developed for different but possibly similar applications.

• Determine the suitability of individual simulation systems to become members of the federation.

• Define a set of specific federation requirements to guide development of the FOM. These requirements are driven by the sponsor's statement of Federation Objectives, and are generally developed collaboratively among all members of the federation.

• Define a methodology for collaborative FOM development. This methodology defines the responsibilities of the individual federation members, and describes how the federation members will work together to produce a unified FOM.

4.1.1.5 Federation Development Phase

The purpose of Federation Development is to instantiate the methodology for collaborative FOM development defined during the Federation Design phase.

Tools that provide intra-FOM consistency checking, interface definition language syntax checking, auto-generation of user-defined complex datatypes and auto-generation of RTI Initialisation Data could facilitate and simplify this phase.

The activities to be performed during this phase are:

• Extract the classes of information from the SOM of each federation member that are believed to be relevant to the goals of the federation application.

• Integrate the material extracted from the individual SOMs into a coherent, unified framework for FOM construction.

4.1.1.6 HLA FOM Development Phase

The purpose of HLA FOM Development is to capture and record the information generated during the FOM development in the Object Model Template (OMT) formats described in the HLA OMT and OMT Extensions Documents.

Tools that provide FOM editing and input/export of different file formats for FOM representation could facilitate and simplify this phase.

4.1.1.7 Federation Execution Phase

The purpose of Federation Execution is to:

- Achieve scenario domain specific goals (e.g.: training of personnel, validating technical design, etc.).
- Collect all the data required for further validation and analysis. Both simulation executive domain and scenario domain specific data may be collected.

The HLA Run-Time Infrastructure (RTI) is a basic component required to perform this phase. Although RTI supports essential services required for federation execution (and, thus, acts as a "back-end" component), it does not provide "front-end" functionality like runtime monitoring, management and data collection.

4.1.1.8 Post-processing Phase

The purpose of Post-processing is to facilitate validation and verification of federation (or federates) and analysis of simulation results.

4.1.2 CORBA

4.1.2.1 Overview

CORBA (Common Object Request Broker Architecture) is a standard architecture from the OMG consortium that allows communication among distributed software objects and components [87]. CORBA is a middleware that separates communication and implementation details of the distributed system from the applications that use it. CORBA automates many common network programming tasks such as object registration, location, and activation; request demultiplexing; framing and error-handling; parameter marshalling and demarshalling; and operation dispatching.

The ORB (Object Request Broker) is the middleware that establishes the client-server relationships between objects. Using an ORB, a client can transparently invoke a method on a server object, which can be on the same machine or across a network. The ORB intercepts the call and is responsible for finding an object that can implement the request, pass it the parameters, invoke its method, and return the results. The client does not have to be aware of where the object is located, its programming language, its operating system, or any other system aspects that are not part of an object's interface. In so doing, the ORB provides interoperability between applications on different machines in heterogeneous distributed environments and seamlessly interconnects multiple object systems.

Additional information can be found at the http://www.corba.org URL address.

4.1.2.2   Architecture

From the CORBA specification documents [61] we have:

Figure 1 shows a request being sent by a client to an object implementation. The Client is the entity that wishes to perform an operation on the object and the Object Implementation is the code and data that actually implements the object.

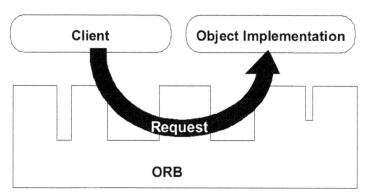

Fig. 1. A request being sent through an ORB

The ORB is responsible for all of the mechanisms required to find the object implementation for the request, to prepare the object implementation to receive the request, and to communicate the data making up the request. The interface the client sees is completely independent of where the object is located, what programming language it is implemented in, or any other aspect which is not reflected in the object's interface.

Figure 2 shows the structure of an individual Object Request Broker (ORB). The interfaces to the ORB are shown by striped boxes, and the arrows indicate whether the ORB is called or performs an up-call across the interface.

To make a request, the Client can use the Dynamic Invocation interface (the same interface independent of the target object's interface) or an OMG IDL stub (the specific stub depending on the interface of the target object). The Client can also directly interact with the ORB for some functions.

The Object Implementation receives a request as an up-call either through the OMG IDL generated skeleton or through a dynamic skeleton. The Object Implementation may call the Object Adapter and the ORB while processing a request or at other times.

Definitions of the interfaces to objects can be defined in two ways. Interfaces can be defined statically in an interface definition language, called the OMG Interface Definition Language (OMG IDL). This language defines the types of objects according to the operations that may be performed on them and the parameters to those operations. Alternatively, or in addition, interfaces can be added to an Interface Repository service; this service represents the components of an interface as objects, permitting run-time access to these components. In any ORB implementation, the Interface Definition Language (which may be extended beyond its definition in this document) and the Interface Repository have equivalent expressive power.

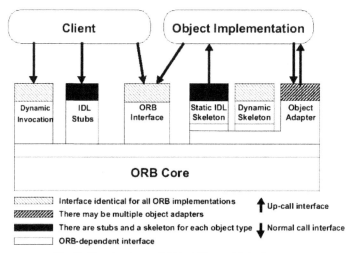

Fig. 2. The structure of Object Request Interfaces

The client performs a request by having access to an Object Reference for an object and knowing the type of the object and the desired operation to be performed. The client initiates the request by calling stub routines that are specific to the object or by constructing the request dynamically (Figure 3).

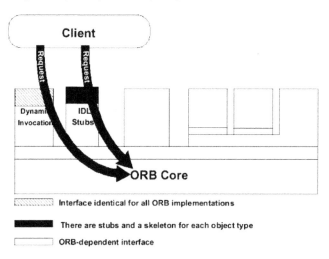

Fig. 3. A client using the stub or a Dynamic Invocation Interface

The dynamic and stub interfaces for invoking a request satisfy the same request semantics, and the receiver of the message cannot tell how the request was invoked. The ORB locates the appropriate implementation code, transmits parameters, and transfers control to the Object Implementation through an IDL skeleton or a dynamic skeleton (Figure 4). Skeletons are specific to the interface and the object adapter. In performing the request, the object implementation may obtain some services from the ORB through the Object Adapter. When the request is complete, control and output values are returned to the client.

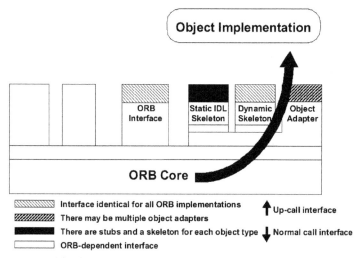

Fig. 4. An object implementation receiving a request

The Object Implementation may choose which Object Adapter to use. This decision is based on what kind of services the Object Implementation requires.

Figure 5 shows how interface and implementation information is made available to clients and object implementations. The interface is defined in OMG IDL and/or in the Interface Repository; the definition is used to generate the client Stubs and the object implementation Skeletons.

The object implementation information is provided at installation time and is stored in the Implementation Repository for use during request delivery.

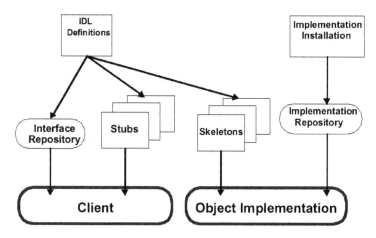

Fig. 5. Interface and implementation repositories

4.1.2.3 CORBA Services

This section lists the set of CORBA services defined by the OMG group [64].

Naming Service

The Naming Service provides the ability to bind a name to an object relative to a naming context. A naming context is an object that contains a set of name bindings in which each name is unique. To resolve a name is to determine the object associated with the name in a given context.

Through the use of a very general model and dealing with names in their structural form, naming service implementations can be application specific or be based on a variety of naming systems currently available on system platforms.

Graphs of naming contexts can be supported in a distributed, federated fashion. The scalable design allows the distributed, heterogeneous implementation and administration of names and name contexts.

Because name component attribute values are not assigned or interpreted by the naming service, higher levels of software are not constrained in terms of policies about the use and management of attribute values.

Through the use of a "names library", name manipulation is simplified and names can be made representation-independent thus allowing their representation to evolve without requiring client changes.

Application localization is facilitated by syntax-independence name and the provision of a "kind" attribute name.

Event Service

The Event Service provides basic capabilities that can be configured together in a very flexible and powerful manner. Asynchronous events (decoupled between suppliers and consumers), event "fan-in," notification "fan-out," and (through appropriate event channel implementations) reliable event delivery are supported.

The Event Service design is scalable and is suitable for distributed environments. There is no requirement for a centralized server or dependency on any global service.

The Event Service interfaces allow implementations that provide different qualities of service to satisfy different application requirements. In addition, the event service does not impose higher level policies (e.g., specific event types) allowing great flexibility on how it is used in a given application environment.

Both push and pull event delivery models are supported: that is, consumers can either request events or be notified of events, whichever is needed to satisfy application requirements. There can be multiple consumers and multiple suppliers events.

Suppliers can generate events without knowing the identities of the consumers. Conversely, consumers can receive events without knowing the identities of the suppliers.

The event channel interface can be subtyped to support extended capabilities. The event consumer-supplier interfaces are symmetric, allowing the chaining of event channels (for example, to support various event-filtering models). Event channels can be chained by third parties.

Typed event channels extend basic event channels to support typed interaction.

Because event suppliers, consumers and channels are objects, advantage can be taken of performance optimizations provided by ORB implementations for local and remote objects. No extension is required to CORBA.

Life Cycle Service
The Life Cycle Service defines conventions for creating, deleting, copying and moving objects. Because CORBA-based environments support distributed objects, life cycle services define services and conventions that allow clients to perform life cycle operations on objects in different locations.

The client's model of creation is defined in terms of factory objects. A factory is an object that creates another object. Factories are not special objects. As with any object, factories have well-defined OMG IDL interfaces and implementations in some programming language.

The Life Cycle Service defines an interface for a generic factory. This allows for the definition of standard creation services.

The Life Cycle Service defines a LifeCycleObject interface. This interface defines remove, copy and move operations.

Persistent Object Service
The Persistent Object Service (POS) provides a set of common interfaces to the mechanisms used for retaining and managing the persistent state of objects.

The object ultimately has the responsibility of managing its state, but can use or delegate to the Persistent Object Service for the actual work. A major feature of the Persistent Object Service is its openness. In this case, it means that there can be a variety of different clients and implementations of the Persistent Object Service, and they can work together. This is particularly important for storage, where mechanisms useful for documents may not be appropriate for employee databases, or the mechanisms appropriate for mobile computers do not apply to mainframes.

Transaction Service
The Transaction Service supports multiple transaction models, including the flat (mandatory in the specification) and nested (optional) models.

The Object Transaction Service supports interoperability between different programming models. For instance, some users want to add object implementations to existing procedural applications and to augment object implementations with code that uses the procedural paradigm. To do so in a transaction environment requires the object and procedural code to share a single transaction.

Network interoperability is also supported, since users need communication between different systems, including the ability to have one transaction service interoperate with a cooperating transaction service using different ORBs.

The Transaction Service supports both implicit (system-managed transaction) propagation and explicit (application-managed) propagation. With implicit propagation, transactional behavior is not specified in the operation's signature. With explicit propagation, applications define their own mechanisms for sharing a common transaction.

The Transaction Service can be implemented in a Transaction Processing monitor environment, so it supports the ability to execute multiple transactions concurrently, and to execute clients, servers, and transaction services in separate processes.

Concurrency Control Service

The Concurrency Control Service enables multiple clients to coordinate their access to shared resources. Coordinating access to a resource means that when multiple, concurrent clients access a single resource, any conflicting actions by the clients are reconciled so that the resource remains in a consistent state.

Concurrent use of a resource is regulated with locks. Each lock is associated with a single resource and a single client. Coordination is achieved by preventing multiple clients from simultaneously possessing locks for the same resource if the client's activities might conflict. Hence, a client must obtain an appropriate lock before accessing a shared resource. The Concurrency Control Service defines several lock modes, which correspond to different categories of access. This variety of lock modes provides flexible conflict resolution. For example, providing different modes for reading and writing lets a resource support multiple concurrent clients on a read-only transaction. The Concurrency Control Service also defines Intention Locks that support locking at multiple levels of granularity.

Relationship Service

The Relationship Service allows entities and relationships to be explicitly represented. Entities are represented as CORBA objects. The service defines two new kinds of objects: relationships and roles. A role represents a CORBA object in a relationship. The Relationship interface can be extended to add relationship-specific attributes and operations. In addition, relationships of arbitrary degree can be defined. Similarly, the Role interface can be extended to add role-specific attributes and operations.

Type and cardinality constraints can be expressed and checked: exceptions are raised when the constraints are violated.

The Life Cycle Service defines operations to copy, move, and remove graphs of related objects, while the Relationship Service allows graphs of related objects to be traversed without activating the related objects.

Distributed implementations of the Relationship Service can have navigation performance and availability similar to CORBA object references: role objects can be located with their objects and need not depend on a centralized repository of relationship information. As such, navigating inside a relationship can be a local operation.

The Relationship Service supports the compound life cycle component of the Life Cycle Service by defining object graphs.

Externalization Service

The Externalization Service defines protocols and conventions for externalizing and internalizing objects. Externalizing an object is to record the object state in a stream of data (in memory, on a disk file, across the network, and so forth) and then be internalized into a new object in the same or a different process. The externalized object can exist for arbitrary amounts of time, be transported by means outside of the ORB, and be internalized in a different, disconnected ORB. For portability, clients can request that externalized data be stored in a file whose format is defined with the Externalization Service Specification.

The Externalization Service is related to the Relationship Service and parallels the Life Cycle Service in defining externalization protocols for simple objects, for arbitrarily related objects, and for facilities, directory services, and file services.

Query Service

The purpose of the Query Service is to allow users and objects to invoke queries on collections of other objects. The queries are declarative statements with predicates and include the ability to specify values of attributes; to invoke arbitrary operations; and to invoke other Object Services.

The Query Service allows indexing. It maps well to the query mechanisms used in database systems and other systems that store and access large collections of objects. It is based on existing standards for query, including SQL-92, OQL-93, and OQL-93 Basic.

The Query Service provides an architecture for a nested and federated service that can coordinate multiple, nested query evaluators.

Licensing Service

The Licensing Service provides a mechanism for producers to control the use of their intellectual property. Producers can implement the Licensing Service according to their own needs, and the needs of their customers, because the Licensing Service does not impose it own business policies or practices.

A license in the Licensing Service has three types of attributes that allow producers to apply controls flexibly: time, value mapping, and consumer. Time allows licenses to have start/duration and expiration dates. Value mapping allows producers to implement a licensing scheme according to units, allocation (through concurrent use licensing), or consumption (for example, metering or allowance of grace periods through "overflow licenses.") Consumer attributes allow a license to be reserved or assigned for specific entities; for example, a license could be assigned to a particular machine. The Licensing Service allows producers to combine and derive from license attributes.

The Licensing Service consists of a LicenseServiceManager interface and a ProducerSpecificLicenseService interface: these interfaces do not impose business policies upon implementers.

Property Service

- Provides the ability to dynamically associate named values with objects outside the static IDL-type system.
- Defines operations to create and manipulate sets of name-value pairs or name-value-mode tuples. The names are simple OMG IDL strings. The values are OMG IDL anys. The use of type any is significant in that it allows a property service implementation to deal with any value that can be represented in the OMG IDL-type system. The modes are similar to those defined in the Interface Repository AttributeDef interface.
- Designed to be a basic building block, yet robust enough to be applicable for a broad set of applications.

- Provides "batch" operations to deal with sets of properties as a whole. The use of "batch" operations is significant in that the systems and network management (SNMP, CMIP...) communities have proven such a need when dealing with "attribute" manipulation in a distributed environment.
- Provides exceptions such that PropertySet implementers may exercise control of (or apply constraints to) the names and types of properties associated with an object, similar in nature to the control one would have with CORBA attributes.
- Allows PropertySet implementers to restrict modification, addition and/or deletion of properties (read-only, fixed) similar in nature to the restrictions one would have with CORBA attributes.
- Provides client access and control of constraints and property modes.
- Does not rely on any other object services.

Time Service
- Enables the user to obtain current time together with an error estimate associated with it.
- Ascertains the order in which "events" occurred.
- Generates time-based events based on timers and alarms.
- Computes the interval between two events.
- Consists of two services, hence defines two service interfaces:
    - Time Service manages Universal Time Objects (UTOs) and Time Interval Objects (TIOs), and is represented by the TimeService interface.
    - Timer Event Service manages Timer Event Handler objects, and is represented by the TimerEventService interface.

Security Service
The security functionality defined by this specification comprises:
- Identification and authentication of principals (human users and objects which need to operate under their own rights) to verify they are who they claim to be.
- Authorization and access control - deciding whether a principal can access an object, normally using the identity and/or other privilege attributes of the principal (such as role, groups, and security clearance) and the control attributes of the target object (stating which principals, or principals with which attributes) can access it.
- Security auditing to make users accountable for their security related actions. It is normally the human user who should be accountable. Auditing mechanisms should be able to identify the user correctly, even after a chain of calls through many objects.
- Security of communication between objects, which is often over insecure lower layer communications. This requires trust to be established between the client and target, which may require authentication of clients to targets and authentication of targets to clients. It also requires integrity protection and (optionally) confidentiality protection of messages in transit between objects.
- Non-repudiation provides irrefutable evidence of actions such as proof of origin of data to the recipient, or proof of receipt of data to the sender to protect against subsequent attempts to falsely deny the receiving or sending of the data.
- Administration of security information (for example, security policy) is also needed.

Object Trader Service
The Object Trader Service provides a matchmaking service for objects.

The Service Provider registers the availability of the service by invoking an export operation on the trader, passing as parameters information about the offered service.

The export operation carries an object reference that can be used by a client to invoke operations on the advertised services, a description of the type of the offered service (i.e., the names of the operations to which it will respond, along with their parameter and result types), information on the distinguishing attributes of the offered service. The offer space managed by traders may be partitioned to ease administration and navigation. This information is stored persistently by the Trader. Whenever a potential client wishes to obtain a reference to a service that does a particular job, it invokes an import operation, passing as parameters a description of the service required. Given this import request, the Trader checks appropriate offers for acceptability. To be acceptable, an offer must have a type that conforms to that requested and have properties consistent with the constraints specified by an import. Trading service in a single trading domain may be distributed over a number of trader objects. Traders in different domains may be federated. Federation enables systems in different domains to negotiate the sharing of services without loosing control of their own policies and services. A domain can thus share information with other domains with which it has been federated, and it can now be searched for appropriate service offers.

Object Collections Service
Collections are groups of objects, which, as a group, support some operations and exhibit specific behaviors that are related to the nature of the collection rather than to the type of object they contain. The purpose of the Collection Object Service is to provide a uniform way to create and manipulate the most common collections generically. Examples of collections are sets, queues, stacks, lists, binary, and trees. For example, sets might support the following operations: insert new element, membership test, union, intersection, cardinality, equality test, emptiness test, etc. One of the defining semantics of a set is that, if an object O is a member of a set S, then inserting O into S results in the set being unchanged. This property would not hold for another collection type called a bag.

4.1.2.4 Meta Object Facility
The Meta Object Facility (MOF) [55] specification provides a set of CORBA interfaces that can be used to define and manipulate a set of interoperable metamodels. The MOF is a key building block in the construction of CORBA-based distributed development environments.

This specification enhances meta data management and meta data interoperability in distributed object environments in general, and in distributed development environments in particular. The MOF also defines a simple meta-metamodel with sufficient semantics to describe metamodels in various domains starting with the domain of object analysis and design. Integration of metamodels across domains is required for integrating tools and applications across the life cycle using common semantics. The main purpose of the OMG MOF is to provide a set of CORBA interfaces that can be used to define and manipulate a set of interoperable metamodels.

The Meta Object Facility represents the integration of work currently underway by the OMG members in the areas of object repositories, object modelling tools, and meta data management in distributed object environments. The MOF specification uses the Unified Modelling Language (UML) notation. Typically, the MOF will be used for manipulating meta objects to provide integration of tools and applications across the life cycle using industry standard metamodels, such as the Object Analysis and Design (OA&D) UML.

The Repository Common Facility is positioned within the Information Management Common Facility and is composed of a number of common facilities and object services, including the MOF and the Change Management Facility.

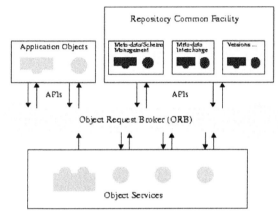

Fig. 6. OMG Architecture and the Repository Common Facility

The standardization of the MOF provides a solid foundation of the OMG architecture in moving toward a unifying architecture for defining and managing metadata in distributed environments. Figure 6 illustrates the positioning of the MOF as a key component of the CORBA architecture as well within the Common Facilities Architecture.

The traditional framework for meta-modelling is based on architecture with four layers. These layers are conventionally described as follows:

- The user object layer is comprised of the information that we wish to describe. This information is typically referred to as "data".
- The model layer is comprised of the meta-data that describes information. Meta-data is informally aggregated as models.
- The meta-model layer is comprised of the descriptions (i.e. meta-meta-data) that define the structure and semantics of meta-data. Meta-meta-data is informally aggregated as meta-models. A meta-model can also be thought of as a language for describing different kinds of data.
- The meta-meta-model layer is comprised of the description of the structure and semantics of meta-meta-data. In other words, it is the language for defining different kinds of meta-data.

The MOF meta-data architecture, shown in Figure 7 below, is based on the traditional four-layer meta-data architecture described above.

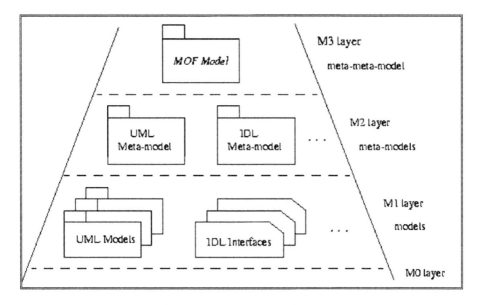

Fig. 7. MOF Meta-data Architecture

The MOF meta-data architecture has a few important features that distinguishes it from earlier meta-modelling architectures:

- The MOF Model is object-oriented, supporting meta-modelling constructs that are aligned with (though a bit simpler than) UML object modelling constructs. Hence, the Figure 7 diagram uses UML style Package icons to denote MOF-based meta-models as well as UML models.
- The MOF Model is self-describing. In other words, the MOF Model is formally defined using its own meta-modelling constructs. Hence, the MOF Model is also denoted by a UML style Package icon.

The self-defining nature of the MOF Model has some important consequences:

- It helps to validate the MOF's meta-modelling constructs. Since the MOF Model can describe itself, it should be adequate for describing other meta-models of similar complexity.
- It allows the MOF's interfaces and behaviour to be defined by applying the MOF IDL mapping to the MOF Model. This provides uniformity of semantics between computational objects that represent models and meta-models. It also means that when a new technology mapping is defined, the APIs for managing meta-models in that context are implicitly defined as well.

4.1.2.5 Real-Time CORBA

Real-Time CORBA (RT-CORBA) is an optional set of extensions to CORBA tailored to equip ORBs [62], [71]. It defines standard features that support end-to-end predictability for operations in fixed-priority CORBA application.

The goals of the specification are to support developers in meeting Real-Time requirements by facilitating the end-to-end predictability of activities in the system and by providing support for the management of resources.

To provide specialist capabilities for specialist application without over constraining non Real-Time development, Real-time CORBA is positioned as a separate Extension to CORBA. The set of capabilities provided by Real-time CORBA constitutes an optional, additional compliance point.

Real-time CORBA is defined as extensions to CORBA 2.2 and the Messaging Service specification). It is necessary to look beyond CORBA 2.2 because the policy framework used in Real-Time CORBA is that from the Messaging Service. Secondly, deferred synchronous, asynchronous and one-way invocations are important tools in developing Real-Time systems.

In particular, RT-CORBA makes use of the features of GIOP/IIOP and the Messaging specification's QoS policy framework. CORBA 3.0 integrates all these features [63].

The RT-CORBA specification identifies capabilities for network interface (to application layer) and for peer-to-peer communications. These must be integrated and managed by ORB end-systems to ensure end-to-end predictable behaviour for activities (information and requests stream) that flow between CORBA clients and servers. These capabilities are listed below:

• Communication infrastructure resource manager
• OS scheduling mechanisms
• Real time ORB end-systems
• Real time services and applications

4.1.2.6   UML for Real-Time

UML (Unified Modelling Language) for Real-Time is not a part of CORBA [65]. But it is strongly connected to CORBA ideas and submits modelling basis for CORBA design.

UML for Real-Time is an extension to the UML 1.1 visual modelling language. UML 1.1 was submitted to the OMG for consideration and adopted in the fall of 1997.

UML for Real-Time has been specifically fine-tuned for the development of complex, event-driven, real-time systems, such as those found in telecommunications, aerospace, defence, and automatic control applications. Its modelling constructs (i.e., role models, capsules, ports, connectors, and state machines) have rigorous formal semantics that provide for model execution, and can be used to generate code for complete, mission critical, real-time applications.

There are unique challenges faced in real-time software development. Every real-time software developer recognises that the requirement for latency, throughput, reliability, and availability are far more stringent than for general purpose, or business software. For real-time system developers, understanding the impact of design decisions and effectively communicating functionality can be a daunting task. An overriding concern is the architecture of the software. This refers to the essential structural and behavioural framework on which all other aspects of the system depend.

To facilitate the design of good architectures, it is extremely useful to capture the proven architectural design patterns of the domain as first-class modelling constructs.

UML for Real-Time combines UML, role modelling, and ROOM concepts to deliver a complete solution for modelling complex real-time systems. UML, role modelling and ROOM are briefly described below.

UML is a general-purpose modelling language for specifying, visualizing, constructing and documenting the artefacts of software systems, as well as for business modelling and other non-software systems. UML has a strong set of general purpose modelling language concepts applicable across domains.

ROOM is a visual modelling language with formal semantics, developed by ObjecTime Limited. It is optimized for specifying, visualizing, documenting, and automating the construction of complex, event-driven, and potentially distributed real-time systems. It incorporates the role modelling concepts that enable the capture of architectural design patterns.

Role modelling captures the structural communication patterns between software components in UML 1.1 collaboration diagrams, which form the basis of structural design patterns, became first class modelling entities. ObjecTime was a member of the UML 1.1 definition team and contributed the role modelling capabilities of ROOM to the UML standard.

UML for Real-Time was co-developed by ObjecTime and Rational Corporation which combined UML 1.1 modelling concepts, and special modelling constructs and formalisms originally defined in the ROOM language and implemented in ObjecTime Developer.

ObjecTime Developer (see section 4.2.11) is a software automation tool that provides model execution capabilities, and automatically generates complete code for complex real-time applications from these modelling constructs. UML for Real-Time supports all of the automation capabilities that are available in ObjecTime Developer today.

This section introduces the important Capsule, Port, and Connector, stereotypes that have been introduced into UML for Real-Time to support the modelling of complex real-time systems. Figure 8 shows a UML for Real-Time collaboration diagram containing these three components.

Capsules correspond to the ROOM concept of actors. Capsules are complex, potentially concurrent, and possibly distributed active architectural components. They interact with their surroundings through one or more signal-based boundary objects called ports. Collaboration diagrams are used to describe the structural decomposition of a Capsule class.

Capsules export their interfaces to other capsules. The functionality of simple capsules is realized directly by finite state machines, whose transitions are triggered by the arrival of messages on the capsule's ports. Capsules themselves can be decomposed into internal networks of communicating sub-capsules. The state machine and network of hierarchically decomposed sub-capsules allow the structural and behavioural modelling of arbitrarily complex systems.

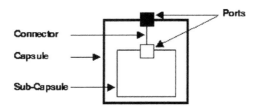

Fig. 8. A capsule collaboration diagram

A **port** is a physical part of the implementation of a capsule that mediates the interaction of the capsule with the outside world—it is an object that implements a specific interface.

Protocols are abstract interface specifications that are realised by ports. In a sense, a protocol captures the contractual obligations that exist between capsules. Ports provide a mechanism for a capsule to export multiple different interfaces; each tailored to a specific role. They also provide a mechanism to explicitly connect an exported interface of one capsule directly to the interface of another capsule.

By forcing capsules to communicate solely through ports, it is possible to fully de-couple their internal implementations from any direct knowledge they have about the environment. This de-coupling makes capsules as well as protocols highly reusable.

Connectors capture the key communication relationships between capsules. These relationships have architectural significance since they identify which capsules can affect each other through direct communication.

The functionality of simple capsules is realised directly by the state machine associated with the capsule. More complex capsules combine the state machine with an internal network of collaborating sub-capsules joined by connectors. These sub-capsules are capsules in their own right, and can themselves be decomposed into sub-capsules. This type of decomposition can be carried to whatever depth is necessary, allowing modelling of arbitrarily complex structures with just this basic set of structural modelling constructs. The state machine (which is optional for composite capsules), the sub-capsules, and their connections network represent parts of the implementation of the capsule, and are hidden from external observers.

4.1.2.7 CORBA and XML Integration

This paragraph provides a brief overview on what is happening in OMG with respect to a possible integration of two ways for data representation (XML and OMG IDL) [17]. "The OMG is integrating XML into the CORBA technical infrastructure, so that new XML-based applications will plug and play with current applications including C, C++, Java, COBOL, Ada as well as future new technologies" (Richard Soley, chairman of the OMG). XML Metadata Interchange Format (XMI) was adopted as a recommended technology by the OMG on March 23, 1999 [28].

XML is an open standard built by W3C standardisation body. It defines a common data format for document interchanges (mainly through the web). Documents are structured by means of tagged metadata (the well-known HTML is an example of such a tag set for describing documents structure).

A common language to be used by application developers for specifying, building, visualising and documenting distributed objects is needed. Standard object oriented model definition and design has to be integrated with XML to provide developers with a common infrastructure for object-oriented information (programming data) exchange. UML (Unified Modelling Language) was chosen to take the advantages of object-oriented data models.

The XML Metadata Interchange Format (XMI) specifies an open information interchange model that is intended to give developers working with object technology the ability to exchange programming data over the Internet in a standardised way, thus bringing consistency and compatibility to applications created in collaborative environments. By establishing an industry standard for storing and sharing object-programming information, development teams using various tools from multiple vendors can still collaborate on applications. The proposed standard will allow developers to leverage the web to exchange data between tools, applications, and repositories to create secure, distributed applications built in a team development environment.

XMI covers the transfer of UML models. It identifies standard XML DTDs to allow the exchange of UML. XMI will also enable the automatic generation of XML DTDs for each meta-information model.

Application areas involved in open interchange with XMI are:

- Design
- Development tools
- Repository
- Database schema
- Reports
- Software assets.

Each product developed for the above application area needs to add a XMI support to access all the other tools.

XMI acts as a bridge among applications. Suppose we have a general system to build, this system will be defined as a set of subsystems and objects. The definition of each object and relations among them is done using UML formalism (by means of a suitable tool). XMI provides XML DTD (Document Type Declaration) and XML document to represent such objects. Thus, if you can represent the system (or more generally a knowledge) using UML, you'll be able to transfer that information to an interested peer using XMI representation. The XML DTD needed to represent a specific UML model is automatically generated using rules defined by XMI. A XMI document may be viewed as an instantiation of a class model (represented by a XMI DTD) this instance will be exchanged among heterogeneous tools.

Beyond UML XMI can work with several formats like Java and C++ class definitions, and IDL.

XMI Companies and Products

IBM and Unisys lead the XMI standardisation effort and are joined by other key members of the software industry. In addition, IBM is incorporating XMI in several products and will have a formal announcement. Proof of concept demonstrations (below) has included WebSphere, VisualAge for Java, VisualAge TeamConnection Enterprise, DB/2, and the XML for Java parser from AlphaWorks.

The 29 submitting and supporting companies are: (submitters) International Business Machines Corporation, Unisys Corporation, Cooperative Research Centre for Distributed Systems Technology (DSTC), Oracle Corporation, Platinum Technologies, Inc., Fujitsu, Softeam, Recerca Informatica, Daimler-Benz, and (supporters) Cayenne Software, Genesis Development, Inline Software, Rational Software, Select Software, Sprint Communications Company, Sybase, Inc., Xerox, MCI Systemhouse, Boeing, Ardent, Aviatis, ICONIX, Integrated Systems, Verilog, Telefonica I+D, Universitat Politecnica de Catalunya, NCR, Nihon Unisys, NTT.

XMI Proof of Concept
Nine products from five vendors were demonstrated working together using XMI technology at the OMG meeting in November 1998, just three weeks after the final XMI specification was made available. The demonstration showed a round trip exchange, starting from a UML design of an electronic commerce application in Rational Rose, converted into an XMI document, stored as components in IBM's TeamConnection running on a DB2 database, then imported into VisualAge for Java and also into WebSphere Enterprise Component Broker, all using IBM's XML for Java parser. Select imported the same XMI document into Select Enterprise, modified the XMI document, and passed the file to Unisys which read, modified and wrote the XMI using Universal Repository. The modifications were shown in Rational Rose. The process was repeated in Oracle Designer and the updated XMI was sent back to IBM which showed the final XMI contents in Java XML software available from the AlphaWorks site. All this interchange resulted in very long round trip. These cross-product, cross-vendor demonstrations underscore the commitment of the submitting companies to XMI, as well as the practical value of XMI in delivering open solutions to real customer problems.

4.1.3 Web-Based Technologies

A great deal of software applications development is moving toward "universal solutions" based on Internet standards. The enabling technologies involved include HTTP and HTML/DHTML, JavaScript, Common Gateway Interface (CGI), Java and Java Beans, ActiveX, CORBA/DCOM.

A navigator communicates with a Web server using HTTP, a data transfer protocol. HTTP is a connectionless protocol and the Web server is thus unable to manage sessions.

The evolution of HTML and HTTP basically concerns:
- the client program (e.g. the web-browser) by improving the interactivity of Web pages thanks to DHTML concepts and Java applets (including for example presentation and pre-treatment features)
- the treatment of HTTP requests on the server using CGI scripts, ASP, JSP servlets, etc.

4.1.3.1 Dynamic HTML

Dynamic HTML (DHTML) is the name given by both Netscape and Microsoft to the use of the Document Object Model (DOM), Cascading Style Sheets, and client-side scripting to make Web pages more interactive (http://www.w3.org). By using these technologies, developers can make their Web pages change on-the-fly and interact with users without having to reload.

The World Wide Web Consortium (W3C) is currently reviewing proposals related to the standardisation of the Document Object Model. On the other hand, both CSS and JavaScript have achieved W3C Recommendation and European Computer Manufacturer Association (ECMA) Standard status, respectively.

The Document Object Model defines the properties and methods for the various elements on an HTML page. There is a W3C's standardisation activity, but the models currently supported by Netscape and Internet Explorer are not the same, Internet Explorer model being somewhat more sophisticated.

By modifying the properties of HTML elements on a page via client-side scripting, using JavaScript for example, you can make your page interactive. Just as it is possible to modify the properties of individual HTML elements using scripting and the DOM, you can also change the appearance of elements using Cascading Style Sheets. For example, by modifying an HTML element's style settings it is easy to make it appear and disappear on command.

4.1.3.2 JavaScript

It is a language developed by Netscape and standardised by the European Computer Manufacturers Association (ECMA) (http://java.sun.com). The language can be defined by the three following parts:

- Core language, a core set of objects, operators, control structures and statements
- Client-side extensions objects to control a browser as well as a Document Object Model
- Server-side extensions: objects to e.g. access a database, provide continuity across invocations, and manipulate server files.

JavaScript programs are in particular used for providing animations, dynamically create and modify windows and documents or form validity checks.

4.1.3.3 Java Applets

Java applets are special Java programs located at server's side (http://java.sun.com). There are downloaded by the navigator with built-in a Java Virtual Machine (JVM) for executing the corresponding bytecode. The JVM class loader is in charge of retrieving all classes necessary to the execution of the applet. This necessitates a Java plugging in the navigator.

Each class of the applet is downloaded through several requests to the server (HTTP being connectionless). This can lead to performance problems when applets are not carefully designed.

4.1.3.4 Common Gateway Interface

The Common Gateway Interface (CGI) is a standard (standardised by NCSA) for interfacing external applications with information servers, such as HTTP or Web servers. It defines how a server-activated program receives information from the server: a plain HTML document that the Web daemon retrieves is static, which means it exists in a constant state: a text file that doesn't change. A CGI program, on the other hand, is executed in real-time, so that it can output dynamic information.

The server must be configured to activate a CGI program for certain URLs.

The simplest example of CGI use, is the possibility of processing queries on database management systems and of providing their results to the client browser.

Many people prefer to write CGI scripts instead of programs, since they are easier to debug, modify, and maintain than a typical compiled program. Most current languages used are Perl and Tcl or any UNIX shell.

With CGI, each script is run as an executable in its own process. As a result, each time a script is requested the server must create new process, run the script, kill the (just created) process. This is inefficient and can severely impact the performance of the Web server. In comparison, ASP or JSP implementations are not re-launched with every script access and is therefore much more efficient.

4.1.3.5 Active Server Pages

Active Server Pages (ASP) are a language-independent framework designed by Microsoft for efficient coding of server-side scripts that are designed to be executed by a Web server in response to a user's request for a URL (http://msdn.microsoft.com/net/aspnet/default.asp). ASP scripts are similar to other server-side scripting like Perl. ASP are developed and maintained by Microsoft and are not approved by any standard organisation.

Active Server Pages are currently available mainly only for Microsoft Internet Information Server (IIS) or WebSite professional from O'Reilly Software. Chili Soft ASP products allow to run ASP for Web servers on Unix platforms, like Apache or Netscape's iPlanet, including Solaris, HP-UX, AIX, Linux.

As said, ASP (and JSP) overcomes performance and load problems of classical CGI solutions. Additionally, ASP is designed to rely heavily on Microsoft COM components for its extensibility. As a result, it is very easy to use any COM component from within an ASP script.

ASP provides built-in session management functionality that allows developers to persist data and also COM component instances (like database connections) for the duration of a session. It keeps track of data between page accesses by a user.

Active Server Pages are actually an ActiveX Scripting Host and, therefore, can use any compatible ActiveX Scripting Engine. Scripting engines for VBScript and JScript (Microsoft's JavaScript variant) come pre-configured with ASP when installed as part of Microsoft's Internet Information Server.

4.1.3.6 Java Server Pages (JSP) and Servlets

ASP and JSP deliver similar functionality (http://java.sun.com). They both use component objects, tags to allow embedded code in an HTML page, session tracking, and database interaction. ASP uses ActiveX components, while JSP uses JavaBeans as the component architecture.

ASP is mostly putting into practice through Microsoft's Visual Interdev tools, gaining from a polished and approachable GUI. JSP developments are mainly done using Sun development tools (Figure 9).

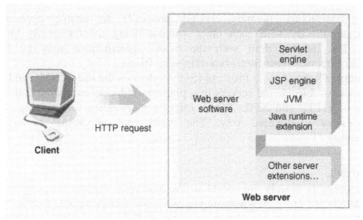

Fig. 9. Request to JSP

The source code of a JSP page is essentially just HTML (or text—or even XML) sprinkled here and there with either special JSP tags and/or Java code enclosed in these tags. JSP define new tags usable directly in HTML pages. They are analysed by a JSP engine.

Servlets are extensions of the Web server and provide a Java Interface and implementation: unlike CGI applications, the servlet code stays resident in memory when a request terminates. A servlet can also connect to a database when initialised and then retain its connection across requests. These features make servlets a good workaround for many CGI limitations.

The file's extension of JSP pages is *.jsp rather than the usual *.html or *.htm, and it tells the server that this document requires special handling. The special handling, accomplished with a Web server extension or plug-in, involves four steps:

- The JSP engine parses the page and creates a Java source file.
- It then compiles the file produced in Step 1 into a Java class file. The class file created in Step 2 is a servlet, and from this point on, the servlet engine handles the class file in the same manner as all other servlets.
- The servlet engine loads the servlet class for execution.
- The servlet executes and streams back the results to the requestor.

If the developer happens to modify the JSP, the servlet will be re-generated and compiled. Some JSP engines are able to interpret directly some JSPs.

Newest versions of Web servers all support servlet mechanisms either natively or through dedicated extensions. As developer kit, one can cite TOMCAT Web server.

JavaBeans are Java's answer to Microsoft's ActiveX components. A JavaBeans is the architecture for using and building components in Java. JavaBeans are a public available API for reusable Java-based components provided by Sun but have never been approved by an independent standard body. A bean can be either a visual object (for example, you can change the properties of a component by changing a radio button or similar object) or a non-visual object.

4.1.3.7 Simple Object Access Protocol
The Simple Object Access Protocol (SOAP) is the part of Microsoft DNA (Distributed interNet Applications) 2000 project. It is an attempt to use the existing

Internet infrastructure (namely, HTTP protocol) to enable applications to communicate directly with each other without being unintentionally blocked by firewalls. The internet draft with the SOAP specification may be found on www.ietf.org/internet-drafts/draft-box-http-soap-01.txt.

The Simple Object Access Protocol (SOAP) defines the use of XML and HTTP to access services, objects, and servers in a platform-independent manner. If developer can agree on HTTP and XML, SOAP offers a mechanism for bridging competing technologies in a standard way. The main goal of SOAP is to facilitate interoperability.

SOAP and RPC

This technology is closely connected to the Microsoft remote scripting technology (see details on www.msdn.microsoft.com/scripting/default.htm?/scripting/remotescripting/) and realize the point-to-point WEB-application interaction. The peculiarity of SOAP technology lies in the XML-manner description of the calling procedure (URL and name) and the list of its variables.

Dave Winer, Microsoft and DevelopMentor drafted the original SOAP specification in spring of 1998. Soon after, Dave established his XML-RPC web site (www.xmlrpc.com) to support the effort. The XML-RPC specification that is on that site is quite similar to the original SOAP specification. The current SOAP specification is (a) more HTTP-focused and (b) more terse XML than the original specification.

SOAP and XML

The XML specification (www.w3.org/XML/) mandates that all XML processors must accept character data encoded using the UCS Transformation Formats UTF-8 or UTF-16. Therefore, any XML data stream encoded in UTF-8 or UTF-16 can be understood regardless of platform or programming language. (Note that since the first 256 character codes of UTF-8 match up with ASCII, an UTF-8-capable processor can understand straight ASCII text files).

This makes XML a good choice for describing method invocations in a platform and language-neutral fashion.

The utilization of the concept of XML scheme and XML URI mechanism provide the supporting of different specific frameworks. BizTalk server project may be considered as an example of such XML standardization activity.

SOAP and Interoperability

Combining HTTP and XML into a single solution gives you a whole new level of interoperability. For example, lathered with SOAP, clients written in Microsoft Visual Basic can easily invoke CORBA services running on UNIX boxes, JavaScript clients can easily invoke code running on the mainframe, and Macintosh clients can start invoking Perl objects running on Linux.

The SOAP client parts for VBScript (Microsoft W95, W98 and NT) are realized as special ActiveX "Microsoft.XMLHTTP" installed simultaneously with XML parser (ActiveX "Microsoft.XMLDOM").

As to other computing environment one can download:

- SOAP/Perl 0.23 bits for UNIX from http://soapl.develop.com/SOAP-0.23.tar.gz ;
- SOAP/Perl 0.23 bits for Win32 from http://soapl.develop.com/SOAP-0.23.zip
- SOAP/Java 0.3 bits for UNIX/Win32 from http://www.develop.com/soap/soap.jar.

SOAP and Firewalls
Since SOAP relies on HTTP as the transport mechanism, and most firewalls allow HTTP to pass through, you'll have no problem invoking SOAP endpoints from either side of a firewall. Don't forget that SOAP makes it possible for system administrators to configure firewalls to selectively block out SOAP requests using SOAP-specific HTTP headers.

SOAP and Predecessors
In the following table (Table 1) we present the preliminary results of comparing XML-SOAP tandem with such venerable age predecessors as CORBA and Enterprise JavaBeans and much younger Microsoft DCOM. By presenting the table we realize that comparing SOAP and these products are now the same as comparing VBScript+Active Server Pages and C++ but nevertheless...

Table 1. Comparison between SOAP and CORBA, EJB, DCOM

Criteria	XML-SOAP	CORBA, EJB, DCOM
Complexity and demand for qualified programmers to develop	Seems to be rather simple for anybody familiar with VBScript, Java Script and ASP, CGI	Demand hi-level professionals skilled in CORBA architecture, C++, Java
Perfect architecture and object model	Only those from XML and almost nothing from SOAP	Hi-level standard of object modelling and programming
Firewalls transparency	Good because of being based on HTTP protocol	May be some problems
XML as standard	Inherent feature	Becoming the part of OMG Meta Object Framing as XMI meta-data model.

4.1.3.8 SyncML

Synchronization Markup Language Protocol (SyncML) is a new industry initiative to develop and promote a single, common data synchronization protocol that can be used industry-wide. Driving the initiative are IBM, Lotus, Motorola, Ericsson, 3Com, Nokia, Palm Inc., Psion, Starfish Software. Additional companies are being recruited to join and participate (http://www.syncml.org/index.php3).

A data synchronization protocol defines the workflow for communication during a data synchronization session when the mobile device is not permanently connected to the network. The protocol must support naming and identification of records, common protocol commands to synchronize local and network data, and it can support identification and resolution of synchronization conflicts.

Being only the initiative may be useful in future for Distributed System Engineering in simulation framework containing remote equipment (sensors, test bench) not permanently connected to the net.

The new standard will support various transport protocols and media:

- HTTP (i.e. the Internet)
- WSP (the Wireless Session Protocol, part of the WAP protocol suite)
- OBEX (i.e. Bluetooth, IrDA, and other local connectivity)

It can also be deployed over:

- SMTP, POP3, and IMAP
- Pure TCP/IP networks
- Proprietary wireless communication protocols.

The following data presentation will be supported:

- Relational data
- XML (the Extensible Markup Language) and HTML documents
- Binary data, binary large objects, or "blobs"

4.1.3.9 HTTPS

One of the problems arising in Distributed System Engineering infrastructure is to provide secure data exchange. In this section we discuss the practice of ciphered plain-text-data (e.g., HTML and/or XML document) transmission (http://www. netscape.com/eng/ssl3/; http://www.symbiandevnet.com/techlib/tech-comms/tech-papers/papers/v6/over/gt2 index.html).

There exists Secure HTTP (HTTPS), that uses the Secure Socket Layer (SSL) protocol on port 443 by default. HTTPS encrypts all traffic, so you can be confident that your content will not be intelligible to anyone snooping Internet packets. In fact, even the HTTP headers and all images will be encrypted.

HTTPS is based on Public Key PGP scheme (Figure 10).

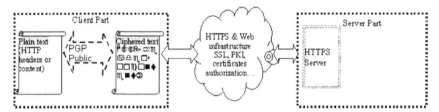

Fig. 10. HTTPS data transmission scheme

HTTPS uses public-key encryption just long enough to exchange keys, and then it switches to private-key encryption for better performance. See PGP: Pretty Good Privacy, by Simson Garfinkel (O'Reilly & Associates), for more information on public versus private key encryption. HTTPS has a significant performance penalty associated with it that can be as high as tenfold for small transmissions. The problem is the exchange of certificates at the beginning of the secure connection rather than the overhead of encrypting and decrypting the data sent across the wire. In fact, I ran some load tests using 40-bit data encryption versus 128-bit data encryption and found no difference at all.

If your site makes use of SSL, you should seriously consider using a cryptographic accelerator card. This is a board that plugs into your server and does the 1024-bit key pair generation for SSL connection setup in hardware. The two dominant cards seem to be nCipher (http://www.ncipher.com/) and Rainbow (http://www.rainbow.com/).

Digital Certificates

One issue with public key crypto-systems is that users must be constantly vigilant to ensure that they are encrypting to the correct person's key. In an environment where it is safe to freely exchange keys via public servers, man-in-the-middle attacks are a potential threat. In this type of attack, some "hacker" can declare himself as a server, offering you his public key to encrypt your private data.

In a public key environment, it is vital that you are assured that the public key to which you are encrypting data is in fact the public key of the intended recipient and not a forgery. Digital certificates, or certs, simplify the task of establishing whether a public key truly belongs to the purported owner.

A digital certificate consists of three things:

* a public key,
* certificate information. ("Identity" information about the user, such as name, user ID, and so on.),
* one or more digital signatures.

The purpose of the digital signature on a certificate is to state that some other person or entity has attested to the certificate information. The digital signature does not attest to the authenticity of the certificate as a whole; it vouches only that the signed identity information goes along with, or is bound to, the public key.

Thus, a certificate is basically a public key with one or two forms of ID attached, plus a hearty stamp of approval from some other trusted individual.

Certificate Distribution

Certificates are utilized when it's necessary to exchange public keys with someone else. As to HTTPS technology public key is sent from server to client, it is necessary to put systems into place that can provide the necessary security, storage, and exchange mechanisms.

These can come in the form of storage-only repositories called Certificate Servers, or more structured systems that provide additional key management features and are called Public Key Infrastructures (PKIs).

Certificate Servers

A certificate server, also called a cert server or a key server, is a database that allows users to submit and retrieve digital certificates. A cert server usually provides some administrative features that enable a company to maintain its security policies—for example, allowing only those keys that meet certain requirements to be stored.

Public Key Infrastructures

A PKI contains the certificate storage facilities of a certificate server, but also provides certificate management facilities (the ability to issue, revoke, store, retrieve, and trust certificates). The main feature of a PKI is the introduction of what is known as a Certification Authority, or CA, which is a human entity—a person, group, department, company, or other association—that an organization has authorized to issue certificates to its computer users. (CA's role is analogous to a country's government's Passport Office.) A CA creates certificates and digitally signs them using the CA's private key. Because of its role in creating certificates, the CA is the central component of a PKI. Using the CA's public key, anyone wanting to verify a certificate's authenticity verifies the issuing CA's digital signature, and hence, the integrity of the contents of the certificate (most importantly, the public key and the identity of the certificate holder).

Certificate Formats
A digital certificate is basically a collection of identifying information bound together with a public key and signed by a trusted third party to prove its authenticity. A digital certificate can be one of a number of different formats.

Pretty Good Privacy (PGP) recognizes two different certificate formats:
• PGP certificates
• X.509 certificates.
The main difference between the two formats is that PGP certificate can contain multiple signatures. Several or many organization may sign the key/identification pair to attest to their own assurance that the public key definitely belongs to the specified owner. X.509 format states only one signature and, consequently, requires hierarchically PKI structure.

X.509 certificates today are most widely used in web browsers. For example on the following Figure 11 you can see an example of certificates attached to HTTPS connection with www.e-vis.com web site. (More information about e-vis.com as Product Data Management (PDM) environment see in 5.1.3.5)

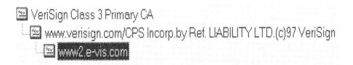

Fig. 11. Example of hierarchically X.509 certificates

Some Details of X.509 Certificate Format
All X.509 certificates comply with the ITU-T X.509 international standard; thus (theoretically) any application complying with X.509 can use X.509 certificates created for one application. In practice, however, different companies have created their own extensions to X.509 certificates, not all of them which work together.

There are many differences between an X.509 certificate and a PGP certificate, but the most salient are as follows:
• you can create your own PGP certificate; you must request and be issued an X.509 certificate from a Certification Authority
• X.509 certificates natively support only a single name for the key's owner
• X.509 certificates support only a single digital signature to attest to the key's validity
To obtain an X.509 certificate, you must ask a CA to issue you a certificate. You provide your public key; proof that you possess the corresponding private key; and

some specific information about yourself. You then digitally sign the information and send the whole package—the certificate request—to the CA. The CA then performs some due diligence in verifying that the information you provided is correct, and if so, generates the certificate and returns it. You might think of an X.509 certificate as looking like a standard paper certificate (similar to one you might have received for completing a class in basic First Aid) with a public key taped to it. It has your name and some information about you on it, plus the signature of the person who issued it to you.

4.2 Products

4.2.1 Defense Modelling and Simulation Office (DMSO) RTI 1.3

General Description
The DMSO RTI 1.3 is an implementation of the HLA Interface Specification 1.3 [33] (http://sdc.dmso.mil). First version of this product was released in 1998 and since that time six further versions were also released. Latest (and last) version of the DMSO RTI 1.3 is 7. This Run-Time Infrastructure (RTI) is a first complete implementation of the HLA Interface Specification. It is widely used by simulation community and still serves as a reference for other RTI implementations.

RTI software is currently comprised of the RTI Executive process (RtiExec), the Federation Executive process (FedExec) and the libRTI library, which also serves as a Local RTI Component (LRC). Each executable containing federates incorporates libRTI. Federates may exist as independent processes or be grouped into one or more processes. A federate may participate in more than one federation.

RTI software can be executed on a standalone workstation or executed over an arbitrarily complex network. The RtiExec process manages the creation and destruction of Federation executions. A single, global FedExec characterizes each Federation executing. The FedExec manages federates joining and resigning the Federation. The libRTI library extends RTI services to federate developers. Services are accomplished through encapsulated communications between libRTI, RtiExec, and the appropriate FedExec.

- RtiExec

RtiExec is a global process. Each federate communicates with RtiExec to initialize RTI components. The RtiExec's primary purpose is to manage the creation and destruction of FedExecs. An RtiExec supplies federates with data necessary to find and join appropriate Federation execution. RtiExec ensures that each FedExec has a unique name.

- FedExec

Each FedExec manages a Federation. It allows federates to join and to resign, and facilitates data exchange between participating federates. A FedExec process is created by the first federate to successfully invoke the "Create Federation Execution" service for a given Federation Execution name. Each federate joining the Federation is assigned a unique handle.

- libRTI

The C++ library, libRTI, provides the services specified in the HLA Interface Specification to federate developers. Federates use libRTI which communicates with the RtiExec, a FedExec, and other federates to invoke HLA services.

The HLA Interface Specification identifies services libRTI provides to federates and obligations each federate bears to the Federation. Within libRTI, the class RTIambassador bundles the services provided by the RTI. All requests made by a federate on the RTI take the form of an RTIambassador method call. The abstract class FederateAmbassador identifies the callback functions each federate is obliged to provide.

Available Functionality
The DMSO RTI 1.3 implements the following services:
• Federation management
Federation management includes such tasks as creating federations, joining federates to federations, observing federation-wide synchronization points, effecting federation-wide saves and restores, resigning federates from federations, and destroying federations.
• Declaration management
Declaration management includes publication, subscription, and supporting control functions. Federates that produce objects (or object parts) or that produce interactions must declare exactly what they are able to publish (i.e., generate).
• Object management
Object management includes instance registration and instance updates on the object production side and instance discovery and reflection on the object consumer side. Object management also includes methods associated with sending and receiving interactions, controlling instance updates based on consumer demand, and other miscellaneous support functions.
• Ownership management
The RTI allows federates to share the responsibility for updating and deleting object instances with a few restrictions. It is possible for an object instance to be wholly owned by a single federate. In such cases, the owning federate has responsibility for updating all attributes associated with the object and for deleting the object instance. It is possible for two or more federates to share update responsibility for a single object instance. When update responsibility for an object is shared, each of the participating federates has responsibility for a mutually exclusive set of object attributes. Only one federate can have update responsibility for an individual attribute of an individual object at any given time. In addition, only one federate has the privilege to delete an object instance at any given time.
• Time management
The focus of time management is on the mechanics required to implement time management policies and negotiate time advances.
• Data Distribution management
Data distribution management provides a flexible and extensive mechanism for further isolating publication and subscription interests – effectively extending the sophistication of the RTI's switching capabilities.

Type of Applications
- Distributed interactive simulation;
- Command and control systems.

Future Evolutions
The Defense Modelling and Simulation Office (DMSO) is transitioning support from the RTI 1.3 implementation to the newer RTI-NG (Next Generation) implementation. It was announced that all RTI 1.3 distributions should be removed from DMSO Software Distribution Centre. The removal of the older distributions will help prevent new users from starting work with software scheduled for retirement.

The DMSO RTI Help Facility is available to assist the migration of federates and federations to the RTI-NG implementation and for will remain available to answer questions on 1.3. RTI 1.3v6 and RTI 1.3v7. Users are advised that there is no plan for a general release of any additional upgrades or patches to the RTI 1.3v7 implementation. The DMSO RTI Help Facility will continue to be available to assist in determining if a perceived problem is RTI-related or is federate code manifested.

Reliability
Latest version (7) of the DMSO RTI1.3 is considered as stable software. Only minor software problems are discovered and reported to date.

Maintainability and Support
The RTI software is easy to install. However, modification of RTI Initialization Data (RID) file requires deep knowledge of RTI parameters and their cross-dependencies. Comprehensive support of the RTI users is available free of charge from DMSO RTI Help Desk.

The RTI 1.3 is well documented. Training courses are provided by DMSO as well as by commercial organisations.

Availability of Localised Versions
Not available and not planned for implementation.

Impact of Utilisation
If the RTI is used, DSE middleware shall be based on the HLA principles and all the applications, which utilise it, shall meet the HLA rules.

Platform
It is available on Windows NT, Linux, and major UNIX platforms including Solaris and IRIX.

Price
Freely distributed product.

4.2.2 Defense Modelling and Simulation Office (DMSO) RTI 1.3-NG

General Description
The DMSO RTI 1.3-NG is another implementation of the HLA Interface Specification 1.3 [34] (http://sdc.dmso.mil). First version of this product was released in 1999 and since that time a newer version 2 was also released. The RTI 1.3-Next Generation (NG) release represents a "from scratch" implementation that builds upon the lessons learned from its predecessors. Architecture and components of the RTI 1.3-NG are identical to RTI 1.3 (described above). However, in contrast with RTI 1.3, this RTI implementation utilises IIOP.

Available Functionality
The DMSO RTI 1.3-NG implements the same services as DMSO RTI 1.3.

Type of Applications
- Distributed interactive simulation;
- Command and control systems.

Future Evolutions
DMSO will support this RTI implementation and further versions will be provided in year 2000.

Reliability
Latest version (2) of the DMSO RTI1.3-NG is considered as stable software. However, some software problems are discovered and information about them is available from DMSO RTI Help Desk.

Maintainability and Support
The RTI software is easy to install. However, modification of RTI Initialization Data (RID) file requires deep knowledge of RTI parameters and their cross-dependencies. This file format is even more complex than one used in RTI 1.3. Comprehensive support of the RTI users is available free of charge from DMSO RTI Help Desk.
    The RTI 1.3-NG is well documented. Training courses are provided by DMSO as well as by commercial organisations.

Availability of Localised Versions
Not available.

Impact of Utilisation
If the RTI is used, DSE middleware shall be based on the HLA principles and all the applications, which utilise it, shall meet the HLA rules.

Platform
It is available on Windows NT, Linux, and major UNIX platforms including Solaris and IRIX. Also, VxWorks real-time OS is supported.

Price
Freely distributed product.

4.2.3 OSimFramework

General Description
OSimFramework is a product of OriginalSim, Inc.

OSimFramework is an extensible integrated environment for the rapid development and deployment of HLA compliant simulation components. It standardises and automates the simulation development process and supports the entire simulation development life cycle, from proof of concept to final application. The OSimFramework object oriented development environment reduces the amount of hard coding required to develop applications or to integrate legacy components.

OSimFramework achieves HLA compliance by:

• Automatically generating an Object Model Template (OMT) DIF file.

• Creating classes for the interface to the DMSO-sponsored Runtime Infrastructure (RTI), version 1.3 and 1.03, in accordance with the HLA Compliance Checklist and RTI Interface specification.

The OSim collaborative simulation development environment provides an integrated model-view-controller framework that automatically generates JAVA code, automatically generates C++ simulations, and automatically generates HLA compliant federates.

OSim effectively facilitates the development of interoperable simulations and reusable simulation components.

Available Functionality
The OsimFramework is composed of several components, which provide different functions and cover several HLA FEDEP phases:

• OSim Builder GUI

The Builder GUI is the primary user interface for OSim and is designed to support a collaborative spiral development process. Within the Builder GUI, analysts, domain experts, and programmers can work together to define the simulation application by defining its object oriented structure, class relationships, attributes, and detailed functionality. The Builder also allows the user to document the code blocks and create on-line help automatically.

The OSim Builder GUI also allows object models and class libraries built using HLA Object Model Development Tools (OMDT) or object oriented CASE tools such as Rational Rose to be imported to create OSim class libraries.

The component supports the following HLA Federation Development and Execution Process (FEDEP) phases:

• Conceptual Analysis
• Federation Design

- Federation Development
- OSim BulletinBoard

The OSim BulletinBoard is the internal distributed object communication facility provided for OSim development and application deployment. The BulletinBoard uses an object-proxy scheme to allow external processes to communicate with a local replica of the simulation object by publishing and subscribing for information.

Because external processes only communicate with simulation objects through their proxies, the process does not care where the data comes from or to where it is being sent. This design supports advanced capabilities such as object attribute ownership transfer between simulation models, distribution of simulation models on multiple computers, and resource balancing during runtime execution.

- Allows objects to post and subscribe for data
- create proxies to allow external processes to communicate with local replica of simulation object created by OSim
- multicast data to subscribers

The component supports the following HLA FEDEP phases:

- Federation Development
- OSim Generator

Customisable code generator using the application description specified through the OSim Builder GUI.

The OSim Generator is the extensible multi-code generation facility within OSim that takes the class library description and automatically generates the complete C++ code for the simulation application. The generated C++ code incorporates the classes and code for the distributed execution engine as well as the distributed object communication.

The automatically generated application is ready to run, by itself, without OSim, in a real-time distributed environment.

In addition to C++ code, OSim automatically generates both X/Motif and JAVA code so those local and remote users can initialise and interact with the simulation using JAVA applets and WWW resources. OSim automatically inserts the comments in the generated code to create fully documented code. OSim creates a documented class library in HTML.

To support HLA, OSim automatically generates classes that interface the federate to the run-time infrastructure, and it generates a simulation object model (SOM) for the federate in the DIF format.

Functionality:

- Generation of C++, JAVA, HTML, SOM and .h files corresponding to the application
- Generation of HLA-specific classes
- Insertion of Comments
- Generation of InstanceEditor Windows
- Generation of Executor and BulletinBoard

The component supports the following HLA FEDEP phases:

- Federation Development
- OSim Executor

The OSim Executor is the hybrid time/event based distributed execution engine built into the OSim Framework. The existing executor is optimised for real-time man-in-the-loop types of simulation applications.

The Executor takes the information contained in the class library description defined in the OSim Builder, including function execution rates and execution constraints and automatically creates the frame-based execution table.

- Generated from execution constraints defined by developer
- Produced by C++ code generator
- Extensive use of Dynamic Shared Objects

Type of Applications
Distributed simulation systems

Impact of Utilisation
It is highly integrated package. All component tools use uniform GUI of OSim Builder. Use of a separate tool from package is impossible.

HLA interface is only one of many functionality of OSimFramework. This package is 7adapted to HLA simulation applications generation and does not strongly follows FEDEP guidelines.

Platform
Versions for several major platforms (NT and UNIX) are available.

4.2.4 IONA Technologies: Orbix 3.0 Family

General Description
This paragraph intends to give a summary information about one of the existing CORBA architecture implementation. The overview will be supported both by information taken by Iona company itself and by lesson learnt in using IONA products (Orbix 2) during past projects.

Components of Orbix3.0 family are Orbix and OrbixWeb, Orbix Object Transaction Monitor, Orbix for OS/390 and OrbixTalk.

Orbix and OrbixWeb are C++ and Java-based CORBA application development and deployment products. Orbix comprises all the CORBA functionality, as well as Microsoft COM integration, naming services, and firewall traversal functionality. Orbix Object Transaction Monitor (OTM) offers the flexibility of a CORBA ORB along with the integrity of Transactions. The Orbix OTM comprises system management, naming, messaging, security and transactions. Orbix for OS/390 is a full integration with the IBM mainframe. Orbix for OS/390 supports COBOL and PL/1 languages, and has adapters for IMS and CICS transaction systems. Our Messaging products extend the base communication of the ORB to allow asynchronous messaging. OrbixTalk, Events and Notification bring enterprise strength messaging functionality to the CORBA environment.

Available Functionality

- COM-CORBA Integration with COMet

OrbixCOMet Desktop is an exciting development in Making Software Work Together™. It combines the best of CORBA and DCOM, giving developers the ability to build systems using both COM and CORBA components. This high performance bi-directional dynamic bridge enables DCOM applications, written using tools such as Visual Basic, PowerBuilder, Delphi, MS Office or Active Server Pages, to access CORBA applications running on Windows, Unix, and MVS.

IONA Technologies and Microsoft have entered into a technology agreement under which Microsoft provides IONA with the source code for the Microsoft DCOM product. This consolidates their leading position in the market place in providing bridging solutions between CORBA and DCOM.

- Location Transparency and Load Balancing with OrbixNames

OrbixNames is IONA's implementation of the CORBA Naming Service. The role of this service is critical in large scale distributed applications. It acts as a central repository of objects which clients use to locate server applications. A CORBA server that holds an object reference can register it with OrbixNames, giving it a fixed name that can be used by any client to subsequently find that object. If the server is moved, it can associate its new object reference using the same fixed name, providing location transparency to the client.

OrbixNames extends the CORBA naming model, providing load balancing of servers through replication. Developers can chose from a variety of server side selection algorithms to optimize the performance of their system in deployment.

- Rapid Application Development with the Orbix Code Generation Toolkit

Orbix's code generation toolkit is a powerful addition to any CORBA programmer's tool kit. Ready-to-run scripts called Genies aid in the development of Orbix and OrbixWeb applications. This Rapid Application Development (RAD) tool dramatically reduces development time by automating many repetitive coding tasks. IONA's Genies are easy to extend and customize to suit the exact requirements of your task. Alternatively, you can write your own Genie that can be used with IONA's Code Generation Tool. Using this tool you can autogenerate gateways to COTS (commercial off-the-shelf) applications, create demos quickly or easily modify your existing CORBA applications.

- Built-in Internet Security with Orbix Wonderwall

Orbix Wonderwall, IONA's industry-leading IIOP firewall technology, can provide the protection required for Internet CORBA systems. Wonderwall filters IIOP messages to provide fine-grained access control for back-end objects and also provides transparent traversal on the client side. Wonderwall features a powerful logging facility for tracing the history of suspicious message exchanges. Orbix Wonderwall is the IIOP proxy technology of choice for many leading software companies, including Application Server vendors such as Netscape Communications Corporation and Internet Firewall vendors such as Raptor and Secure Computing.

Orbix and OrbixWeb support callbacks using bi-directional IIOP and both ORBS integrate with OrbixSSL which provides authentication, privacy and integrity for IIOP traffic on the Internet.

- OrbixOTM

OrbixOTM is an application container, which is the basis of IONA's enterprise product range. Object Transaction Monitor (OTM) 3 combines the functionality of

Orbix3, the leading implementation of the CORBA standard with an integrated suite of services: management, security, naming, messaging, fault tolerance, load balancing and distributed transactions.

This combination, in conjunction with the Orbix family of products, forms an unparalleled set of component services, enabling OrbixOTM to work not only as an enterprise application server, but also as the basis for web-commerce solutions; a backbone for the desktop; or as a gateway to the mainframe. OrbixOTM's adherence to CORBA standards protects today's software investment for the future; applications are coded to an open, standardized set of service interfaces rather than to vendor-specific models.

OrbixOTM 3 now has extended Java and Internet supports. OrbixOTM is built to be flexible. Although the base container has a full set of enterprise services, extra functionality may be required for specific needs. The following products were designed with this in mind; they all plug straight into the OrbixOTM system.

• Advanced Security with OrbixSecurity

A full implementation of the CORBA security service (Level 1), OrbixSecurity provides developers with the ability to add a comprehensive, enterprise strength infrastructure to Object Transaction Monitor (OTM) systems. With OrbixSecurity, an OTM system can be enhanced to support the five prime security features: encryption, authentication, authorization (object level), delegation and auditing/logging.

• Advanced Resource Location with OrbixTrader

OrbixTrader allows the client to 'browse' service applications and choose the most appropriate server. Examples of such scenarios include telecommunication networks or Internet commerce applications with dynamic service provision. OrbixTrader is an implementation of the CORBA Trader service.

Type of Applications
The Orbix 3.0 product family offers standards-based integration of software from desktop to server, mainframe to web browser.

Impact of Utilisation
Orbix enables an organization's software development team to eliminate or reduce the time spent on solving integration issues that are created by the organization's variety of hardware platforms, network protocols, application tools, programming languages, operating system or compiler versions. By using Orbix to eliminate these issues, the development team can focus its energies on providing the business logic so vital for successful information systems.

Platform
Solaris, HP-UX, Windows NT, Windows 95/98.

4.2.5 IONA iPortal Suite

General Description
The IONA iPortal Suite supports the creation, integration, and management of enterprise portals, orchestrating the content, interactions, transactions, and functions

drawn from many sources to service portal users over time. In this, IONA iPortal Suite provides the access, delivery, linkage, integration, services, and personalization enterprise portals require. The IONA iPortal Suite includes four products (see Figure 12):

- IONA iPortal Application Server, a server for the application logic required by enterprise portals, which supports Sun's Enterprise Java Beans and Java2 Enterprise Edition (J2EE) standards;
- IONA iPortal Integration Server, a CORBA 3.0-based environment for integrating the applications required to support enterprise portals in a flexible but deep way;
- Orbix 2000, a CORBA 3.0 server based on a new modular architecture designed for the dynamic operations of enterprise portals;
- IONA iPortal Server, a portal access and control point that manages customized views of all internal applications, provides reliable, secure and scalable access to internal applications, and provides access to Internet applications such as search and profiling/personalization.

Each of the members of the IONA iPortal Suite is based on a new IONA framework called Adaptive Runtime Technology (ART). ART is a microkernel architecture that supports dynamic configuration of the underlying services of a request broker, name resolution, security, and other core services, as well as of the layered services and application components that run atop the core services. The common foundation provided by ART enables the easy integration and cooperation of the members of the iPortal Suite.

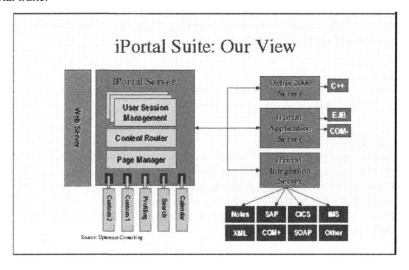

Fig. 12. The IONA iPortal Suite

Available Functionality
- IONA iPortal Application Server

The iPortal Application Server is designed for the many developers that are using Sun's Enterprise Java Beans (EJB) and the Java2 Enterprise Edition (J2EE) platform as the basis for their portal architectures. These developers have been forced to use generalized application servers with EJB components (boltons) for their applications until now. They've been forced to hand-code both the logic and the assembly of the server-based components they build.

IONA's iPortal Application Server supports EJB 1.1 and J2EE hosting on a solid CORBA foundation, provides a server builder for EJB development, assembly, deployment and administration; and incorporates an XML EJB provision mechanism that makes integration of third party EJBs into the environment easy. The result is a scalable platform for EJB application development and deployment that is open and manageable.

The IONA iPortal Application server is designed to support the dynamic assembly, configuration, and deployment requirements of enterprise portals. Developers can change applications running on the server without having to stop the server first. The iPortal Application server employs a policy-based EJB assembly and deployment approach that allows developers to focus on business logic, eliminating the need for system-level code governing security, transaction access, and other low-level functions. The IONA iPortal Application Server will work well with third party integrated development environments (IDEs) and easily accommodates the use and ongoing administration of third party EJBs. Lastly, the IONA iPortal Application Server is built on a robust CORBA foundation for reliability and scalability.

- Orbix 2000

Orbix 2000 is IONA's new CORBA engine, based on the ART framework, a modular architecture designed for scalability, performance, and deployment flexibility. Initially for C++ developers, Orbix 2000 will support the CORBA 2.3 standards at general release, including Portable Object Adapter, DynAny type, Object by Value semantics, and the new Persistent Storage Service (PSS). Orbix 2000 will bundle an Object Transaction Service. Orbix 2000 will support all of the CORBA 3.0 specifications, including XML payloads in IDL interfaces.

IONA has thousands of Orbix customers and for them, Orbix 2000 will be the next step in a product line with a 9-year history. In addition, Orbix 2000 will give these customers a platform for applying their skills in CORBA design, development, and deployment to the construction of enterprise portals. In addition to support for the latest CORBA specifications, Orbix 2000 will support policy-based binding, which allows selection of binding types based on client-side policy and Microsoft's Simple Object Adapter Protocol (SOAP), an XML-based standard for communications with Microsoft's COM+.

Orbix 2000 offers the dynamic deployment and runtime administration features that builders of enterprise portals require. Every system component and every application interface deployed in the environment can be added, removed, and changed without having to shut down the server first. Policy-based binding allows developers to implement different quality of service levels for requests and operations, a level of control that previously required custom coding. Orbix 2000 supports the full range of load balancing and failover strategies, supports transactions and transactional operations, and provides centralized server configuration and management facilities.

Lastly, Orbix 2000's Code Generation Toolkit saves time and resources in the construction of sophisticated application code by generating TCL scripts for complete clients and servers.

- IONA iPortal Integration Server

The IONA iPortal Integration Server is an integration broker based on CORBA messaging that automates linkage and integration between the elements of enterprise portals, including the application servers, the back-office systems within the corporation, external systems, and the portal server itself.

The iPortal Integration Server will be best for deep integration of applications running on IBM mainframes, Microsoft environments, major Enterprise Resource Planning (ERP) systems and other large, dynamic environments. IONA plans to provide pre-built adapters for IBM's CICS and IMS; Microsoft's DCOM, and SAP's R/3 at general release, and others later. These adapters will support data, process, and semantic integration of target systems. IONA plans to support third-party rules engines for the translation, filtering, and routing of messages and payloads between systems. The iPortal Integration Server supports the dynamic requirements of enterprise portals with an architecture that allows changes to running systems and incorporates a policy-based development approach that supports rapid reconfiguration of running applications.

• IONA iPortal Server

The IONA iPortal Server is the administrative control point for an enterprise portal. In an enterprise portal, an application server capable of supporting one or two applications will be inadequate as a platform for administrative control of portal operations. The iPortal Server interfaces with the web server and manages user sessions, content routing, and user profiles. Organizations will define the iPortal Server's operations through a configuration, policy-based interface, as opposed to a programming interface. Thus, the product will be accessible to system administrators. The iPortal Server provides Internet and internal content routing based on standard messaging protocols, including CORBA messaging, HTTP, and IIOP. Lastly, the iPortal Server will provide a single control and integration point for user (customer) profile management, integrated with third party profiling engines.

IONA designed its iPortal Suite as a modular product set so that it can accommodate the wide variety of demands leading up to enterprise portals. For example, an organization might start with the iPortal Application Server as the basis for an Intranet unification application, and then expand the range of content and function sources by interleaving the iPortal Integration Server into their architecture. As the architecture grows, users can add the iPortal Server to manage the workloads and administer a complex environment. Over time, enterprise portals will have multiple application servers and multiple integration servers for reasons of scale, flexibility, history, and culture.

Type of Applications
IONA iPortal Suite, a collection of server products designed to support large-scale, dynamic Enterprise Portals based on Internet standards (including XML) and Java with a CORBA foundation.

Future Evolutions
Orbix 2000 is IONA's next-generation CORBA platform. Over time, the full suite of CORBA services and connectors that IONA provides will become available on the Orbix 2000 platform, gaining flexibility and improved performance in the process. Orbix 2000 can coexist and interoperate with Orbix 3 and OrbixWeb applications today, so you can start to build Orbix 2000 components that are integrated with

existing Orbix 3 and OrbixWeb based systems and gradually migrate to the Orbix 2000 platform over time. IONA encourages its customers to migrate existing Orbix 2.x applications to Orbix 3 so that these applications can interoperate with newly developed Orbix 2000 applications.

IONA iPortal Application Server is built on a POA-based Java language implementation of the Adaptive Runtime Technology architecture. As a result, iPortal Application Server lets you combine the ease of development offered by a Java application server with the high-performance of C++ CORBA, while sharing common configuration, location, and administrative information across the entire system.

Reliability
IONA has a strong track record in support of scalable, reliable, standards-based solutions for mission-critical systems at such companies as American Airlines, Boeing, SouthwesternBell, Bank of America, and Motorola.

Maintainability and Support
The configuration and location domain architecture of Orbix 2000 is similarly open to future enhancements. The locator daemon architecture lets you apply highly scalable load balancing and fault tolerance strategies to application services that are completely transparent to the clients that use them. New configuration plug-ins can allow the ORB to get configuration information transparently from other configuration management systems. Comprehensive information is available on IONA Technologies Web site http://www.iona.com/support. Training and consulting courses are provided. Comprehensive information need for developers is available on IONA Technologies Web site http://www.iona.com/developer.

Impact of Utilization
IONA iPortal Suite provides:
- New high-performance CORBA engine.
- IONA Adaptive Runtime Technology architecture for dynamic deployment and configuration of core services as well as application code.
- Policy-based binding allows selection of binding types based on client-side policy.
- Support for CORBA Portable Object Adaptor (POA), DynAny type, and Object by Value semantics, Persistent Storage Service (PSS), and XML payloads in IDL.
- Support for CORBA Object Transaction Service, with integral transaction engine.
- Support for Microsoft's Simple Object Adapter Protocol (SOAP), an XML-based standard for communications with Microsoft's COM+.
- Support for CORBA/COM object interoperation through IONA' s OrbixCOMet.

Platform
Orbix 2000 is available on Windows NT, Linux, and major UNIX platforms including Solaris and HP.

Price
Orbix 2000 is currently in Beta, with plans to make it generally available in Q1 2000.

4.2.6 Component Broker

General Description
Component Broker is an enterprise solution for distributed object computing that includes an operational environment and toolset (Figure 13).

Component Broker Release 3.0 is included with WebSphere Application Server, Enterprise Edition Version 3 IBM®. WebSphere™ Application Server Enterprise Edition enables full e-business transactions over the Web. Using open standards-based technologies like interoperable CORBA and Enterprise JavaBeans™ (EJBs), Enterprise Edition provides comprehensive, high quality middleware runtime services for distributed component applications. It also contains the industry's most complete support for integrating existing IT applications and resources for reuse on the Web.

Available Functionality
The Enterprise Edition offers comprehensive support by providing:
- The ability to compose new business applications that provide transactional commit and recovery – including full two-phase commit – across disparate back-end systems, such as XA-compliant relational database management systems (RDBMSs) and transaction processing (TP) monitor applications using IBM CICS® and IBM IMS™ systems
- A full complement of EJB-based interfaces to existing resource managers (databases, messaging and queuing systems, TP monitors and other vendor Enterprise Resource Planning (ERP) systems through IBM's common connectivity approach
- Tuneable, queryable, cacheable, performance-enhancing technology for interfacing with existing back-end datastores

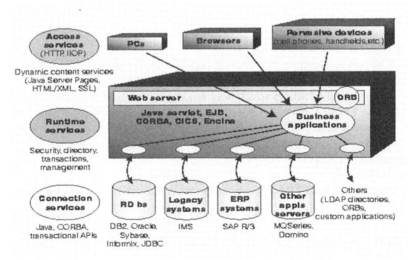

Fig. 13. WebSphere Application Server enables powerful Web interactions

In addition, the Enterprise Edition offers the highest levels of scalability, performance availability and configurability:

- Extensive horizontal and vertical scalability:
  - Provides configuration of application servers on a single processor or across multiple processors
  - Allows multiple servers to share workloads within a configurable WebSphere server managed by agents from a single management console
  - Provides the best platform coverage - from Microsoft® Windows NT® to IBM OS/390®
- Fast performance:
  - Optimizes for extremely complex, high-volume transactional workloads
  - Provides workload management in the base architecture of the product
  - Offers other Web application servers for less transaction-oriented needs (through WebSphere Application Server Standard and Advanced editions)
- High availability:
  - Allows for easy reconfiguration without bringing down the system
  - Allows new servers and hosts to be brought online without adversely impacting the system while it is running
  - Creates a responsive environment where capacity can be added dynamically
  - Provides workload management that does not rely on server clustering technology
  - Offers dynamic management and configuration of software for flexibility to optimize hardware resource use
  - Brings mature runtimes with years of rigorous testing on some of the largest systems, greatly reducing the frequency of outages
  - Brings flexibility so that many component environment choices can be made at deployment time, rather than hard coded into or around the component

The Enterprise Edition also brings:

- Comprehensive application integration support
- Open, standard, distributed component-based application support
- High-volume, high-performance transaction support

- Application integration support

The Enterprise Edition provides comprehensive application integration through its support of a standard, portable, Java™-based Web application server (WebSphere Application Server, Advanced Edition) that hosts and executes Java servlets, JavaServer™ Pages (JSPs) and EJBs while interacting with enterprise databases, transaction processing systems and other applications to produce dynamic Web content. The value and versatility of this server is enhanced by:

  - Complete Java and Enterprise Java support including a server for applications built to the EJB specification for relational database transaction management. The server can be used in highly transactional environments in conjunction with dynamic Web content generation and Web-initiated transactions.
  - Inclusion of an Apache-based HTTP Server as well as support for other major Web servers providing top security and control.
  - A new site analysis tool to help obtaining detailed analysis of Web content integrity and site performance. With many predefined, ready-to-use reports, the

site analysis tool will help you make the best e-business decisions based on customer usage.

- Performance and scaling attributes with support for bean-managed and container-managed persistence, with relational database transaction management and monitoring. Container management and persistent storage (through the IBM DB2® Universal Database™) helps provide a high-performance transactional environment using servlets and EJBs.
- Seamless integration between IBM VisualAge® for Java and WebSphere allowing developers to incrementally develop and debug their business logic, including EJBs, Java servlets and JSPs, from within the integrated development environment.
- Tivoli Ready™ enablement (www.transarc.com/News/press/tivolitx-9809.html) which builds upon the Tivoli™ scalable infrastructure and consistent end-to-end management solutions.
- Extensible Markup Language (XML) Document Structure Services to develop e-business applications that interchange data through XML to parse, generate, manipulate and validate content created to the XML and Extensible Style Language (XSL) specifications.
- Reduced cost of deploying applications on all WebSphere-compliant platforms with the use and reuse of industry-standard tools in an enhanced administration and interface environment.
- Support for Intel®- and UNIX®-based platforms including Windows NT, Sun Solaris and AIX on HTTP servers from IBM, Apache, Microsoft and Netscape.

- Component-based application support
  The Enterprise Edition's component-based application development, runtime execution and management is the most complete and integrated implementation of the open standards contained in the Object Management Group's Common Object Request Broker Architecture (CORBA) initiative. The distributed component technology (formerly called IBM Component Broker) addresses the needs of business-critical applications by providing server-based support for customers to build, execute and manage applications across heterogeneous network computing environments. This technology includes:
  - A programming model that enables data access to be partitioned from business logic
  - A CORBA 2.0 compliant ORB, using the widely accepted Internet Interoperability Protocol (IIOP) standard to communicate with other complying ORBs
  - An application runtime environment, providing integration and management of object services
  - Management of distributed application interactions with networked computing hardware and software resources (for monitoring, resource allocation, unit of work)
  - Support for Web (Java™) clients, traditional CORBA clients, ActiveX clients and an ever-increasing number of non-traditional clients, including kiosks, ATMs and others
  - Multitier visual development tools for the major object oriented languages

- Transaction support

The Enterprise Edition supports high-volume, high-performance transactions using two leading transaction-processing monitors:

- CICS
- IBM Encina.

CICS and Encina are elements drawn from the product formerly called IBM TXSeries™, winner of the Well-Connected Award from Network Computing in 1998. The Enterprise Edition offers an Object Transaction Monitor in Component Broker. You can create business solutions with any of these systems, and those solutions will be able to communicate and cooperate with one another. The gateways, clients and other software needed for extensive enterprise and e-business connectivity may be also included.

- CICS TP monitor technology

CICS technology derives from a family of products that offer online transaction processing and transaction management for applications on both IBM and non-IBM platforms. It offers many services for application development, communications, recovery, presentation, data management, security and intercommunication.

- Encina TP monitor technology

Encina technology provides a complete infrastructure for developing, running and administering transaction-processing applications. This infrastructure includes:

- A full-featured API that shields the programmer from the complexities of distributed computing
- A reliable execution environment that provides high performance and transactional integrity
- A comprehensive management environment that enables widely distributed monitor-based systems to be administered as a single, logically defined system

Encina provides an open modular system that is scalable and that interoperates with existing computing resources such as IBM mainframes running CICS. It supports interoperation among a number of components – the operating system, DCE, the Encina Toolkit, third party relational database management systems such as Informix and Oracle, third-party front ends (user interfaces) and networks – for application development.

Type of Applications
Middleware runtime services for distributed component applications.

Reliability
Encina technology provides a reliable execution environment that delivers load balancing, scheduling and fault-tolerance across heterogeneous environments to guaranty high performance and transactional integrity.

IBM WebSphere Performance Pack provides a combination of load balancing, caching, proxy and filtering functions, file content management and replication in a single Internet hosting infrastructure offering. This software product provides high performance in both local and global environments and enables e-business applications to handle peak loads efficiently and helps maintain 24x7 availability.

Key features:

- Optimal server load balancing for traffic surge protection and scalability
- Accelerated server performance through caching, quality of service
- Fault-tolerant architecture and distributed content management for high availability

Maintainability and Support
Easy configurability:

- Supplies management tools supporting the configuration of components onto servers and server clusters on multiple hosts
- Offers GUI configuration tools and does not require hand-editing of properties files or other manual configuration techniques
- Enables management and configuration of remote systems from a central console
- Separates development and deployment roles, so that developers do not need to worry about production configurations

All customers purchasing WebSphere Application Server Enterprise Edition, V3.0 will receive a prerelease version of WebSphere Application Server Advanced Edition, V3.0. All Enterprise Edition customers of record will automatically receive the global application version of the Advanced Edition when it becomes available later year 2000.

Support information for Component Broker Release 3.0 as well as Release 2.0 is available at http://www-4.ibm.com/software/webservers/appserv/cb/support/.

A list of classes for the WebSphere family is available at http://www.ibm.com/software/webservers/education.html

Visit the following Web site for additional information:
http://www.ibm.com/services/learning/

Platform
WebSphere Application Server Enterprise Edition runs on AIX, Solaris and Windows NT.

Following in Tables 2, 3 and 4 are the minimum software requirements for WebSphere Application Server Enterprise Edition, V3.0.

Table 2. Software prerequisites for AIX

Operating system	IBM AIX/6000® Version 4.3.2 or higher
Communications	TCP/IP and network interface support (provided by the operating system)
Web browser	Netscape Navigator Version 4.07 or higher or Microsoft Internet Explorer Version 4.01 or higher and JDK 1.1.5-capable, or later
Web server (one of the following)	Apache Server, Version 1.3.6
	Netscape Enterprise Server, Version 3.51 and Version 3.60
	Lotus® Domino™ Application Server Release 5
	Domino Go Webserver Release 4.6.2.5 and 4.6.2.6
	IBM HTTP Server V1.3.6

Table 3. Software prerequisites for Solaris

Operating system	Sun Solaris Version 2.6 or 2.7
Communications	TCP/IP and network interface support (provided by the operating system)
Web browser	Netscape Navigator Version 4.07 or higher or Microsoft Internet Explorer Version 4.01 or higher and JDK 1.1.5-capable, or later
Web server	Apache Server, Version 1.3.6 Netscape Enterprise Server, Version 3.51 and Version 3.60 Lotus® Domino™ Application Server Release 5 Domino Go Webserver Release 4.6.2.5 and 4.6.2.6 IBM HTTP Server V1.3.6

Table 4. Software prerequisites for Windows NT

Operating system	Microsoft Windows NT Workstation 4.0 Microsoft Windows NT Server 4.0 Note: The component feature requires Microsoft Windows NT 4.00 Service Pack 4 with either operating system
Communications	TCP/IP and network interface support (provided by the operating system)
Web browser	Netscape Navigator Version 4.07 or higher or Microsoft Internet Explorer Version 4.01 or higher and JDK 1.1.5-capable, or later
Web server (one of the following)	Apache Server, Version 1.3.6 Netscape Enterprise Server, Version 3.51 and Version 3.60 Microsoft Information Server Version 4.0 Lotus Domino Application Server Release 5 Domino Go Webserver Release 4.6.2.5 and 4.6.2.6 IBM HTTP Server V1.3.6

Price
WebSphere Application Server, Enterprise Edition is available since September 2000 on NT and AIX in November on Solaris, at a price of $35,000 per processor. The package will include early code for WebSphere Advanced Edition 3.0.

In addition, VisualAge Component Development is available in September 2000 on NT and AIX, at a price of $7,500 per development seat. The package will include early code for VisualAge for Java Version 3.0 Enterprise Edition.

Customers are entitled to free upgrades to generally available versions for WebSphere Advanced Edition 3.0 and for Visual Age for Java Version 3.0 Enterprise Edition upon their availability.

More information about the WebSphere product line is on the Web at www.ibm.com/software/websphere.

4.2.7 VisiBroker 4.0

VisiBroker 4 provides full support for CORBA 2.3, including: Portable Object Adapters (POA), Objects By Value (OBV), RMI over IIOP Clustering and Load-Balancing.

General Description
VisiBroker is a complete CORBA 2.3 Object Request Broker (ORB) that supports the development, deployment, and management of distributed object applications across a variety of hardware platforms and operating systems. VisiBroker 4 now provides full support for CORBA 2.3, including:
• Portable Object Adapters (POA)
• Objects By Value (OBV)
• RMI over IIOP
• Clustering and Load-Balancing
• GIOP 1.2 support
• New property manager
• Quality of Service (QoS)
• VisiBroker Console
In addition to VisiBroker (the ORB), three other components are available with this product. They include:
• Naming Service
• Event Service
• Gatekeeper

Available Functionality
• Complete OMG CORBA Implementation
   – Full support for CORBA 2.3 specifications
   – Portable Object Adapter (POA), which provides for sophisticated management of server object lifetimes, and allows server source code portability across ORB products
   – Objects By Value (OBV), for passing of arbitrary complex objects and graphs of objects by value across processes, machines, and languages
   – Valuetypes, the OMG-specified mechanism for encoding and passing objects by value, which allows interoperability of OBV across ORB products
   – RMI over IIOP and the Java-to-IDL reverse mapping allows Java developers to write CORBA applications without having to learn IDL and other CORBA

features, and allows existing RMI applications to be migrated to the VisiBroker high-performance CORBA runtime.
- A very high-performance, robust implementation of IIOP, which has become the de-facto industry-standard IIOP protocol implementation against which other IIOP implementations are judged
- GIOP 1.2 for enhanced interoperability. Fragmentation for enhanced performance by enabling large requests to be interleaved seamlessly with smaller ones.
- Quality of Service (QoS) APIs, for configuring or modifying the behaviour of the ORB runtime & services, to allow developers to make engineering trade-offs
- ORB Property Management, a uniform scheme for managing the numerous configurable aspects of VisiBroker
- Support for Multi-homed Hosts, to allow effortless deployment of VisiBroker applications on machines with multiple network cards, such as firewall machines or high-end servers
- Interface Repository (IR) for storing descriptions of CORBA Object Interfaces, and other Type information for runtime discovery by clients
- Implementation Repository and the Object Activ
- Separately Available Options for VisiBroker 4
    - Complete range of CORBA Services (from Prism Technologies)
    - OpenFusion Trading Service
    - OpenFusion Notification Service
    - OpenFusion LifeCycle Service
    - OpenFusion Property Service
    - OpenFusion Collection Service
    - OpenFusion Concurrency Service
    - OpenFusion Relationship Service
    - OpenFusion Time Service

Type of Applications
VisiBroker 4 is a complete CORBA 2.0 ORB environment for building, deploying and managing distributed Java and C++ applications that interoperates across multiple platforms.

Reliability
Inprise VisiBroker - The Leading Deployed ORB Technology Inprise's VisiBroker for Java and VisiBroker for C++ CORBA Object Request Brokers are designed to facilitate the development and deployment of distributed enterprise applications that are scalable, flexible, and easily maintained. Industry affiliations with Oracle Corporation, Sun Microsystems, Hitachi, Informix, Intershop, Novell, Netscape, Silicon Graphics, Sybase, and others have played a key role in making VisiBroker the leading deployed and adopted ORB in the computer industry, with over 30 million licenses world-wide.

Testing results are on the site: http://www.beust.com/virginie/Benchmarks.

Maintainability and Support

VisiBroker provides a complete set of tools for administering your VisiBroker environment. These tools can be used within scripts, giving you greater flexibility and control over administration tasks.

Training and consulting courses are provided. Comprehensive information need for developers is available on Imprise Web site http://www.inprise.com/services.

Impact of Utilization

Compatibility with VisiBroker for C++ 3.x: VisiBroker 4.0 is not binary- or source-compatible with previous releases. Please regenerate your stubs and recompile your applications.

Platform

Supported Platforms:

- Microsoft Windows (Intel)
- Sun Microsystems Solaris (SPARC)
- RedHat Linux (Intel)
- Hewlett Packard HP-UX (PA-RISC) (Available soon)
- IBM AIX (RS/6000) (Available soon)

More detailed information on site:

  http://www.borland.com/techpubs/visibroker/platforms/platform.html

4.2.8 TAO

General Description

TAO (The ACE ORB) [30] by Washington University is an ORB Endsystem Architecture that contains the network interface, operating system, communication protocol, and CORBA middleware mechanisms.
(http://theaceorb.com/; http://www.cs.wustl.edu/~schmidt/TAO.html;)

TAO is a high-performance, real-time ORB with the current focus on policies and mechanisms for dispatching CORBA requests in hard real-time avionics systems. It contains an optimized IIOP engine, support for the portable object adapter, Naming, Trader and a real-time Event Service.

TAO is open source software that is compliant with features and components in the CORBA 2.2 specification, as well as many features and components in the 2.3 specification.

TAO enhances the standard CORBA Event Service to provide important features, such as real-time event dispatching and scheduling, periodic event processing, efficient event filtering and correlation mechanisms, and multicast protocols required by real-time applications.

Available Functionality

The current release of TAO contains the components shown in Figure 14.

Each component in TAO is outlined below:

- IDL Compiler. TAO's IDL compiler is based on enhanced version of the freely available SunSoft IDL compiler.
- Inter-ORB Protocol Engine. TAO contains a highly optimized protocol engine that implements the CORBA 2.x Internet Inter-ORB Protocol, version 1.0 and 1.1.
- ORB Core. TAO's ORB Core provides an efficient, scalable, and predictable two-way, one-way, and reliable one-way synchronous and asynchronous communication infrastructure for high-performance and real-time applications. TAO's ORB Core is based on patterns and components in ACE. The key patterns used in TAO include the Acceptor and Connector, Reactor, Active Object, Half-Sync/Half-Async, and Service Configurator.
- Portable Object Adapter. TAO's implementation of the CORBA Portable Object Adapter (POA) is designed using patterns that provide an extensible and highly optimized set of request demultiplexing strategies, such as perfect hashing and active demultiplexing. These strategies allow TAO's POA to provide constant-time lookup of servants based on object keys and operation names contained in CORBA requests.
- An Implementation Repository that automatically launches servers in response to client requests.

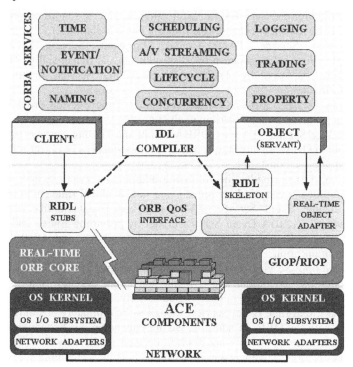

Fig. 14. The TAO ORB Endsystem Architecture

- CORBA Object Services (COS) Support. TAO provides many of the standard CORBA services, including the following:

1. Audio/Video Streaming Service. TAO's CORBA-compliant A/V Streaming Service implements the standard Control and Management of Audio/Video Streams Specification.
2. Concurrency Service. CORBA-compliant Concurrency Service provides a mechanism that allows clients to acquire and release various types of locks in a distributed system. Note that TAO only currently supports a subset of the Concurrency Service, i.e. the non-transactional part.
3. Event Service. TAO's CORBA-compliant Event Service supports decoupled communication among multiple suppliers and consumers using the standard GIOP/IIOP protocol.
4. Lifecycle Service. TAO's CORBA-compliant Lifecycle Service provides a standard means to locate, move, copy, and remove objects.
5. Logging Service. TAO's implementation of the OMG's Telecom Log Service allows applications to send logging records to a centralized logging server.
6. Naming Service. TAO's CORBA-compliant Naming Service supports both persistent and non-persistent hierarchical mappings between sequences of strings and object references. In addition, TAO supports the Interoperable Naming Service, which defines a standard way for clients and servers to locate the Naming Service, as well as any other CORBA service.
7. Notification Service. TAO's Notification Service is a more powerful form of the Event Service that supports filtering and correlation.
8. Property Service. TAO's CORBA-compliant Property Service allows applications to associate properties with objects dynamically. The Property Service is used by TAO's A/V Streaming Service to transmit QoS information.
9. Time Service. TAO's CORBA-compliant Time Service provides globally synchronized time to distributed clients.
10. Trading Service. TAO's CORBA-compliant Trading Service implements a mapping between attribute constraints and sequences of object references that match those constraints.

In addition, TAO provides the following additional services, which demonstrate TAO's capabilities in various deterministic and statistical real-time environments:

1. Real-time Event Service. TAO's real-time Event Service augments the standard CORBA Event Service model by providing source and type-based filtering, event correlation, real-time dispatching, and UDP/IP multicast communication.
2. Scheduling Service. TAO's real-time Scheduling Service supports static rate monotonic scheduling and dynamic maximum urgency first scheduling to assign priorities and validate schedulability. It is currently integrated with TAO's Real-time Event Service, though we're ultimately planning to integrate this with the ORB. In addition, we are enhancing our Scheduling Service to conform to the Scheduling Service defined in the new Real-time CORBA specification, as well as the forthcoming dynamic scheduling specification.

Type of Applications
TAO is a high-performance, real-time ORB with the current focus on policies and mechanisms for dispatching CORBA requests in hard real-time avionics systems.

Future Evolutions

The following evolutions are forthcoming:

- Additional ORB concurrency models, e.g., asynchronous thread pool using the Proactor, thread-per-request and thread-per-object.
- The Interface Repository, which provides run-time information about IDL interfaces.
- The CORBA/DCOM integration.
- Various protocols for TAO's forthcoming Pluggable Protocols framework, including UNIX domain sockets, TP4, SS7, ATM, GSMP, shared memory, and Fibrechannel.
- Support for Minimum CORBA, which will reduce the footprint of TAO.
- The forthcoming CORBA Fault Tolerance specification, which ensures that client applications are largely insulated from management of redundant copies, failure masking, and recovery.
- The forthcoming CORBA Wireless Access and Control specification, which will provide CORBA service in the presence of personal and terminal mobility.
- Adding CORBA Security Service features to TAO.
- Adding the CORBA Component Model (CCM) support to TAO.

Reliability

TAO's efficiency, scalability, and predictability have been measured on many different real-time operating systems with different features.

Maintainability and Support

Commercial support, documentation, training, and consulting for TAO are available from Object Computing, Inc. (OCI). See the TAO Press Releases for more information on TAO's use in commercial projects.

Availability of Localised Versions

TAO can be downloaded from the Internet and freely used and redistributed without developer or run-time licensing costs.

Impact of Utilisation

Developers got TAO to work with other ORBs (e.g., Orbix, COOL, CORBAPlus, and VisiBroker); the result is that its IIOP implementation is robust and interoperable.

Platform

TAO has been ported to OS platforms including Win32 (i.e., WinNT 3.5.x, 4.x, 2000, and Win95/98 using MSVC++, Borland's C++ Builder, and IBM's VisualAge on Intel and Alpha platforms), many versions of UNIX (e.g., Solaris 1.x and 2.x on SPARC and Intel, SGI IRIX 6.x, HP-UX 10.x and 11.x, DEC/Compaq UNIX 4.x, AIX 4.x, SCO, and freely available UNIX implementations, such as Debian Linux 2.x, RedHat Linux 5.2 and 6.0, FreeBSD, and NetBSD), real-time operating systems (e.g., LynxOS, VxWorks, QnX Neutrino, and Chorus ClassiX 4.0), and MVS OpenEdition.

TAO is planned to port to all OS platforms that ACE runs on.

Price

TAO is freely available.

4.2.9 LiveContent BROKER 3.2

General Description

LiveContent BROKER was formerly known as DAIS. It is based on the Common Object Request BROKER Architecture (CORBA), which has been defined and refined by the Object Management Group (OMG), is a set of CORBA based software tools for creating distributed applications.

LiveContent BROKER is built on a set of architectural principles including separation and distribution, diversity and heterogeneity, scalability, and federation. Also covered are transparency, concurrence, configuration, and evolution. LiveContent BROKER delivers powerful run-time services including Trader, Alerting, Factory, and Recovery.

It supports a wide selection of platforms and tools. Using IDL, it can link together components built using any development tool, which can call or be called by C, C++, Java, Eiffel, or ActiveX. This effectively means support for most development tools.

LiveContent BROKER allows a wide range of manufacturers' systems to work together, including ICL, IBM, HP, Sun, SCO, and Digital. The various systems supported are described in the LiveContent BROKER product description.

It offers full client and server support on Windows NT and 95, including multithreading which enables applications to make and accept several calls in parallel. LiveContent BROKER applications can be integrated with Windows development tools, including ActiveX and Visual Basic.

Available Functionality

LiveContent BROKER is a high performance, distributed ORB that provides essential management services and the communications infrastructure for distributed applications. Its product set includes: the LiveContent BROKER, LiveContent BROKER Core Services, and additional Component Object Services.

- LiveContent BROKER Component Object Services

Naming Service simplifies object location by allowing distributed application components to associate meaningful names with advertised object references. Hierarchical name storage, context, and namespace federation provide enterprise scalability. Persistent naming ensures system resilience when failures occur.

Transaction Service provides complete transactional integrity to distributed object applications. LiveContent Object Transaction Service (OTS) enables correlated updates and transactional semantics in a distributed object infrastructure. All resources are grouped and managed with all communications optimized within the distributed two-phase commit.

Event Service supports asynchronous messaging using the CORBA compliant push model for scalable publish & subscribe applications. Producers publish information, and consumers subscribe to that information. Multicast support allows messages to be sent to subsets of subscribers. The Event Service orders, reschedules, and guarantees delivery of messages and maintains a persistent record of events.

- LiveContent BROKER Core Services

Trader provides a directory for advertising and dynamically locating services offered by objects. Traders can be federated or linked to any number of additional Traders to ensure system resilience.

Node Manager creates, monitors, and terminates objects for complete lifecycle management. The Node Manager starts inactive services on request using the Factory Service.

Factory Service is responsible for the mechanics of creating and terminating objects.

Alert allows LiveContent Broker applications to redirect warnings, status, and error messages.

Recovery enables backup servers to be nominated and promoted, ensuring high availability and fault-tolerance.

- LiveContent BROKER Performance and Scalability Features:
  - Multi-threading. LiveContent BROKER supports multi-threading, concurrent processing and asynchronous processing on all platforms—even on those operating systems that do not offer native thread support.
  - High Availability. LiveContent BROKER applications can be distributed around the network to avoid any single point of failure. Essential services can be replicated for added resilience.
  - Optimal Performance. Communications resources can be optimized either through the use of connectionless protocols or by multiplexing over connection-oriented protocols. Data flow is automatically matched to the server's ability to respond.
  - System Management. Using Extended Objects, applications are easy to write and run. Developers and system managers can create, delete, and "start-up" sets of objects automatically or on demand. Multiple copies can be scheduled to achieve the required throughput.
  - Common API. A Portability Library that is identical on all platforms provides a platform independent interface to the host's native operating system services. This allows LiveContent BROKER applications to run unchanged on all supported platforms.

Type of Applications
The DAIS is a set of CORBA based software tools to create and run a distributed application.

Future Evolutions
LiveContent BROKER is expected to:
- Work with and influence the OMG to develop new standards
- Expand the number of supported platforms
- Work with major development tools
- Deliver those features required for the commercial market, including:
  - Java integration
  - Persistent objects
  - Improved system management
  - Additional CORBA Services

Reliability
LiveContent Broker implements the OMG's CORBA standard and offers IIOP interoperability and enterprise robustness. It detects when components have failed and can take remedial action, also offering facilities for standby components to be

constructed. The System Administrator can map requests for a particular service onto another, for example, to avoid an overloaded or failing service. LiveContent BROKER provides dependable messaging over connectionless transport protocols.

Maintainability and Support

Existing applications can be integrated into LiveContent BROKER systems by writing a program, called a wrapper, which makes them appear as LiveContent BROKER components. Any type of application can be connected in this way — even if the target application does not run on a platform supported by LiveContent BROKER.

Using gateways, it can also connect to applications written using another distributed paradigm, such as Microsoft's Common Object Model (COM)-based technology, ActiveX, X/Open's Distributed TP, or OSF's DCE. Currently, gateways are written for each application, with the exception of ActiveX; however, standard gateways will be developed. LiveContent BROKER supports CORBA IDL to ActiveX automation mapping as dictated in the COM-CORBA interworking specification produced by the OMG.

LiveContent BROKER supports CORBA 2.0 interoperability protocols, such as the Internet Inter-Orb Protocol (IIOP), enabling applications to interwork with other CORBA implementations. The ability to work with other ORBs allows it to adopt a comprehensive and flexible approach for supporting objects distributed across multiple CORBA-compliant ORBs.

Training and consulting courses are provided. Comprehensive information need for developers is available on PeerLogic Web site http://www.peerlogic.com

Platform

Development Environments
    Visual Basic, Visual C++, Borland C++, Optima, and Gupta.
    Informix, Oracle, and Sybase RDBMS.
    Paradigm Plus, Select Enterprise, System Architect, and Galaxy.
Supported Environments
    Operating Systems: AIX, HP-UX, OpenVMS, SCO, UnixWare, Stratus VOS, Solaris, Windows 95, and NT.
    Transports: IIOP, TCP/IP, UDP/IP, and IPC

4.2.10   BEA WebLogic Enterprise 5.1

General Description

BEA WebLogic Enterprise™ is a proven platform for building rock-solid, easy-to-manage e-commerce systems (Figure 15). BEA WebLogic Enterprise offers a flexible development environment that features component-based development, simplified deployment, reliable transaction management, and rigorous support for Enterprise Java, CORBA, and industry standards.

As the industry-leading e-commerce transaction platform, BEA WebLogic Enterprise provides a number of features critical to developing and deploying mission-critical e-commerce applications across distributed, heterogeneous computing environments.

BEA WebLogic Enterprise is the only integrated application server platform that allows you to develop solutions based on any combination of J2EE and EJB, CORBA Java, CORBA C++, Tuxedo ATMI with C, C++, or COBOL. It delivers the high productivity benefits of component-based development for building e-commerce solutions, leveraging industry standards — CORBA and Java — for greater interoperability, portability, and tools support.

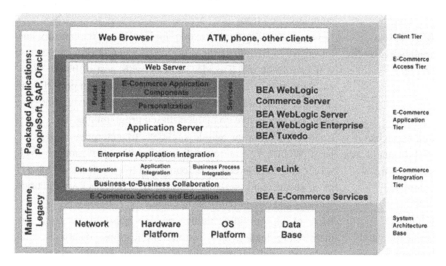

Fig. 15. BEA WebLogic Enterprise Architecture

Available functionality (Table 5)

Table 5. BEA WebLogic functionalities

Feature	Benefit
The industry leading server for Web and transaction technology	One product does it all. BEA WebLogic Enterprise delivers completeness and choice, featuring the convergence of BEA's industry leading technologies for Web servers, Java application servers, and industrial-strength back-end transaction servers.
Comprehensive transaction management system	Protect your transactions. BEA WebLogic Enterprise supports high-performance heterogeneous transaction management. It protects transaction integrity by ensuring that database updates are done accurately, even across a variety of heterogeneous databases.

Feature	Benefit
Choice of programming languages and models	Choice in business logic: BEA WebLogic Enterprise supports component-based programming with its support of J2EE and CORBA; it also supports the procedural model with the Tuxedo ATMI container. Your programmers can code in Java, C++, C, or Cobol. With BEA WebLogic Enterprise you have a broad choice in business logic, developing and deploying in many programming languages and models for highly scalable e-commerce solutions.
BEA Tuxedo application hosting (ATMI)	Leverage existing BEA Tuxedo applications. You can mix and match BEA Tuxedo services with EJB and CORBA objects; or you can front-end Tuxedo services with best-of-breed Web-enablement in BEA WebLogic Enterprise. You can protect your investment in Tuxedo personnel and applications while moving to highly productive component-based programming.
Fully scalable Web-to-mainframe solutions for e-commerce	Connect Internet or wireless clients to enterprise resources. BEA WebLogic Enterprise features a high-performance Web server and a comprehensive foundation to extend these requests in a secure and scalable fashion to your back-transactions services and other enterprise applications.
Enterprise application and business process integration via BEA eLink	BEA eLink provides highly scalable connectivity from the mainframe, legacy and custom applications, databases, and packaged applications. BEA eLink Adapters for Mainframe provide bi-directional mainframe connectivity services that enable BEA WebLogic Enterprise applications and IBM OS/390-based CICS or IBM Management System Version 6 Transaction Manager application components to operate as one integrated application across distributed systems. Support for two-phase commit helps ensure your transactions in Web-to-mainframe e-commerce solutions.
Robust client/server communications system	Support thousands of clients with greater performance, scalability, and high availability — for servlets, JSPs, EJB components, CORBA objects, and BEA Tuxedo services. Eliminate the risk of outgrowing the business solution. And when your application calls for integration with your existing NES, IIS or Apache Web servers, BEA WebLogic Enterprise has plug-ins ready to integrate with fault tolerance and scalability.
Robust fault management infrastructure	Provide continuous access for your e-commerce customers. BEA WebLogic Enterprise minimizes downtime and keeps your applications running. It supports clustering and replicated server groups that ensure continuous processing when planned and unplanned outages.

Feature	Benefit
Robust security infrastructure	Secure your application resources. BEA WebLogic Enterprise features many services for end-to-end security from the browser to the back-end transaction and data management systems. It supports end-to-end single sign-on for Java; CORBA or procedural applications; SSL (Secure Socket Layer) encryption, and LLE (Link Level Encryption) are also supported. BEA WebLogic Enterprise delivers Service Provider Interfaces (SPIs) to facilitate integration of "best-of-breed" third-party security solutions for user authentication, application access control and auditing. BEA WebLogic Enterprise also supports integration with Unix NIS, NT and LDAP security environments.
Data-center caliber administration capabilities	Automate your administration and management. BEA WebLogic Enterprise automates many of the key management functions in a distributed system, minimizing operator intervention. With BEA WebLogic, you can use industry-standard SNMP MIBs or BEA value-add APIs for programmatic interface in your total management strategy.
A wide variety of clients and servers	Choose from many clients and server options supported by BEA WebLogic Enterprise to deploy your e-business solution.

Type of Applications

BEA WebLogic Enterprise is a flexible development environment that features component-based development, simplified deployment, reliable transaction management, and rigorous support for Enterprise Java, CORBA, and industry standards.

Reliability

BEA WebLogic Enterprise provides a superior architecture for distributed mission-critical systems. The architecture allows the development of Java-based e-commerce applications that meet the Web's most demanding performance and availability requirements, and support emerging technologies such as XML and Wireless Markup Language (WML). It also supports the deployment of flexible component-based applications on a proven system infrastructure. Features such as client connection management, reliable message routing, load balancing and distributed transaction management provides mainframe levels of system manageability, reliability and scalability.

Maintainability and Support

BEA WebLogic Enterprise provides complete capabilities for dynamically configuring, monitoring, and tuning your distributed applications — minimizing operator intervention. With BEA WebLogic Enterprise, you can use industry-standard SNMP MIBs in conjunction with leading management consoles or you can leverage BEA value-add APIs for designing programmatic interfaces in your total management strategy.

Training and consulting courses are provided. Comprehensive information need for developers is available on BEA Systems: http://www.beasys.com/services.html.

Impact of Utilization
BEA WebLogic Enterprise (WLE) provides third party ORB Interoperability. The WLE C++ ORB supports the IIOP 1.2 protocol, and the WLE Java ORB supports the IIOP 1.0 protocol. Both ORBs interoperate with client products from other vendors that support the IIOP 1.2 (or earlier) protocol.

WLE provides transactional and security support for the following third-party client products:

- ActiveX;
- Netscape Communicator;
- VisiBroker C++ Version 3.3 (not clients using the VisiBroker Java ORB);
- Orbix 2.3c02 (with patch 26 or greater).

However, BEA does not provide environmental objects for these clients, so these products cannot directly access to transactional and security capabilities inside the WLE domain. These client products can connect to a WLE server application using a "stringified" object reference.

Platform
BEA WebLogic Enterprise supports the following server platforms:

- HP-UX 11.0 (32 bit)
- Solaris Sparc 2.6 and Solaris Sparc 7
- Windows NT 4.0 on Intel
- Compaq Tru64 4.0f
- IBM AIX 4.3.3
- Windows 2000
- SCO UnixWare 7.1.1
- OS/390 Unix System Services

For more specific information on WebLogic Enterprise platform support see: http://www.beasys.com/contact/sales1.html.

Supported client platforms include:

- Browser clients
- Wireless clients
- CORBA clients
- RMI clients
- Tuxedo clients
- COM clients

4.2.11   ObjecTime Developer

General Description
Framework: simulation and middleware

ObjecTime Developer is a product of ObjecTime Limited, Canada. It is an object-oriented application generation toolkit designed specifically for event-driven, real-time systems. ObjecTime Developer (a software automation tool which implements UML for Real-Time constructs) enables software developers to build applications using component-based visual design models. TotalCode™ application generation automatically generates complete production quality C and C++ executables for UNIX, NT and a variety of real-time operating systems directly from system or component models. Application generation of fully or partially complete designs, plus animated visual and symbolic debuggers, encourage early and continuous design refinement and validation.

ObjecTime Developer is used for developing a wide variety of complex, real-time, event-driven applications in telecommunications, data communications, defense, aerospace, and other industries. The world's leading telecommunications, data communications, defense, aerospace and industrial control companies including Nortel, Lucent, Motorola, Lockheed-Martin, and Kodak use ObjecTime Developer to accelerate real-time software delivery, and to improve the quality and functionality of their real-time products.

Available Functionality
Key capabilities are:
- a robust graphical modelling environment to manage the complexity of real-time software executable models to eliminate design defects
- TotalCode™ application generation to automatically generate complete applications from the design model

Type of Applications
Real-time simulators and control systems.

Future Evolutions
New versions will be more oriented to distributed computing concept.

Reliability
No information available.

Maintainability and Support
Applications developed by means of ObjecTime Developer do not require a run-time environment and incorporate all necessary code.

Availability of Localised Versions
Training and consulting courses are provided. Comprehensive information needed for developers is available on ObjecTime Web site http://www.objectime.com

Impact of Utilisation
ObjecTime Developer supports all phases of software lifecycle and facilitates development of the real-time systems. It utilises true object-oriented approach and proprietary modelling language. However, it does not provide any middleware functionality, but only allows using third party RTI, which uses different object modelling representation (OMT).

Platform
Development platforms: MS Windows NT and most commercial UNIX implementations.

Target platforms: more than 30.

Price
1 to 4 licenses: DM 54050
5 to 9 licenses: DM 47320

4.2.12   Exceed WEB

General Description
Exceed Web is a centrally managed, Java-based Thin X solution that allows corporations to use standard Web-based technologies and a familiar browser interface to provide end users with access to X Window applications (Figure 16). Exceed fully supports the X.Org's X Window System Release 6.4 (X11R6.4) which has been integrated into Exceed as X Web. X Web remotely launches and displays X clients from within a Web browser, either across a corporate Intranet or the Internet. It uses LBX (low bandwidth X) for increased performance across WANs and slow dial-up connections. X Web offers the ability to centrally deploy and manage X application access while eliminating the costs associated with training users on the X Window system's protocol. Exceed ensures wide X Web compatibility by supporting virtually any Web browser.

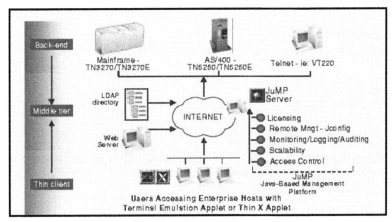

Fig. 16. ExceedWeb Architecture

Hummingbird JuMP uses a scalable architecture that consists of modular components that are built on standards-based technologies to ensure interoperability, compatibility, and platform independence. The standards used include TCP/IP, CORBA/IIOP and Java along with an integrated Web Server and LDAP Server. At the desktop, JuMP supports Microsoft's Internet Explorer 4.01 and Netscape 4.05 (or later) to access JuMP and the Hummingbird applets. The result is an integrated set of services that Java applets use to provide users familiar access to core enterprise applications and enterprise information.

Available functionality (Table 6)

Table 6. Exceed WEB functionalities

Key Features	Benefits
JuMP	Deploys and centrally manages all Hummingbird Java-based applications enterprise wide (HostExplorer Web and Exceed Web) JuMP Technical Brief (pdf) - For more information
Jconfig	Remote and centralized desktop application management Provides a common user interface for thin and fat client connectivity users, decreasing training requirements and increasing user productivity
License Metering	Greatly simplifies license management
User and Group Access Control	Enhanced security with JuMP's integrated access control support
Central Host Profiles	Create and manage host profiles for centralized control
SOCKS integration	Simple and secure firewall traversal
SSL (Secure Socket Layer)	Encryption provides controlled and secure host access through a Web browser
X Proxy Manager	Provides scalability and load balancing for multiple JuMP servers
TXP (Thin X Protocol)	Improves performance of X on LANs, WANs and dial-up connections
Multiple X Display Support	Easier and greater flexibility when accessing multiple environments simultaneously
Enterprise Toolkit for JuMP (ETK)	Develop and test third party Java 2 compatible applets in a segregated environment
Intuitive Web Desktop	Improves user productivity and decreases user learning curves
DirectStart	Instantly start X clients from a desktop shortcut or URL link on a Web page

Maintainability and Support
Hummingbird's unique system administration tools, Jconfig and Sconfig, allows administrators to centrally deploy, configure, and maintain all Hummingbird connectivity products.

UniPress provides consulting, and support services.
(Additional information, see at

http://www.unipress.com/hbird/exceedweb/support.html)

Platform (Table 7)

Table 7. Platform

Desktop System Requirements	
Platform	Pentium
Operating System	Windows NT 4.0 (with Service Pack 3 or higher) Windows 95/98
Browser	Internet Explorer 4.01 or higher (with Service Pack 1) Netscape 4.05 or higher
Memory	64 MB (min. recommended)
JuMP Server Requirements	
Platform	Pentium II, 400 MHz or faster recommended Sun SPARC HP PA-RISC
Operating Systems	Windows NT 4.0 (with Service Pack 3 or higher) Sun Solaris 2.5.1/2.6 HP - UX 10.20
Java Runtime Environment	Windows NT - Java Runtime Environment (supplied with software) SPARC Solaris - Java Runtime Environment (supplied with software) HP-UX - Java Runtime Environment (supplied with software)

Price
Exceed Web 10 Pack: $3449
JuMP Server Starter Kit for Exceed Web: $1529

4.2.13   BizTalk Server

General Description
The continued project is to provide middleware framework supporting interoperability on the base of XML schemas and SOAP protocol. The project is realizing on non-profit basis under the aegis of Microsoft Corporation. More than 40 organisation are involved now into the BizTalk initiative.

The BizTalk Framework itself is not a standard. XML, XSL (XML Stylesheet Language) and SOAP (Simple Object Access Protocol) are standards. The goal of the BizTalk Framework is to regulate the use of XML.

Microsoft BizTalk Server is developing and advertising as the tools and infrastructure that companies require to interchange business documents among various platforms and operating systems regardless of the application being used to process the documents. Being based on "XML-XSL-SOAP backbone" BizTalk Server also may provide a standard framework for workflow via the Internet (in point-to-point manner).

The flexible nature of XML and the existence of XML Style Sheets (XSL) simplify the programming tasks associated with data transformation to a degree that allows the need to manage transforms within an adapter or glue layer unnecessary. With XSL, vendors can publish their XML data schemas that describe the information that is created or consumed as a result of business events (this is one purpose of www.biztalk.org.)

One can to draw an analogy with XML-XSL schemas and CORBA MOF (Meta Object Facility) approach. XML-XSL schemas specified by different fields of "distributed" activity (e-commerce, engineering, manufacturing etc.) may be used like repository of MOF metaobjects in the construction of distributed development environment.

The BizTalk.Org Web site serves as the online reference for the BizTalk Framework specifications, schemas, reference materials, tools, sample applications and a community newsgroup. The Web site is a public library for finding and publishing XML schemas - which are technical descriptions of business documents and messages expressed in XML.

Up to day there are already more than 250 different XML-XSL schemas corresponding to 13 kinds of business. In particular there are some relating directly to the Distributed System Engineering subjects: Construction, Information, Management of Companies and Enterprises. All schemas are (still) open for utilization in the free-of-charge manner by means of URI (Universal Resource Identifier) and URL mechanism supported in XML.

Type of Applications
Now available in the following form:
- the set of the XML-XSL schemas libraries specified for different kinds of e-business (more than 250 schemas relating to 13 frameworks) freely available on www.biztalk.org/Library/schema_search.asp;
- the BizTalk Jumpstart Kit v.2 (sources and documentation). Freely available on www.microsoft.com/biztalk/. Some assembly required.
  Software required:
Microsoft Windows NT, version 4.0; Microsoft SQL Server or MSDE; Microsoft Message Queue; Microsoft Internet Information Server; Microsoft Visual Studio 6; Visual Basic; Visual C++
  PERL version now is INCLUDED (no available information)

Availability of Localised Versions
BizTalk schemas vendors and users community are based on www.biztalk.org. Comprehensive information needed for developers is available on the www.microsoft.com/biztalk/.

Impact of Utilisation
  Based on XML-XSL standard, which is becoming industrial one.
  Can utilise third party RTIs and inherits their middleware-specific performance.

Platform
  Development platforms: MS Windows NT 4, MS Windows 2000.
  Target platforms: all supporting XML and SOAP protocol.

Price
  Up today free downloadable BizTalk Jumpstart Kit is available.

Chapter 5. Product Data and Workflow Management

K. Drira, M. Molina, O. Nabuco, L.M. Rodriguez-Peralta, and T. Villemur

5.1 Product Data Management, Exchange, and Interoperability

Product Data Management (PDM) is an increasingly important technology for engineering and manufacturing enterprises. The information technology that supports Product Data Management requires standards in order to allow interoperability between systems and the sharing of product information between organizations. Two important sources of standards in this area are the Object Management Group (OMG) and the International Organization for Standardization (ISO) STEP community (officially ISO TC184/SC4 Industrial Data). This document will show how these two standards work together to support engineering and manufacturing processes in today's business environment.

5.1.1 General Presentation

A Product Data Management System is a set of coordinated tools that traces and controls product information from development throughout manufacturing, tests and recycles phase. Such systems are known generically as Engineering Data Management (EDM) systems. There are many types of systems within the generic class of EDM systems such as those ones known as Product Data Management (PDM) systems, and those known as Engineering Document Management Systems (EDMS). Also Enovia and MatrixOne refuse the PDM logo using instead eBusiness Solutions and collaborative product commerce (CPC) or Virtual Product Development Management known as PDMII.

The challenge is to maximize the time-to-market benefits of concurrent engineering while maintaining control of the data and distributing it automatically to the people whom need it - when they need it. The way PDM systems cope with this challenge is that master data is held only once in a secure 'vault' where its integrity can be assured and all changes to it monitored, controlled and recorded.

They manage engineering data and provide improved management of the engineering process through better control of engineering data, of engineering activities, of engineering changes and of product configurations. PDM systems also provide support for the activities of product teams (also collaborating teams, web enable teams) and for techniques, such as Concurrent Engineering, that aim to improve engineering workflow. They provide tools for management of web supply chain manufacturing.

They allow companies to get control of engineering information, and to supervize activities in several departments. In the long term, PDM systems could allow companies to get control of all their engineering information, and manage the overall engineering process.

K. Drira, A. Martelli, T. Villemur (Eds.): Cooperative Environments, LNCS 2236, pp. 107-151, 2001.
© Springer-Verlag Berlin Heidelberg 2001

PDM systems provide a backbone for the controlled flow of engineering information throughout the product life cycle. Other systems using engineering data, such as CAD, ERP and field service, will be integrated to this backbone (that's why standards interfaces are for). PDM systems address both information and workflow issues. As such they intend to be true integration tools. In particular, within the engineering environment, they are central to the integration of previously separated systems such as CAD, CAM, CSM, Electronic Publishing, Configuration Management, Process Planning, Document Scanning and Project Management.

From information warehouse to workflow management, they have to perform data and process management.

Data management systems should be able to control attribute and documentary product data, as well as relationships between them, through database system. With so much data being generated, a technique needs to be established to classify this information easily and quickly.

Process management controls the way in which people create and modify data by using active procedures. It is like a distributed operational system focusing in product development from the engineering point of view.

A PDM system offers a solution by acting as the engineer's working environment, meticulously capturing all new and changed data as it is generated. It maintains a record of which version the data is, recalling data on demand and effectively keeping track of the engineer's every move. PDM systems vary widely in how they perform these functions.

According Stark [79] there are nine components in PDM Systems:

5.1.1.1 Information Warehouse
This is where the data is located, acting as a single source of all engineering information in the company. It can be distributed across different departments of the company and some with suppliers and customers.

Typical data are draws, CAD data, computer programs to be used in shop floor, bills of materials, product specification, technical manuals, standards (international, national and company-specific), process design, process specific and order specific information (with time and costs information included).

The role of the Information warehouse module is to store engineering data. Other names for the warehouse are Electronic Library, Electronic Vault, Information Vault, and Data Repository.

The Information warehouse will contain information about information. To track a customer order it could include information of his requirements and engineering change orders.

5.1.1.2 Information Management
It controls the flow of data to and from Information warehouse. It uses metadata to manage data. It has a pointer containing the attributes of different files such CAD, numerical results, engineering drawings, etc. and manages from simple files to relational/object-oriented/hierarchical databases.

The Information management module is aware of the various stages of the life cycles of the different information types. It knows how they are created, used modified, stored, and archived. It knows the possible release and revision levels of documents, and the steps they go through to be signed-off, released and changed.

The module knows the users and their privileges The Information management module is responsible for the security of information in the system. Security can be applied at different levels and on different categories such as per-user, per-information item, per-activity, or per-product. The module only provides access to authorized users, and refuses access to unauthorized users. It provides security information on any unauthorized attempts to access data.

The module can provide an audit trail of all actions taken on data. The audit trail shows who has accessed and changed both data and metadata.

The Information management module is responsible for the integrity of the warehouse preventing simultaneous update of information. It can manage the backup and archival of data and recover any information lost as the result of computer or human problems.

It is possible to use metadata items as search criteria. The module can search for the existence, location and status of particular information on the basis of pre-defined classification codes and characteristics such as physical properties, manufacturing processes, and part numbers. It can use metadata items for information browsing and navigation.

5.1.1.3 Infrastructure

All kind of operating systems including proprietary and all kind of computers may be present in an engineering platform. Also application packages of various sources, databases of different vendors, in-house developments and all sort of peripherals.

The environment varies from single user to multi-user geographically dispersed connected by WAN, LANs over Internet, Extranet or Intranet links.

5.1.1.4 Interface

The Interface module is made up of four sub-modules:
- user interface,
- program interface,
- data interface,
- information presentation.

This interface allows access to people working in different stages of product life cycle, from shop floor to engineering. It should be easy to understand and use; suitable for casual and frequent users and offer an on-line help facility. It should include icon-driven, forms-driven and menu-driven approaches. Users must be able to tailor icons, forms and menus to their specific needs.

The data interface sub-module provides efficient and secure data exchange and data translation functionality for data that may be either in the PDM environment or outside it. For example, the PDM system may be managing data files on a CAD system and on a structural analysis system. If the data on the two systems are compatible, the data interface sub-module may be used to transfer data from the CAD system directly to the structural analysis system. If the data are not compatible, the data interface sub-module may be used to translate the CAD data to a suitable format, and then transfer it to the structural analysis program. The data interface sub-module should provide a set of translators, some standard, and some direct embedded in the module.

5.1.1.5 Information Structure Definition

The Information structure definition module is used to create the information structure of a product, and to create, by modification, the information structure of derivative product versions. It can support a hierarchy of classifications such as part, sub-assembly, assembly, component, product, and system, or segment, macro, function, and program.

5.1.1.6 Information Structure Management

The Information structure management module is used to maintain and work with information structures created by the Information structure definition module. Throughout the product life cycle, it maintains the relationships between the information structure and the information items.

At each stage of the life cycle, the Information structure management module is aware of the exact state of the associated information items describing product information such as specifications, drawings, parts lists, test results, and field information. It maintains a complete history of the product through design, manufacture and delivery to field use. It is aware of the status of all information (e.g. in-process, in-review, released), and can distinguish between the as-specified, as-designed, as-built, as-installed, and as-maintained configurations of the product.

As a design progresses, or product use evolves, the Information structure management module keeps track of modifications and of status. It tracks relationships within a particular product, among different versions of a product, and across product lines. It is aware of the relationships between the basic structure and the different views of the product structure, and allows user to work with information in any of the views. It can be used to provide structural information such as Bills of Materials, goes-into lists and belongs-to relationships.

At any time, the information structure of a product can be browsed through (or 'navigated' by paging down and across) to look for a specific part. The Information structure management module is at the heart of the PDM system, and it is aware of the status and relationships of all information in the system.

5.1.1.7 Workflow Structure Definition

The Workflow structure definition module is used to define the structure, flow and content of engineering activities. It defines the various tasks that make up each engineering activity, the relationships between activities, and the order and attributes of each task. The Workflow control module will later use these definitions to control the flow of work through engineering activities and tasks.

A wide range of engineering activities has to be defined. And they vary in size and complexity from lengthy and complex activities such as multi-year multi-disciplinary projects to short and simple activities such as document release. For program management, the activities to be defined could entail all the engineering processes that make up the entire life cycle for a particular product. In other cases the workflow structure definition module may be used to define an activity that is effectively an individual task. The Workflow structure definition module is used to define the structure and flow of all these activities.

The Workflow structure definition has to include all the information required to make workflow control possible. The structure of the workflow may be defined in different ways. Sometimes the workflow will already be well known in which case it can immediately be laid out in detail. In other cases, it may be possible to define the workflow for a particular activity by copying and modifying the workflow of an existing activity. Sometimes the workflow can be reconstructed by taking a finished product and working backwards to identify the activities used to produce it. In other cases the only solution may be to start with a blank sheet, and work forward to identify the individual activities that will occur. Once an activity has been started, it may be necessary to change the workflow, so the Workflow structure definition module has to be flexible enough to handle workflow changes.

5.1.1.8 Workflow Control

For each activity in the product life cycle, the product information and the workflow structures are defined using the Information structure definition module and the Workflow structure definition module.

The Workflow control module will keep status information up-to-date, and ensure that design information is handled as planned. It tracks product information moving through the various tasks. At any time, the Workflow control module will be able to display the exact status of each task it is managing. It will track, and be able to report, the status of all tasks in progress. It can produce progress reports at specified times, showing for example, how much lead-time has been used up, if bottlenecks are developing, and which resources are available.

It is event driven based, meaning that, when an event occurs, it flags the module which starts the subsequently activity. Events are pre-programmed in the workflow module.

When a process is well know, a particular workflow/product pair can be initiated. It assigns tasks to individuals, informs them of the resources to be used and the procedures to be followed, initiates the associated actions, and maintains status information. It manages the review, approval, communication and archival of information.

5.1.1.9 System Administration

The System Administration module of the PDM system is the module that allows the initial configuration and environment of the system to be described, and the system to be set up, installed and put into use. This module will also be used to handle the changes that will occur when the environment evolves, and when the use of PDM becomes more extensive.

The System Administration module will be used to define users to the system, identify applications in the environment, and initialize project creation rights. It will be used to define the access rights to particular data files. The module will also be used to define and modify the access rights of individual users to specific data and commands.

5.1.2 Standards and Committees

5.1.2.1 STEP – ISO 10303

STEP, Standard for the Exchange of Product Model Data [80], is the familiar name for ISO 10303, which is an International Standard for the computer-interpretable representation and exchange of product data. The objective is to provide a neutral mechanism capable of describing product data throughout the life cycle of a product, independent from any particular system. The nature of this description makes it suitable not only for neutral file exchange, but also as a basis for implementing and sharing product databases and archiving.

This International Standard is organized as a series of parts, each published separately. The parts of ISO 10303 fall into one of the following series: description methods, integrated resources, application-integrated constructs, application protocols, abstract test suites, implementation methods, and conformance testing. The series is described in ISO 10303-1.

5.1.2.2 STEP AP233 - Application Protocol for System Engineering
This part of ISO 10303 is a member of the application protocol series.

The System Engineering Application Protocol (AP) aims at the systems design processes. This application protocol defines the context, scope, and information requirements for various development stages during the design of a system and specifies the integrated resources necessary to satisfy these requirements. This application protocol shall be applicable to any forms of systems, such as aircraft, cars, marine, and plants.

In the context of aerospace and aircraft for instance, the term system comprises: avionics systems (e.g. mission, communication, navigation, human/system interface); and airframe systems (e.g. crew/passenger escape, power generation and distribution, environment control, fuel management). These systems are made up of a set of predominantly active components, sensors, displays and actuators that are interconnected via dedicated direct links or by communication means. Systems cannot be simply considered as a sum of the single components; rather, their integrated behaviour, which in most cases is real-time dependent, has to be defined, validated and verified.

5.1.2.3 STEP SDAI - Accessing Data in the STEP Framework
This part of ISO 10303 specifies an implementation method for a functional interface to data repositories that logically separates a computer application from the data storage technology. The interface is specified by the operations available to the application for purposes of acquiring and manipulating data whose structure is modelled in the EXPRESS (ISO 10303-11) language. SDAI is specified in a way independent of a programming language. STEP also specifies the binding between this neutral definition and specific programming/definition languages like C++ or CORBA IDL.

5.1.2.4 XML
XML Genesis (Predecessor, family and future)
The following scheme (see Figure 1) illustrates the genesis and possible future of XML (eXtensible Markup Language).

It is a simplified subset of a previous markup language standard called SGML (Standard Generalised Markup Language), and was devised by a committee of the

World Wide Web consortium (W3C) in response to the need for a generalisation of HTML, the Hypertext Markup Language used for formatting Web pages.

The WWW native language HTML may be considered as "brother" of XML (being based on the same SGML basis). But XML instead of HTML is intended for data structuring not for data presentation.

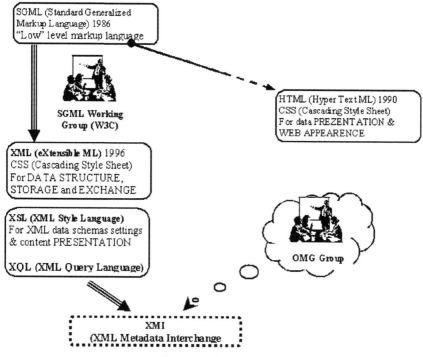

Fig. 1. XML Genesis

An XML document is a text file representing textual description of some hierarchical information.

The text in the left column of Table 1 is an example of weather report in XML-form with <WEATHERREPORT> uppermost node, two second-level node <STATE> with 3-d level nodes <CITY> and 4-th level nodes <SKIES>, <HI> and <LOW> (temperature).

Any node may have:
1. named attributes (e.g. nodes STATE have attribute NAME; nodes HI have attributes C and F);
2. the content (e.g. the content of the node <CITY NAME="Los Angeles"> is "Partly cloudy").

XML Parsing and Validating

Because every XML file is simply a text it should be imported into memory for further processing. There are special programs, so-called "parsers", intended for this procedure. These programs are middleware providing the interoperability of the XML format for different computer environments. A number of parsers already exists for different computing environment, e.g. Microsoft Win9*&NT as ActiveX ("Microsoft.XMLDOM"), as C++ and Java for Unix.

As a result of XML text file parsing (in case of success) the parser returns some object containing methods and properties providing access to the graph tree corresponding to the data structure described in XML file.

Table 1. Examples of XLM files

WeatherReport.xml file content	WeatherSchema.xml file content

<?xml version="1.0"?>
<WEATHERREPORT   xmlns="x-schema:WeatherSchema.xml">
  <STATE NAME="California">
    <CITY NAME="Los Angeles">
      <SKIES VALUE="PARTLYSUNNY"/>
      <HI C="31" F="87"/>
      <LOW C="18" F="65"/>
      Partly cloudy
    </CITY>
    <CITY NAME="Sacramento">
      <SKIES VALUE="SUNNY"/>
      <HI C="36" F="97"/>
      <LOW C="17" F="64"/>
      Sunny and hot.
    </CITY>
  </STATE>
  <STATE NAME="New Jersey">
    <CITY NAME="Newark">
      <SKIES VALUE="PARTLYSUNNY"/>
      <HI C="36" F="97"/>
      <LOW C="21" F="71"/>
      Partly sunny, breezy and humid
    </CITY>
    <CITY NAME="Trenton">
      <SKIES VALUE="PARTLYCLOUDY"/>
      <HI C="32" F="90"/>
      <LOW C="18" F="65"/>
      Partly cloudy and humid
    </CITY>
  </STATE>
</WEATHERREPORT>
	<Schema xmlns="urn:schemas-microsoft-com:xml-data"
	    xmlns:dt="urn:schemas-microsoft-com:datatypes">
	 <AttributeType name="C" required="yes" dt:type="string"/>
	 <AttributeType name="F" required="yes" dt:type="string"/>
	 <ElementType name="LOW">
	  <attribute type="C"/>
	  <attribute type="F"/>
	 </ElementType>
	 <ElementType name="HI">
	  <attribute type="C"/>
	  <attribute type="F"/>
	 </ElementType>
	 <AttributeType name="VALUE" required="yes" dt:type="enumeration" dt:values="SUNNY PARTLYSUNNY PARTLYCLOUDY CLOUDY RAIN SNOW"/>
	 <ElementType name="SKIES">
	  <attribute type="VALUE"/>
	 </ElementType>
	 <AttributeType name="NAME" required="yes" dt:type="string"/>
	 <ElementType name="CITY" content="mixed">
	  <attribute type="NAME"/>
	  <element type="SKIES"/>
	  <element type="HI"/>
	  <element type="LOW"/>
	 </ElementType>
	 <ElementType name="STATE" content="mixed">
	  <attribute type="NAME"/>
	  <element type="CITY"/>
	 </ElementType>
	 <ElementType name="WEATHERREPORT" content="eltOnly">
	  <element type="STATE"/>
	 </ElementType>
	</Schema>

During the parsing process, the parser checks the XML syntax and (optionally) checks if the input file content satisfies some additional rules.

E.g. in the "WhetherReport" example element (node) STATE should have attribute NAME and may have element CITY. Further, attribute VALUE is not optional and should take on a value from the following list "SUNNY PARTLYSUNNY PARTLYCLOUDY CLOUDY RAIN SNOW" etc.

Such validating is available and is supported by special DTD and XML schemas mechanism. XML schemas are in turn XML file containing the rule of some XML data structure.

E.g. XML schema corresponding to the WeatherReport example is presented in the second column of Table 1.

XML Schemas

The W3C XML Activity Page states: "While XML 1.0 supplies a mechanism, the Document Type Definition (DTD) for declaring constraints on the use of markup, automated processing of XML documents requires more rigorous and comprehensive facilities in this area. Requirements are for constraints on how the component parts of an application fit together, the document structure, attributes, datatyping, and so on. The W3C XML Schema Working Group is addressing means for defining the structure, content and semantics of XML documents."

As to the Distributed System Environment, the concept of XML schemas and XML namespace may provide the unity and framework specification for the project developed. E.g. one of the main ideas of the BizTalk server Microsoft initiative is to develop a number of XML schemas covering different fields of e-commerce and business. Being adopted these schemas will support the standards for interoperable environment.

The Schema document element can contain any number of top-level declarations. The principal XML Schema elements include ElementType (which declares element types) and AttributeType (which declares attribute types). These elements must have an explicit name attribute that is unique within the schema. The element and attribute elements can appear within the ElementType element to constrain its content and attributes. The ElementType attribute order and the group element allow you to further establish fine-grained definitions. The minOccurs and maxOccurs attributes allow you to define the number of occurrences of an element or group.

The content for an element of a given element type can be defined as one of four categories: empty (no content), text only, subelements only, or a mix of text and subelements. This choice is expressed in the ElementType attribute named content, which can take the values "empty," "textOnly," "eltOnly," and "mixed," respectively.

Element types and attribute types can constrain their values and contents to be instances of a particular data type, referenced from the datatype element namespace. To use the datatype namespace in a schema, it must be declared within the Schema element. The dt:type attribute can then be used to reference data types; in the Internet Explorer 5 implementation, element and attribute types can take "rich" data types.

Finally, note that in XML, schema files are optional and are not required. Some XML applications do not require validation and do not specify a schema file.

XML Schema Elements and Data Types Support
The different elements are listed in the two following Tables 2 and 3.

Table 2. XML Schema elements

ATTRIBUTE "NODE NAME"	Description
Attribute	Refers to a declared attribute type that can appear within the scope of the named ElementType element.
AttributeType	Defines an attribute type for use within the Schema element.
Datatype	Specifies the data type for the ElementType or AttributeType element.
Description	Provides documentation about an ElementType or AttributeType element.
Element	Refers to a declared element type that can appear within the scope of the named ElementType element.
ElementType	Defines an element type for use within the Schema element.
Group	Organizes content into a group to specify a sequence.
Schema	Identifies the beginning of a schema definition.

Table 3. Data Types XML Schema elements

dt: <name>	Description
bin.base64	MIME-style Base64 encoded binary BLOB.
bin.hex	Hexadecimal digits representing octets.
boolean	0 or 1, where 0 == "false" and 1 =="true".
char	String, one character long.
date	Date in a subset ISO 8601 format, without the time data. For example: "1994-11-05".
dateTime	Date in a subset of ISO 8601 format, with optional time and no optional zone. Fractional seconds can be as precise as nanoseconds. For example, "1988-04-07T18:39:09".
dateTime.tz	Date in a subset ISO 8601 format, with optional time and optional zone. Fractional seconds can be as precise as nanoseconds. For example: "1988-04-07T18:39:09-08:00".
fixed.14.4	Same as "number" but no more than 14 digits to the left of the decimal point, and no more than 4 to the right.
float	Real number, with no limit on digits; can potentially have a leading sign, fractional digits, and optionally an exponent. Punctuation as in U.S. English. Values range from 1.7976931348623157E+308 to 2.2250738585072014E-308.
int	Number, with optional sign, no fractions, and no exponent.
number	Number, with no limit on digits; can potentially have a leading sign, fractional digits, and optionally an exponent. Punctuation as in U.S. English. (Values have same range as most significant number, R8, 1.7976931348623157E+308 to 2.2250738585072014E-308.)

dt: <name>	Description
time	Time in a subset ISO 8601 format, with no date and no time zone. For example: "08:15:27".
time.tz	Time in a subset ISO 8601 format, with no date but optional time zone. For example: "08:1527-05:00".
i1	Integer represented in one byte. A number, with optional sign, no fractions, no exponent. For example: "1, 127, -128".
i2	Integer represented in one word. A number, with optional sign, no fractions, no exponent. For example: "1, 703, -32768".
i4	Integer represented in four bytes. A number, with optional sign, no fractions, no exponent. For example: "1, 703, -32768, 148343, -1000000000".
r4	Real number, with seven-digit precision; can potentially have a leading sign, fractional digits, and optionally an exponent. Punctuation as in U.S. English. Values range from 3.40282347E+38F to 1.17549435E-38F.
r8	Real number, with 15-digit precision; can potentially have a leading sign, fractional digits, and optionally an exponent. Punctuation as in U.S. English. Values range from 1.7976931348623157E+308 to 2.2250738585072014E-308.
ui1	Unsigned integer. A number, unsigned, no fractions, no exponent. For example: "1, 255".
ui2	Unsigned integer, two bytes. A number, unsigned, no fractions, no exponent. For example: "1, 255, 65535".
ui4	Unsigned integer, four bytes. A number, unsigned, no fractions, no exponent. For example: "1, 703, 3000000000".
uri	Universal Resource Identifier (URI). For example, "urn:schemas-microsoft-com:Office9".
uuid	Hexadecimal digits representing octets, optional embedded hyphens that are ignored. For example: "333C7BC4-460F-11D0-BC04-0080C7055A83".

XML and Interoperability
Because of its popularity and text representation, XML seems to become the standard for not very large information portion exchange between different computing environment. Figure 2 illustrates possible scheme of communication between some Windows application and Oracle DB over HTTP protocol by XML documents.

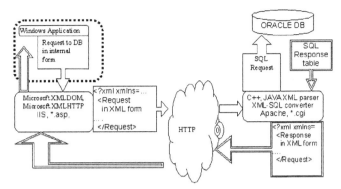

Fig. 2. Interoperability via XML

5.1.2.5 Product Data Markup Language

The DoD's Product Data Markup Language (PDML) [14] is an Extensible Markup Language (XML) vocabulary to support the interchange of Product Data Management (PDM) information. The specification is being developed with the cooperation of several major PDM vendors and the support of a US federal government contract (Department of Defense). The government and its subcontractors have a wide variety of different commercial and in-house developed PDM systems in service. Once completed, the specification will be submitted to an appropriate standards body for comment and approval. PDML group is now participating of SC4 meetings showing its early bind XML Data Type Definition (DTD) onto Express language.

PDML is a neutral format to access and retrieve information from PDM, legacy and other application systems that shares product data. PDML defines Application Transaction Sets (ATS) data requirements for different uses of data. They have an Integration Schema designed based on STEP Integrated Resources which is a vocabulary which could be used across communities. These sets are translators written in XML DTD that takes data from a system and puts it into Integration Schema format.

PDML schemas are specified by Express language (the meaning and constraints). It uses, as source, Product Structure and Product Descriptions of PDM Enablers to write two ATS. According PDML developers this implementation is more general than PDM Enablers and PDM Schema (see Table 4. Source http://www.pdit.com/pdml/PDMLSpecification05.ppt).

5.1.2.6 PDM Enablers

The OMG's PDM Enablers specification [69] establishes a framework for interfaces to PDM services, and a base object model. It exposes most PDM-supported objects in detail and provides "fine-grained" operations to manipulate those objects and their relationships. The last release was a revision of the existing work representing efforts of 6 major PDM vendors – Co-Create, Enovia, Fujitsu, Metaphase, Sherpa, and SAP, four major industrial users and NIST to finalize the reference specification for the first implementations in product and the first interoperability tests. The purpose of the OMG PDM Enablers is to provide access to the services of product data management systems from various application software systems in a manufacturing enterprise. Activities supported by such "client" applications encompass product conception and planning, product design, manufacturing engineering, production, delivery and maintenance.

Table 4. Comparison between PDML, PDM Enablers and PDM Schema

	PDML	PDM Enablers	PDM Schema
Functional Objective	Integration	Access	Interfacing
Implementation Objective	Accommodate: 2549, STEP APs, XML, PDM Enablers, PDM Schema	PDM Vendor	AP203/214
Customer Requirement	Government	PDM Vendors/users	PDES, Inc. & ProSTEP
Scope	Product Data	PDM System Only	Subset of AP203 & AP214
Schema	based on STEP IR	Object Model (UML) based on STEP	STEP Aps
Transaction Sets	XML	IDL	Express/ P21
Data Sharing Method	XML/File exchange	CORBA/Access	P21/SDAI
Validation	During POC - use real world data/ environment	Vendor product based	PDES Inc / ProSTEP Roundtable (pay to play)
Access Method	PDM Enablers, SDAI, XML, SGML, ODBC, etc.	CORBA	SDAI

The PDM Enablers are intended to support manufacturing activities, and particularly engineering activities, operating on specifications in varying stages of completion and release. For this reason the emphasis is on the services of the PDM and other engineering data management systems that implement these interfaces.

The PDM Enablers are a standards-based Application Programming Interface (API), specified in Interface Definition Language (IDL), that makes PDM services available in a CORBA environment to other systems that require them (such as CAD, CAE, CAM systems mentioned above, and even other PDM systems). Following the CORBA model, CAX systems can use the PDM Enablers API and the standard network interfaces to interact directly with any conforming PDM system.

The PDM Enablers provide direct interfaces to support Document management, Product Structure management, Change management, Configuration management

(Product Options), and Manufacturing implementation specifications, and include support for Views, Effectivities, and Baselines. A special Enabler provides for import and export of STEP exchange files. The PDM Enablers are intended to provide interface to the services of a PDM system operating in an arbitrary manufacturing enterprise with an enterprise-specific schema.

The Enablers constitute a model of PDM interfaces that can be mapped to commercially available PDM systems. As such, they are not meant to be a definitive model of PDM Objects or Systems. They are intended to serve Work-in-Process PDM systems as well as Enterprise-level Release Management PDM Systems, and they are intended to support most engineering activities, but not all PDM activities. Interfaces for PDM administration, for example, are not in the scope of the standard.

The main elements of the PDM Enablers' model are the inheritance hierarchy and the relationships among objects. The STEP PDM Schema was used as a reference model in constructing this framework of relationships, and the Enablers adhere to that model, except in a few cases. Where the STEP PDM Schema did not cover an area of functionality, a specific STEP Application Protocol was used to the extent possible.

Most of the differences between the Enablers and the STEP standards arise from the need to support work-in-process PDM services and other dynamic services of the PDM system, and from the need to support enterprise-specific extensions and modifications to the PDM schema.

This work is supported by ATI, The Boeing Company, ERIM, Enovia, EuroSTEP Limited, Ford, IBM Corporation, INSO Corporation, Metaphase/SDRC, MSC.Software Corporation, NCMS PDES Inc., ProSTEP GmbH, NASA and NIST.

5.1.2.7 STEP's PDM Schema

The STEP PDM Schema [70] is a reference information model for the exchange of a central, common subset of the data being managed within a PDM system. It represents the intersection of requirements and data structures from a range of STEP Application Protocols, all generally within the domains of design and development of discrete electro/mechanical parts and assemblies.

The PDM Schema has been established to promote interoperability between STEP APs in the area of product data management [68]. It aims to establish a common schema for PDM vendors to implement and for AP developers to use as building blocks. Establish a core set of entities in STEP that supports the mapping of concepts for Product Data Management. As stated in this section, PDM systems have several modules. PDM Schema addresses some of these like identification, versioning, structures including transformations, approvals and authorization, project work order, work request, effectivity, classification and properties structures to manage the documentation of requests and corresponding orders for engineering action, in support of the change management process. Also included are representations for contract and project identification.

Companies who participate in the consortium are Army, Boeing, British Aerospace, Delphi Automotive Systems, Electric Boat, Ford, General Motors, IBM, Lockheed Martin, MSC Software, NASA, NIST, Northrop Grumman, Parametric Technology Corporation, Rockwell, Rolls-Royce, SDRC, Spatial, Theorem Solutions, United Technologies Corporation, Advanced Technology Institute (ATI).

5.1.2.8 PDX

PDX (located at http://www.pdxstandard.org/) is the Product Definition eXchange standard for the e-supply chain. The PDX standardisation effort is focused on the problem of communicating product content information between Original Equipment Manufacturers (OEMs), Electronic Manufacturing Service (EMS) providers and component suppliers. The standard is based on XML because this provides a simple yet powerful and flexible way to encode structured data into a format that is both human and machine-readable. The PDX standard provides a way to describe product content (Bill of Materials (BOMs), Drawings, etc.), Efficient Consumer Response (ECRs), Efficient Consumer Order (ECOs), Deviations and RFQs in an XML format. This standard will enable dramatic efficiency improvements throughout the supply chain since partners will have a way to exchange product content and changes in a common language.

Supply chain partners benefit directly from a standardized product definition exchange mechanism as they are required to allocate fewer of their valuable resources to normalizing incoming product definitions and importing them into their in-house systems. Even more significant than this however is reduced turnaround time. The adoption of a standard facilitates a more automated product content exchange process which itself accelerates the process but more importantly, it also improves accuracy. Accuracy problems sometimes cause delays of several days or more before the incorrect data is discovered and repaired. By eliminating some of these problems, PDX can significantly reduce the amount of time it takes to get new products into production. In today's highly competitive environment, this reduced time-to-market translates into increased profits for the entire supply chain.

5.1.3 Products

There are several PDM products and they vary in capabilities, from those who allows to define a classification at the time when data base is implemented to others that allows it "on the fly".

There are more than thirty PDM vendors but eight of then has 80% of installed base. Around 75% of the installed base belong to big companies (according Fortune's classification). The costs vary from U$5K to U$100K plus server costs plus seats. The package may include the necessary training to operate these systems. But there is also a movement toward medium and small size companies market because of the supply chain these companies share with the big ones [84].

To understand the matrix Figure 3, a company in the GartnerGroup PDM enterprise leaders quadrant has more than $100 million in annual PDM revenue, growth at or above the industry average, a clean balance sheet (e.g., little or no debt and generating cash), consistently profitable operating performance, and a global installed base of 400 or more installations, with 75 percent or more in full or partial production. Its technology foundation must be fully Web-enabled (read and write) and be proven in large installations (with several hundred to several thousand simultaneous users) across geographically dispersed sites. Also, 25 percent or more of the installations must be using the full-core PDM application suite (e.g., vault, workflow and configuration management), and 50 percent of the implementations must be connected and interoperating with one or more enterprise application (e.g.,

CAD, Enterprise Resource Planning (ERP)) [13]. This matrix shows the leaders companies in PDM's market. There is also a briefing of five products which supplies the aeronautics and defense market.

Source of Figure 3 is the Gartner Group.

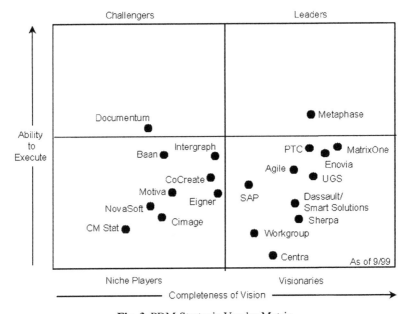

Fig. 3. PDM Strategic Vendor Matrix

5.1.3.1 Enovia Digital Enterprise Solution
Enovia Corporation (http://www.enovia.com/) is a Dassault Systems company and with IBM it forms the Enovia Digital Enterprise Solution. The Portfolio combines ENOVIAVPM and ENOVIAPM digital enterprise solutions to help small and large manufacturers create, manage, communicate, and digitally simulate all aspects of the product life cycle, regardless of existing CAD or ERP systems.

ENOVIAPM

General Description
ENOVIAPM supports business processes including engineering and manufacturing change management, requests for engineering actions, change release, and distribution. It also includes off-the-shelf integration with enterprise resource planning (ERP), computer aided design (CAD), office and other information systems.

Available Functionality
Expanded access to product data through the Java-based Web browser client interface.

Enhancements to ENOVIAPM have extended enterprise support by providing a federated corporate PDM function for central management of distributed ENOVIAPM data and processes.

A powerful Rules Based Configurator (RBC) for managing generic product definition.

Additional life-cycle support in such areas as product serialization and tracking, product and part obsolescence, rules based workflow and approved part usage.

Maintainability and Support
Openness and flexibility to adapt to specific customer requirements through Advanced Customization Environment allowing to extend functionality and to extend or modify the system's data model.

Extensive suite of associated integration solutions with other major industry applications such as CAD, ERP, office automation and components catalog: Integration between ENOVIAPM and Pro/ENGINEER®, CATIA®, MICRO CADAM®, AutoCAD®, and Professional CADAM® enables access to ENOVIAPM from the tools and allows the user to perform some ENOVIAPM functions.

Platform
ENOVIAPM is installed and operated as an open client/server application.

ENOVIAPM server runs on IBM AIX, Sun Solaris and HP-UX and supports either DB2/6000 or ORACLE as the underlying database.

ENOVIAPM client runs on Windows, SGI IRIX, IBM AIX, Sun Solaris, Macintosh, and HP-UX.

Zero-installation Web Interface, based on JAVA technology, accessible from any of the popular Web browsers.

ENOVIAVPM

General Description
ENOVIAVPM allows engineers to design and optimize a product, and its associated processes and resources, during the development stages. Its shared product model captures both product geometry and product behaviour. It also allows customers to build and change multiple product configurations using "engineering actions" that record and trace individual changes made to the product model.

Available Functionality
Private or local vaulting for documents and product information, including product structure definitions.

- Definition of engineering actions. Actions allow, define and trace changes to product data.
- Configuration definition. Designed to allow flexibility and rapid configuration prototyping, configuration mechanisms will support part versioning and roll-up, part-level configurations, configuration mix-and-match, views, parallel designs, instance-level object definition, etc.
- Storage and management of technological links.

- Event notification. A publish/subscribe mechanism can trigger system messages or processes to accelerate user notification and implementation of derived actions.
- Generative document management. Managing associativity between technical documentation and the related products to ensure that documents reflect product changes.
- Profile based pre-packaged applications for: Engineers, Managers/Supervisors, Reviewers, Technical writers, Administrators.

Maintainability and Support
Authoring and visualisation tools plug-ins.

Open programming interfaces and use of industry standards to enable customization, enhancement and interfacing to legacy systems and other applications.

ENOVIA product lines are CAX-independent and require appropriate "plug-ins" supplied by ENOVIA or its partners to connect the tools.

Platform
The ENOVIAVPM server runs on IBM AIX, Sun Solaris, SGI IRIX, and HP-UX and supports either DB2/6000 or ORACLE as the underlying database.

The ENOVIAVPM client side runs on Windows platforms, SGI IRIX, AIX, Sun Solaris, and HP-UX.

Aeronautics' Customers
Boeing Joint Strike Fighter, Alenia Aeronautica, Bombardier Aerospace.

5.1.3.2 Windchill
http://www.ptc.com/products/windchill/productmgmt/ds_pdm.htm

General Description
Windchill is a Parametric Technology Corporation PDM solution based on the universal browser interface and standard Internet technologies such as URLs, HTML and XML. Windchill eliminates the problems associated with developing, deploying and learning proprietary client/server applications.

Available Functionality
Product Structure Management, enables users to create and manipulate various representations of Bill of Materials (BOMs).

Multi-level BOM reporting. This feature creates two kinds of essential HTML reports: a hierarchical report and a summarized parts list report.

BOM view management. Participants need to view BOM information in different formats, based on their role in the organization.

Effectivity provides the ability to indicate when a part is active and is designed to facilitate the progressive definition of a product.

Baseline feature allows users in an organization to take a snapshot of significant parts and documents within product structures at arbitrary milestones throughout the product and process lifecycle.

Document referencing provides the ability to associate documents to parts within a product structure, allowing authors to attach supporting information.

Dynamic hierarchical navigation lets users search for parts, navigate within product structures, and perform operations on selected parts.

Change references. Net change allows a user to select two product structures for comparison and understand how they differ from each other.

Change Management. Change processing is divided into separate phases, including change request, investigation of the root cause, proposal of alternative solutions, and implementation through change orders and activities. In each phase, relevant information is captured and organized for future reference.

Workflow automation.

Platform
Client/Servers OS: Win/NT 4.0, Solaris 2.6, HPUX 10.2, HPUX 11, and IRIX 6.5.1.
- Clients: Win 95 OS and Win 98
- Data Base Server: Oracle8 Server Enterprise Edition
- Server: Netscape Enterprise Server, Internet Information Server, Verity Search97 Information Server, IBM XML 4J Parser, and IBM XSL Processor.
- Clients: Netscape, Internet Explorer, and Adobe Acrobat Reader

5.1.3.3 Metaphase Technology
http://www.sdrc.com/solutions-partners/metaphase

General Description
Metaphase offers a Web-centric information infrastructure that harnesses its customers' intellectual capital to drive product innovation and manage the complete product life cycle. SDRC company is preparing to launch Metaphase Team, a lower-priced and easier-to-install version of its market-leading Metaphase PDM software.

Available Functionality
There are four solutions delivered by Metaphase: a solution to control product information, to configure the entire product life cycle, to enable collaboration between teams and connecting products information from its original system into PDM systems.

To Control, Metaphase uses MetaDM (Metaphase Document Manager) to manager documents widely dispersed from different authoring; MetaChange to track changes in documents based in best practices and standard based change models as CMII, EIA/IS 649, ISO 10007/10303, STEP and MIL-STD 2549; MetaSM (Storage Manager) to maintain relationships between data, to maintain data integrity and to identify data consistency.

To Connect product information Metaphase has interfaces with important CAD vendors (Pro/Engineer, AutoCAD, FrameMaker...), with Enterprise Resource Planning vendors (SAP, Oracle) and commitment with STEP and CORBA standards.

To Configure it uses Slate that is a groupware solution to which supports product design teams to build and describe complex products on a system basis. Metaphase

Configuration capabilities manage the processes associated with taking a product to market and continuing its support after customer purchase.

Metaphase Collaboration capabilities manage works-in-process so companies can increase the innovative content they introduce in new products, gaining greater competitive position. The capability is implemented using MetaVPM (Virtual Product Manager) and MetaSlate.

Price
SDRC completed the acquisition of Sherpa Systems in January 2000 to become the dominant supplier of PDM solutions with an estimated 40% market share and over 340,000 production users world-wide.

The full version of Metaphase is priced at about $2,000 per seat; typical installations cost approximately $500,000 [19].

Aerospace and Defense Customers:
Alliant Techsystems, Boeing, Giat Industries, Holland Signaal, Honeywell, Lockheed Martin, Northrop Grumman, Rockwell, Rolls-Royce, Aerospace Thomson, Tusas Aerospace, Industries UK Ministry of Defense, United Defense.

5.1.3.4   MatrixOne
http://www.matrixone.com

General Description
MatrixOne offers its eMatrix web solution enables worldwide teams to share information across federate databases regardless data model server or location.

Available Functionality
The eMatrix solution has three modules, the Advantage Web server, the Integration Tools and Business Applications.

The web server supports secure data storage, access and control; lifecycle and process management; global dissemination of business operations and procedures. The server has five components: a Navigator's graphical browser that enables to create objects, define relationships among objects and build associate process; a web Navigator client, offering secure access to enterprise information; a business modeller; a system manager; and a business object server which is a CORBA compliant server.

The integration tools uses Adaplets, a technology to interfaces legacy databases and other information sources.

The Business Applications tailors custom business application.

Platforms
   Compaq Tru64 Unix
   Hewlett Packard HP-UX
   IBM AIX
   Microsoft Windows 95/98
   Microsoft Windows NT or Intel
   SGI IRIX
   Sun Solaris

5.1.3.5 e-Vis.com
http://www.e-vis.com

General Description

Web-based workspace for sharing documents, applications and information. e-Vis.com users can store, organize and view project data from different sources including CAD, PDM and ERP systems, receive notification when the data changes, track decisions, communicate via instant messages and conduct virtual conferences over the Internet.

e-Vis.com is not a PDM system. It is an enhancement to PDM systems. It also complements multiple CAD/CAM environments and corporate/project databases. e-Vis.com provides a secure environment (on the base of HTTPS with RSA (512bit) open key). Data from other PDM systems such as Metaphase, INSO, MatrixOne, PTC and Unigraphics can be integrated into and referenced from e-Vis.com.

e-Vis permits to organize different kinds of documents on the base of project concept. The user can create projects and folders within the project. Then registered project participants can upload different files into these folders to share work.

e-Vis.com users can view data in a variety of 2D and 3D formats, including over thirty 2D raster and vector formats and documents. It also reads and displays high-performance DirectModel files that allow users to interact with large models and assemblies. In addition, it supports 3D CAD translators for CATIA, Pro/ENGINEER, I-DEAS, Unigraphics and CADDS as well as neutral file format support for STEP, IGES, VRML, DXF and STL.

Available Functionality

Major features of e-Vis are:

- Secure sharing of product data such as documents, drawings and 3D models that reside in PDM, CAD, ERP or legacy database systems
- Familiar Web browser interface for creating and administering projects and teams
- High-performance, Web-based visualization of 2D and 3D data and documents
- Interactive conferencing for real-time design reviews and shared visualization and markup of documents, drawings and 3D models
- Threaded discussion forum that tracks issues, conflict resolution and decision rationale
- Intelligent indexing and searching of data stored within e-Vis.com and in any user-specified data repository
- Automatic notification of changes in user-defined areas of e-Vis.com
- Application sharing that allows multiple people to view and edit documents created in common applications such as Microsoft Word and Excel
- Instant messaging and real-time chat
- Single configurable visual interface shared across the extended enterprise and supply chain.

- Secure network access via the Internet backed by Hewlett Packard's Praesidium world-wide security infrastructure
- Caching for high-performance data access
- Access to industry news, editorials, Webcasts, training and other topics of interest to the manufacturing community
- Enhancements to e-Vis.com's functionality via "E-services" downloaded from e-Vis.com on a pay-per-use basis

Future Evolutions
Support for UNIX (including HP-UX, IRIX, Sun Solaris, and AIX) is announced.

Maintainability
Updates, upgrades and new features will be made available to registered users via the e-Vis.com portal at http://www.e-vis.com

Impact of Utilization
The product is still "under construction". So, there are some troubles even during running trial versions.

Learnability
Free for 30-day trial client part can be downloaded. Include 2D and 3D assemblies viewer, conferencing and messaging tools.

Help and trial tours also available.

Platform
Windows NT 4.0 (with Service Pack 5, minimum), or Windows 95 (with Year 2000 update), or Windows 98 (with Year 2000 update)

Netscape Navigator (4.08 minimum), or Internet Explorer (4.01 Service Pack 2)
50 MB disk space

Price
Subscriptions to e-Vis.com are available at three levels: Standard, Deluxe and Professional.

The Standard version costs $89 per month, per user, and includes all basic e-Vis.com functionality: Project management, Project Binder, Decision Capture, Change Notification, Search and Instant Messaging in addition to Conferencing features, Product Structure (tree) and 2D and 3D Viewing.

The Deluxe version costs $129 per month per user and includes all the features of the Standard version plus 2D/3D Measurement and Markup.

The Professional version costs $169 per month per user and includes all features of the Deluxe version plus PMI Viewing

VisView or VisMockUp users can upgrade to the Professional version for $39 per month per user.

Disk space is charged at a rate of $30/GB/month based on average usage.

5.1.4 Supporting and Using Industries

5.1.4.1 Systems Integration for Manufacturing Application Programs

National Institute and Standard Technology (NIST) Programs [59] deal with Manufacturing Enterprise Integration and encompass several projects in a manufacturing organization's business processes, structure, and technical systems.

NIST acts as a neutral information repository that can be used by enterprises to make decisions regarding the adoption and deployment of software technologies, used individually or in combination with one another, to integrate people, software, and machines across the manufacturing enterprise. It is deeply related with ISO PDM's program and OMG efforts providing support and working together with their standard activities.

The dominant information standardization activities undertaken by the program are those of the ISO Technical Committee on Industrial Automation Systems and Integration, Sub-committee on Industrial Data (ISO TC184 SC4). The Manufacturing Enterprise Integration program works within ISO TC184 SC4 to develop a broad set of interrelated information standards, it participates in the administration of standards activities, and it contributes to the development of information structure, quality, and management.

This program developed an interface definition for Product Data Management (PDM) software. The interface definition provided a basis for future development of the PDM Enablers interface standard under the auspices of the Object Management Group (OMG). This program currently conducts a large portion of the formal interface standardization within the OMG Manufacturing Domain Task Force.

Enterprise systems whose interface definitions are either under development or review within this program include Supply Chain Management (SCM) systems, Enterprise Resource Planning (ERP) systems, Manufacturing Execution Systems (MES), Machine Control (MC) systems and PDM systems.

The top-level work is conducted largely through participation in the ISO Working Group on Modelling and Architecture (ISO TC/184/SC5/WG1), the IFAC/IFIP (International Federation of Automatic Control / International Federation for Information Processing) Task Force for Enterprise Integration [92]. The approach for this part of the program is to develop a common taxonomy that reflects the domain of enterprise integration, requirements for enterprise representations, a general reference model for enterprise integration, as well as other products that support the development analysis, and operation of top-level enterprise models.

NIST actively participated in initial drafting through adoption of the Product Data Management Enablers interface standard by OMG. It also participates in the development of ISO 184 SC4 information model standards.

5.1.4.2 Using Industries

Table 5 summarizes the main use of Product Data Management by industries.

Table 5. Industries using Product Data Management products

Singapore Technologies Aerospace (ST Aero)	Metaphase product data management software and related services.
Lockheed Martin - Government Electronic Systems	Windchill
Boeing	Metaphase
Lockheed Virtual Fighters	Metaphase
Alcatel Space Industries	WorkManager
Siemens Automotive Streamlines Global Design and Manufacturing	MatrixOne
Northrop Grumman	Metaphase

5.2 Workflow Management

5.2.1 General Presentation

Workflow is defined by the Workflow Management Coalition as "the automation of a business process, in whole or part, during which documents, information or tasks are passed from one participant to another for action, according to a set of procedural rules".

Workflow management systems have their origins in a number of different developments to automate and support business applications, the principals are document management, image processing, electronic mail, GroupWare applications and business process re-engineering.

5.2.2 Standards and Committees

5.2.2.1 Standardization Organizations

The main organizations involved in workflow standards definition are the Object Management Group (OMG) and the Workflow Management Coalition (WfMC).

OMG works in the standardization of IDL interfaces to execute workflow services under CORBA architectures.

The WfMC is a grouping of companies who have joined together to avoid the creation of "islands" of processes automation. It has been recognized that all work flow management products have some common characteristics, enabling them potentially to achieve a level of interoperability through the use of common standards for various functions. The WfMC Coalition has been established to identify these functional areas and develop appropriate specifications for implementation in workflow products. It is intended that such specifications will enable interoperability between heterogeneous workflow products and improved integration of workflow applications with other Information Technology (IT) services such as electronic mail and document management, thereby improving the opportunities for the effective use of workflow technology within the IT market, to the benefit of both vendors and users of such technology.

5.2.2.2 Process Definition

The purpose of modelling is to produce an abstraction of a process (model) that serves as a basis for the workflow specification. The model of a process enables us to understand what activities, dependencies among activities, and roles (human or information system skills) are necessary to the process.

UML Extension

UML has created an extension for business modeling. It consists of the definition of stereotypes that can be used to tailor the use of UML in business modeling. All of the UML concepts can be used for business modeling, but providing business stereotypes for some common situations provides a common terminology for this domain. Note that UML can be used to model different kinds of systems: software systems, hardware systems, and real-world organizations. Business modeling models real-world organizations.

IDEFØ

IDEFØ is a method designed to model the decisions, actions, and activities of an organization or system. IDEFØ was derived from a well-established graphical language, the Structured Analysis and Design Technique (SADT). The United States Air Force commissioned the developers of SADT to develop a function modeling method for analyzing and communicating the functional perspective of a system. Effective IDEFØ models help to organize the analysis of a system and to promote good communication between the analyst and the customer. IDEFØ is useful for establishing the scope of an analysis, especially for a functional analysis. As a communication tool, IDEFØ enhances domain expert involvement and consensus decision-making through simplified graphical devices. As an analysis tool, it assists the modeler by identifying what functions are performed, what is needed to perform them, what the current system does right and wrong. Thus, IDEFØ models are often created as one of the first tasks of a system development effort.

In December 1993, the Computer Systems Laboratory of the National Institute of Standards and Technology (NIST) released IDEFØ as a standard for Function Modeling in FIPS Publication 183.

5.2.2.3 Enactment Service

The workflow enactment service provides the run-time environment in which process instantiation and activation occurs, utilising one or more workflow management engines, responsible for interpreting and activating part or the whole of the process model and interacting with the external resources necessary to process the different activities.

WfMC Workflow Application Programming Interface Protocol
The Workflow Application Programming Interface (WAPI) may be regarded as a set of API calls and interchange functions supported by a workflow enactment service at its boundary for interaction with other resources and applications. Although this architecture refers to 5 "interfaces" within WAPI, a number of the functions within each of these interfaces are common (for example process status calls may be issued from the client application interface or the administration interface). The WAPI is thus being defined as a common core of API calls /interchange formats with specific extensions where necessary to cater individually for each of the five functional areas.

The majority of WAPI functions comprises APIs calls with defined parameter sets / results codes. Where appropriate it also defines interchange data formats, for example for the exchange of process definitions.

OMG IDL Based WF Facilities
OMG evaluates a submission, presented by the WfMC, that specifies interfaces for workflow execution control, monitoring, and interoperability between workflows defined and managed independently of each other. The interfaces are based on a model of workflow objects, which includes their relationships and dependencies with requesters, assignments, and resources. The core workflow interfaces are defined in the WorkflowModel module. The model is graphically represented in UML class and object interaction diagrams, and specified by IDL interfaces. For each interface, its attributes, relationships, state set and its operations are described. Standard patterns are used for operations realizing relationships and access to attributes and object state.

SWAP Working Group
There is no standard way to communicate and interoperate across heterogeneous workflow (WF) engines in order to coordinate and execute work process instances across those WF engines. Most of the solutions existing today are vendor specific. This means that WF vendors need to support multiple protocols to enable interoperability between WF systems.

The goal of the SWAP Working group is to develop the goals and requirements for Workflow systems interoperability.

5.2.3 Products

5.2.3.1 Oracle Workflow
General Description
Oracle® Workflow is a complete workflow management system that supports business process definition and automation. Its technology enables automation and continuous improvement to business processes, routing information of any type according to user-defined business rules. Oracle Workflow is part of the Oracle E-Business Suite, an integrated set of applications, which is designed to transform your business to an e-business.

Available Functionality

Oracle Workflow allows you to provide all parties in a business process with all the information they need to make the right decision in an efficient manner. Oracle Workflow can route summary and detail information to each decision maker in your workflow process, whether that process is a self-service transaction, a standard business document approval, or a software implementation. It also lets you reference documents in your business process that are dynamically generated from data in your Oracle-based application.

Oracle Workflow lets you model and maintain your business processes using a graphical workflow builder. Unlike those workflow systems that simply route documents from one user to another with some approval steps, Oracle Workflow allows you to model and automate sophisticated business processes. You can define processes that loop, branch into parallel flows and rendezvous, decompose into sub-flows, branch on task results, timeout, and more.

Oracle Workflow extends the reach of business process automation throughout your enterprise and beyond to include any e-mail or Web user. It allows people to receive, analyze, and respond to notifications needing their attention via Oracle Applications, any standard e-mail system, or standard Web browser.

The heart of Oracle Workflow is the rules-based workflow engine residing in the Oracle 8i database. Oracle 8i transactional integrity guarantees consistency between your application and workflow.

Oracle Workflow Builder (Figure 4) provides a graphical drag and drop process designer. It allows you to modify existing business processes without changing applications code—a clear reduction in the cost of change and ownership.

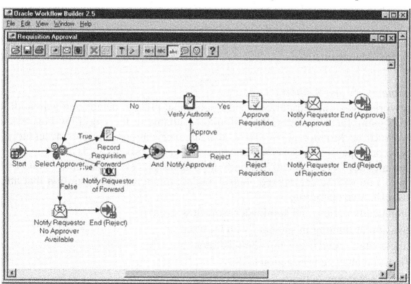

Fig. 4. Oracle WorkFlow process diagrams

- Workflow Builder
  - Graphical Drag and Drop Process Designer
- Workflow Engine
  - Manages business process execution
  - Immediate and deferred execution
  - Generates complete process audit trail
  - Supports sophisticated business rules
  - Incorporates human decision points into process execution
  - Automatically manages process exceptions
  - Maintains multiple active versions of a process
  - Implements new process versions without interrupting active work items
  - Programmatic extensibility using PL/SQL and Oracle 8i Advanced Queues
- Notifications
  - Sends messages to individuals and roles
  - Processes responses from recipients to Workflow Engine
  - Automatic notification forward and response
  - Change participants in a group role without changing the business process
  - Internet-Enabled Standard Web browser to review and respond Drill-down to any URL or Applications screen Available from Oracle Applications, Self-Service Applications, and Business Intelligence System
  - E-mail Standard Mail Protocols (Oracle Internet Messaging, MAPI, UNIX Sendmail) Detail and summary message formats Template and direct response Plain text or HTML message body HTML Attachments

Type of Applications
Workflow Management

Maintainability and Support
As a Workflow administrator, you view additional process details and gain additional controls using the same Workflow Monitor available to the workflow business user. The Workflow Monitor allows easy manual intervention whenever necessary. You can stop or to pause a process while you investigate a processing issue. You can retry or skip any activity. You can "rewind" a business process to an earlier state and re-execute. You get the centralized control and simplicity of administration that are key to cost-effective operation:
- Graphically review and administer workflow events
- Java applet running in standard web browser
- Single site for end users and administrators
- View and analyze transaction history
- Retry or skip any activity
- Rewind and re-execute any process
- Summary of decision makers
- Current decision maker
Oracle provides consulting, education, and support services.
http://www.oracle.com/support

Platform
Microsoft Windows 95/98/NT, Unix

Price
Workflow Enterprise Edition (Part A80464) named User Multi Server $75.00

5.2.3.2 C4 Software - Process Director
http://www.c4software.com

General Description
100% Java based Process Director brings the latest workflow standards (OMG, IETF, WFMC) together to form a development, integration and deployment environment for enterprise-wide process automation applications. The product set includes components for the full life-cycle of the business process including design, deployment, execution, monitoring, reporting and archiving.

Available Functionality
Process Director is packaged in two forms:
   I) A set of Java components for building workflow enabled applications. The product set includes components for the full life-cycle of the business process including design, deployment, execution, monitoring, reporting and archiving. For developers implementing solutions for Internet, Intranet or Extranet deployment Process Director has a rich set of client and server interfaces including integration with JavaBeans and ActiveX components with none or minimal programming. The Process Director environment includes tools and applications, which allow:

- Design of complex business processes spanning multiple organizations using process constructs such as parallel flows, events and timeouts.
- Scheduling of the business processes using a number of different algorithms including by role, group, and priority workload.
- Integration of business processes with existing applications.
- Browser based client interfaces.
- Monitoring of business processes though client tools.
- Feedback through reports and audit trails.
- Administration from a single console.
- Use of standard infrastructure components such as WWW,
- Mail and Directory servers.

   II) An Original Equipment Manufacturer (OEM) program designed specifically to address the needs of organizations that require integrating or embedding workflow technology within their products and solutions. This program offers:

- Assessment of your exact requirements and the integration options best suited for your needs.
- Design and development of your unique processes including
    - GUI components.
    - A choice of a wide variety of protocols such as Sockets, RMI, CORBA, SMTP and HTTP.

- A choice of a wide variety of databases for integration either through JDBC/ODMG interfaces or native Java interfaces.
- Assistance with integration including any bespoke development (e.g. user authentication and security interfaces, optimization of scheduling algorithms, HTML/Java client interfaces, integration with existing administration and reporting tools).
- Access to source code and test suite.
- Maintenance of changed source code and assistance through product updates.
- Flexible licensing policy based on your needs including fixed annual payment or percentage of generated revenue.

5.2.3.3   COSA Solutions - COSA Workflow
http://www.ley.de/cosa/index.htm

General Description
COSA is a product family covering workflow, Business Process Re-engineering (BPR) modelling, analysis, and archiving. It allows for flexible definition and change of business processes and organizational structures using graphical editing and analysis tools. Its interfaces provide many integration possibilities and simplify the work for end users and system integrators. COSA ToolAgents can extend product functionality to other desktop applications such as Lotus Notes, Outlook and ERP products such as SAP and BaaN, and is complemented by COSA Intranet, which extends functionality to the Internet.

Available Functionality
The modelling and control of complex flow definitions - for "Production Workflow" - with structured and process-oriented results are just as possible as are the creation of independent partial flows. The user can select the action. Even so-called, ad-hoc workflows can easily be handled with COSA Workflow.

Type of Applications
COSA Workflow is employed in many specialised areas including insurance, banking and commerce and well as government. The flow organisation developed with the Network Editor and the corresponding organisational structure with the graphical User Editor is fast and easily modelled by means of mouse clicking and by using existing symbol libraries. After short familiarisation, the specified business and branch flows are easily identified.

Reliability
The system design of COSA Workflow is based on the Petri-net, which is acknowledged as the best method for the conversion of logical flow structures. The additional use of logical references guarantee that the COSA Workflow system reacts dynamically to flow related modifications during the whole operation. COSA Workflow adapts itself completely to success-oriented developments of a modern organisation. COSA Workflow provides numerous safety mechanisms, which guarantee access control on one side and data security on the other. COSA Workflow

is backed by many years of mature robust development. Since 1986, significant investment has been made into the research and development of COSA products built upon the know-how of successful major customer projects. Among main clients are the authorities of finance and the Ministry of Defence for the Netherlands, the Mees Pierson Bank, the liability association of industry (HDI), the Deutsche Bibliothek (German library) in Frankfurt, the German patent office, the German post (Deutsche Post) and Karstadt AG.

Maintainability and Support
Following the requirements of large organisations at different locations, COSA Workflow was developed for multi-server operations. The compliance with standards and the availability of numerous interfaces guarantee its openness for the integration of all kinds of applications. Under common market standards, COSA Workflow meets the reference model of the Workflow Management Coalition (WfMC), where LEY GmbH, Business Unit COSA SOLUTIONS is an active member.

Platform
The COSA Workflow modules, developed in client/server architecture, allow any kind of extension. Unlimited variations are possible, from single terminal, system department solutions to business-wide heterogeneous global systems. COSA Workflow enables the developer to reduce development time during the prototyping of flows by a factor of 4, by means of the sophisticated debugging function. The COSA products are executable on all platforms commonly on the market. System environments from HP, IBM, Intel, Sun and SGI are supported on the server side. The availability of COSA clients under Windows (16/32 Bit) 3.X, 95, NT, OS/2 and as "Light" Web clients under HTML is just as natural as the support of relational databases such as Oracle, Informix, Sybase and Microsoft SQL-Server.

5.2.3.4 IBM - EDM Suite
http://www.ibm.com

General Description
IBM – EDM Suite is enterprise document management for e-documents spread across and beyond the enterprise. It includes best-of-breed document imaging; Computer Output to Laser Disk/Enterprise Report Management (COLD/ERM); simultaneous access to diverse repositories; workflow and enterprise process management; and distributed document management.

Available Functionality
MQSeries Workflow (formerly FlowMark) is a workflow engine designed for the client/server environment. It's dedicated to manage the flow of work, allowing companies to integrate the applications required to meet the needs of their business processes. The main MQSeries capabilities are:
- Provides for advanced workflow and process automation.
- Allows you to separate the application logic from the business process rules.
- Ties legacy and client/server applications to business process steps.

- Ties to Business Process Reengineering tools and provides for rapid modelling, animation, and simulation of your business process.
- Process monitoring to show where a specific piece of work is in the process.
- Recording live production process data and presenting it for analysis by management.
- Permits processes to occur across Intranets and the Internet, enabling e-business.

5.2.3.5 JetForm
http://www.jetform.com/

General Description
JetForm Corporation delivers electronic forms software products and support services worldwide. In terms of a workflow solution, JetForm Workflow is targeted at a broad spectrum of business users and applications, helping to make electronic forms and workflow universal. It is an out-of-the-box workflow solution that is built for day-to-day administrative-based business processes such as expense reports, purchase orders and Human Resources (HR) policy forms.

JetForm Workflow is developed to be complementary to production class workflow systems such that workflow processes can be passed between one vendor's engine and another, realizing that many organizations will have the need for both front office and dedicated back office workflow systems.

Available Functionality
The InTempo suite of integrated applications includes the following core software:
- Agent – the multi-threaded workflow engine that coordinates the flow and storage of information for all process instances, and determines the rules for the process instance to create work items. Agent receives, posts and outputs submitted work items; verifies the status of active work items; notifies participants of new work items, deadlines or reminders; and creates and maintains a history of each work item for searching and reporting issues.
- Process Designer – the visual design tool used to create a process map.
- Role Builder – to create the roles and reusable role sets for a process.
- Organization Builder – is a sample organization database (name, department, position, reporting structure, etc.) that can be used for developing sample or test applications.
- Administrator – to manage the InTempo Agent, users, security, database connectivity and e-mail.
- Web Access – a set of Active Server Pages that provides the primary end user interface. They reside on the Web server and provide a direct connection to InTempo Agent across the Web.

Platform
CPU: Pentium II 300 MHz, with 256 MB RAM recommended;
Operating System:
- Microsoft Windows NT Server 4.0 SP 4 for InTempo Agent and InTempo Web Access;

- Windows 9x or Windows NT for Application Development;

Web Server: Microsoft IIS 4.0;

Web Browser:

- Microsoft Internet Explorer 4.x,
- Netscape Communicator 4.x, Netscape Navigator 4.x;

Messaging (optional): Microsoft Exchange 5.x, Lotus Notes 4.5 and 4.6;

Database: Microsoft SQL Server 6.5 or 7.0, Oracle 7.3 or 8.0;

E-forms: HTML and FormFlow 99, FormFlow 2.2, JetForm Filler Pro 4.x or 5.x, JetForm Filler for Windows CE, J-forms.

5.2.3.6 TeamWARE - TeamWARE Flow

http://www.teamw.com/

General Description

TeamWARE Flow is a collaborative workflow product designed for knowledge workers who deal with information and participate in business processes. It offers users tools for modelling and monitoring processes, for participating in processes via work lists, and for creating e-forms.

Available Functionality

TeamWARE Dolphin with MS Exchange and Outlook integration delivers today the benefits of productive, flexible, collaborative work management through the users' familiar desktop interface. TeamWARE Dolphin's strengths include its focus on automating and tracking business processes (together with the relevant documents) rather than just managing the workflow of individual documents or folders.

TeamWARE Dolphin is a work management product, which enables teams to plan, execute, track and manage flexible business processes:

- Clearly structured, intuitive user interface gives access to planning, tracking and enactment of processes
- Planning can be done both graphically and using a list
- The worklist shows the outstanding tasks, with a graphical overview of the entire process
- Optional system integration with Microsoft Exchange or TeamWARE Office
- Processes can be changed even while they are in progress (subject to appropriate authorization)

Platform

Server:

- Minimum Pentium Processor, 64 MB RAM recommended
- TCP/IP
- Disk space 15 MB
- Windows NT 4.0

Databases supported on Windows NT:

- MS SQL Server 6.0, 6.5 or 7
- MS Jet Engine (Installed with TeamWARE Dolphin)

Optional groupware integration on Windows NT:
- MS Exchange V4.0, V5.0 or V5.5
- TeamWARE Office 5.1 Ed7, 5.2 or 5.3 (only with the standard Windows client)

Standard Windows Client Requirements:
- Minimum 80486, with 32 MB RAM and 12 MB disk space
- Windows 95,98 or Windows NT 4.0
- TCP/IP

MS Outlook Client Requirements:
- As above plus Microsoft Outlook 2000 or Outlook 97/98

5.2.3.7 W4

http://www.w4.fr/

General Description

W4 is a workgroup tool combining the power of a proven workflow engine with genuine Internet technology for supporting production, ad-hoc and even serendipitous workflow. It features flexible access to workflow services through industry standard browsers, and applications implementation using a graphic process modelling tool combined with codeless design and HTML page editors. Instantaneous deployment of multilingual concurrent applications including multiple versions is made possible.

Available Functionality

User Functionality

The W4 workflow management features a number of compelling benefits for end-users exceeding the functionality and extent of traditional workflow management systems:

- W4 is an infrastructure workflow supporting the geographical, organisational and security related
- Distribution of work management needed for the world-wide span of business interchange along the Internet phenomenon.
- W4 handles in the same time procedural and structured workflows for automating predefined and recurring administrative or production processes, as well as collaborative workflows, of which the sequences and rules may vary in order to support dynamic processes undergoing exceptions.
- W4 features a hyper-procedure concept where multiple procedure tiers embody various layers of business rules. Individual, basic business processes can be successfully implemented and be consistently governed by a higher-level procedure.
- W4 features flexibility of task assignment, view selection of various workflow instances, as well as building, customising, administration, supervisory and audit tools, interoperability features, multiple language support, etc.
- W4 highlights performance beyond those of a traditional client / server workflow management system. This is achieved by its architecture, which goes along transaction consignment features usually only available on mainframes.

- W4 participants only need an industry-standard Web browser running on any type of workstation including Network Computers and NetPC, to access full functionality. Therefore, it overcomes the limiting factors of traditional client / server workflow management systems.
- W4 supports multiple language terminology throughout each work case and at each working position.

Customer Organisations
For large and internationally spread-out organisations administrating such applications and processes, W4 is the appropriate tool to generate added value, to achieve user satisfaction by delivering them effective and advanced solutions combining workflow with their operational environment:

- W4 sharpens focus on adding value. At process design or adaptation, the graphic W4 Author tool features ease of analysing, modelling, design, building and appraising procedures and processes.
- W4 yields productivity and swiftness at implementation. W4 versioning features help to easily adapt procedures and user interfaces to the changing organisation of processes and company structures. A comprehensive set of application models and templates combining with the use of industry-standard, visual design tools and HTML page editors, providing cost-effective applications implementation and customising.
- W4 provides a wide range of facilities for seamless and effective integration within existing infrastructures according to terminal / host, 2 and 3 tier client / server, and browser / Web server paradigms. It provides client / server APIs and widely available, industry standard interconnection capabilities in most of the existing environments (e-mail, directories, corporate repositories, legacy and office applications).
- W4 offers bottom-up implementation capabilities by supporting the "hyper-procedure" concept where multiple procedure tiers embody various layers of business rules. Accordingly processes can be implemented at a desired pace without involving heavy, time and budget consuming Business Process Re-engineering (BPR) methods, and this without precluding overall consistency. The "can do" user environment leverages user and management commitment through early successes.
- W4 imparts instantaneous exposure and effectiveness to deployment. Since W4 does not require any particular software installation at the client end, all predicaments at system deployment and update are evicted.
- W4 binds only little support and maintenance resources. Since W4 is based on genuine Internet technology and on the use of industry standard protocols, editors and tools, support and maintenance service resources are widely available and can easily be trained. They are not locked up in cumbersome product update jobs distracting them from applications focus. Product persistence is real.

5.2.4 Supporting and Using Industries

This is a non-exhaustive list of corporations involved in the WfMC:
Abbott McCarthy
Action Technologies
Baan Company NV
Computron Software, Inc.
COSA SOLUTIONS Standardsoftware GmbH
Eastman Software, Inc.
Fuego Technology Corp.
GLS Conseil
Hatton Blue Ltd.
Hewlett Packard
IABG
IDS Prof. Scheer GmbH
IMA
InConcert Inc.
Meta Software
Netscape
Optika Imaging Systems, Inc.
Sema Group Sae
SNS Shared Network Systems Inc.
TDI
US DoD Defense Information Systems Agency
Xedoc Software Development, Inc.

5.3 Session Management

A session is the unit of collaborative activity. A session is a collective of users connecting from various locations to work together on shared data or using conferencing tools to communicate ideas. Sessions can consist of individual or multicast groups sharing specific interests [22]. There is different session definition for each system, however all of them converge in the same focus, collaboration.

Session Management is a set of mechanisms by which users may start, find, join and leave a collaboration session, controlling the behaviour of a current system and managing the application that creates the system.

A mechanism of managing sessions involves two things:

• generating the Session Management action, which changes the state of a session;
• displaying the information about the changes in the state of sessions.

In this section several collaborative systems and features of the Session Management mechanisms implemented in these systems will be presented.

5.3.1 Features

The common features of all mechanisms [39] will be presented and compared with regard to the definition of session and possible Session Management actions. We will see in that part, that there are two different ways of defining session:

- Single-type session: a session consists of applications of one type, running on different hosts and exchanging collaboratory data over the network.
- Multi-type session: a session consists of applications of many different types, running on different hosts and exchanging collaboratory data over the network. An application of certain type collaborates only with applications of the same type. That means there are several virtual connections within one session, one virtual connection for each type of application.

We also can divide sessions into two other groups:

- Single session allowed for an application type.
- Multiple sessions allowed for an application type.

In [39] seven possible operations that can be executed to change the state of a session (actions) are distinguished:

1. Creating a session.
2. Joining/Leaving a session.
3. Opening/Closing of an application remotely.
4. Floor Control mechanism.
5. Sending the update information about the state of session to the users.
6. Customizability of Session Management tools – adapt the functionality of the Session Management mechanism and the graphical components of Control Application to the needs of a particular user or a group of users.
7. Saving the state / the definition of a session.

These two classifications have been used as a basis for listing and comparing the retained projects and products, because, to our mind, they precisely reflect the main characteristics expected by session management platforms.

According to this definitions and features, some web-based collaboratory systems written in Java will be described. We focused on the most representative systems that we found in papers and the Web site and conclude our synthesis by presenting an on-going project to manage real-time collaboration.

5.3.2 Products

In this subsection we will present several examples of the distributed systems implemented in the Web environment and the mechanisms for controlling those systems.

5.3.2.1 TANGO

General Description

TANGO (http://trurl.npac.syr.edu/tango/), developed at Northeast Parallel Architectures Center (NPAC), is a Java-based integration platform, which enables implementation of Web-Based collaboratory environments [3]. It is implemented using Internet technologies and protocols and it provides means for fast integration of Web- and non-Web-applications into one multi-user collaborative system [9].

In TANGO, a session is a group of application instances currently working together in a collaborative mode [39]. All applications belonging to the same session exchange information and share behaviour.

TANGO has a master/slave session model. The user who creates a session is automatically the master, but all participants have the same rights to use an application. The master mode may be transferred to another user.

Available Functionality

The Session Management mechanism implemented in TANGO to generate and control the changes of the state of sessions, involves:

- changing the state of a session by generating an action;
- displaying the accurate and consistent information about all established sessions on the GUI panel on all machines using the system.

The Session Management actions are:

- Creating a session: a participant launches a local application to create a session.
- Joining an existing session: selecting a session and sending a message to the Server to join the session.
- Launching an application remotely: the master of a session can connect one or more of the TANGO users to the session by launching an application of the appropriate type on the remote host(s).
- Leaving a session: there are three possible cases:
  1. If the participant is not the master of the session then remove the application from the session.
  2. If the participant is the master of the session but didn't create the session then the master mode is transferred to the creator of session.
  3. If the participant is the current master and the creator of session then the session ends, and all the participants are removed from the session, the application ends and session is deleted.
- Opening / closing an application remotely. It is possible for any subset of users currently logged on.
- Requesting /granting the master mode is possible.

The communication inside TANGO is made by messages and by using applets. It is single-type sessions but multiple sessions per application type is allowed.

The update information about the state of sessions to the user is sent by the server to all users and is displayed in the Control Application window. However, TANGO has no mechanisms to save the state of sessions.

In TANGO, customizability of Session Management tools is not possible unless the code is partially re-written.

Future Evolutions: TANGO 2

This system is based upon the architecture of TANGO, but with several modifications and improvements. It has support for multiple-type sessions (subset of applications types). It introduces the concept of room paradigm with the purpose of encapsulated session for each room. A room reproduces an abstract entity with separate sets of users. TANGO 2 allows multiple sessions per application type.

The Floor Control is based on a lock mechanism, which replaces the master/slave control mechanism from TANGO. The lock approach is more generic. An application in a session may request a lock, become master, and release the lock afterwards.

In TANGO 2, the Session Management tools are fully customisable.

5.3.2.2 Habanero
General Description

The Habanero system (http://havefun.ncsa.uiuc.edu/habanero/) is a software framework of inter-computer object transportation capabilities, which facilitates the construction of software for synchronous communication over the Internet [15]. It also provides an environment for creating and participating in collaborative sessions and a suite of tools, which utilizes the framework and demonstrates many of its capabilities.

Habanero session is defined as a meeting where a user can go to and join the others participants. A user initiates a meeting. A session may encapsulate many applications and multiple participants.

Habanero environment supports multiple sessions. A participant can collaborate in several different sessions currently.

Habanero collaboratory modules are Java applications, not applets, so this system does not support software "downloadability" and hence, is not really a Web-based collaboratory system.

Habanero is built according to client/server architecture. The server stores the session states and distributes events among clients. A client application provides a user with a Graphical User Interface (GUI) to visualize the session. Habanero works by replicating applications across clients and then sharing all states changes in those clients. When a new client joins a session, it is informed about which applications are running in that session. Habanero also ensures that all clients see the same state changing events in the same order, which results in applications appearing the same to all clients.

Available Functionality

The concerned Session Management module owns the following features and mechanisms:

- The floor control object, called an arbitrator, supervises the events that can be performed at a given time. One important class of arbitrator provides locking. Locks are objects, which are used to restrict access to application resources. Locks can conflict with each other, and are thus used to ensure that only one participant has access to a given resource. They also can conflict with actions, so that the creator of the lock can only perform a given action. The Habanero server controls the locks.

- Any number of different types of applications can be opened within a meeting and they will work in a collaborative mode.

- The session control module has access to detailed information about session such as its name, schedule, agenda, and list of current collaborative tools on and who is allowed to participate. It also supports participant anonymity in the session side.

- Joining and creating a session requires defining before the host, the port and the name of the session.

- It provides a notification mechanism to invite participants to join an online session. This system supports both synchronous and asynchronous notification.

- The Session Management tools are not customizable.

The NCSA Software Development Division, that has proposed the Habanero system, has developed a suite of basic tools to establish a remote collaboration. These tools cover some of the three collaborative dimensions: production, coordination and communication. We can distinguish the voting tool as an example of coordination.

5.3.2.3 The Java Collaborative Toolset
General Description
The Java Collaborator Toolset (JCT) of Old Dominion University [40] defines the term session as a group of applications exchanging information, i.e. working in a collaborative mode. Nevertheless, there is not support in JTC for multiple session of the same application type. Only one session of one type can be created in the system, i.e. JCT is single-type sessions and single session per application [2].

JCT uses applets as collaboratory modules. To provide event and data sharing, the Java's Abstract Windowing Toolkit (AWT) of the Java Developers Kit (JDK) is replaced by a custom collaboratory toolkit. The principal advantage of such a system is the simplicity of application porting. However, we consider this approach to be too restrictive: JCT is like an X Window sharing toolkit adapted for Java.

Available Functionality
JCT owns an application, called Collaborator Manager, to manage the sessions. The set of possible actions consists of:
- Joining/Leaving a session by starting/closing an application.
- Displaying information about opened sessions and their participants.
- Floor control actions - a user can request a floor in order to be able to send collaboratory data. One user can have many floors at the same time (one for a session of a particular type).
- Sending the update information about the state of sessions to all users and this information is displayed in the Collaborator Manager window.

The JCT Collaborator Manager is not customizable unless the code is partially re-written and has not support for remote application Opening/Closing. Besides, saving a session state or a session definition is not available.

Java Collaborative Environment (JCE) [3] follows the same philosophy as JCT, but unlike JCT, JCE is based on the replicated tool architecture in which each participant runs a copy of the application and the activity of each user is multicast to all the participants in a conference.

5.3.2.4 CALTECH Infospheres System
General Description

Another example of distributed system is WWW distributed system Java developed at CALTECH (California Institute of Technology). This system is built using Java that supports peer-to-peer (no floor control) communication among processes spread across a network [49].

In this system, the authors introduce two compositional units, dapplets (which are multithreaded, communicating objects) and sessions (which are groups of composed dapplets). The dapplets are composed together, in parallel to form distributed sessions. Furthermore they are composed into temporary networks of dapplets that the authors call a session. A session carries out a task such as arranging a meeting time for a group of people. A session is dynamic; their members may grow and shrink as required by users.

A session is specified in terms of a state transition: the state of component processes at the point in the computation at which it is initiated and the corresponding states at the point at which it terminates.

The task of one session is to arrange a common meeting time. When this task is achieved, the session terminates. It is a goal driven session type.

In this distributed system a session is defined as a network of applets. A session consists of many different types of dapplets. An initial process (an initiator dapplet) is associated with each session. It is responsible for creating a session by sending participating dapplets port addresses to all participants and linking dapplets together into a session. Initiator dapplet controls joining and leaving sessions by connecting and disconnecting dapplets.

A dapplet, on receiving a request to participate in a session, may accept the request and link itself up, or may reject the request. The link is rejected because the requesting dapplet was not on its access control list, or because it is already participating in a session and another concurrent session would cause interference. When a session terminates, component dapplets unlink themselves from each other.

Available Functionality

A session in this system has the following features:
- Dapplets can exist without being linked to any session.
- Create a session means establishing a temporary network of dapplets of any type.
- A dapplet can participate in many different sessions.

In addition to Session Management, we can distinguish the following characteristics:
- Multi-type sessions are supported (different applications can exchange data).
- One application can participate in multiple sessions (or in anyone).
- There is no support for opening and closing applications remotely.
- There is no floor control, strictly peer-to-peer mechanism.
- Update information about the state of sessions is not sent to users.
- The Session Management tools are not customizable.
- There is not support for saving the state or the definition of a session.

Due to a loose integration between a dapplet and a session, this schema of communication remains, however, very generic and flexible.

5.3.2.5 InVerse

General Description

The Java-based InVerse system developed by IBM provides a common infrastructure for deploying a variety of collaborative applications over the Internet [77].

InVerse is a platform that supports real-time interactive applications (such as audio, video, text and motion) on the Internet. It provides a common backplane for disseminating and managing multiple real-time data streams. Within this general-purpose structure, the InVerse system maximizes scalability by implementing a hybrid communication architecture that adapts itself to available network bandwidth, observed network latency, installed network security measures, and available services such as multicast.

A user can define a set of receivers for a particular piece of data coming from his/her application. This set is encapsulated in a Group object. Group may represent any one of the following options:

- Individual: a single user
- Proximity: all users to whom the sender is "visible"
- Private Group: a distribution list created locally and only visible to the creator.
- Public Group: a system-wide user group managed by the server.
- Broadcast: all registered users.

The term Group is similar to the notion of a session. Nevertheless, the InVerse Group offers a capability to divide users into subgroups. Another security feature is Data Security, by installing security firewalls around some user hosts. InVerse permits applications to establish secure communication sessions. Data may be encrypted before sending. This system offers means for encryption by setting a PacketFilter interface. The interface might be used to encrypt and decrypt all data packets. In addition, it can modify all incoming packets before they are processed by applications.

Furthermore, within the definition of a Group type, which is necessary for transmitting data, the sender has to indicate whether the data should be sent reliably or unreliably. The InVerse communication layer is responsible for determining how to transport the data to the destination to ensure the required type of transport.

InVerse contains a Graphical User Interface that serves as the Session Management tool in the system. Though its use, a group member performs the following actions:

- Locate other registered users by sending a query server, because there is no automatic sending of update information from the server
- Get the information about the public sessions by sending a query to the server
- Join public groups
- Create private groups

Available Functionality

There is no flexible floor control mechanism, however, creating a private group ensures that information is sent one-way. The customizability of the Session Management tools is not supported.

Finally, InVerse supports only single type sessions, but multiple sessions per application type are allowed. For creating a session, a group in the server is registered and it defines reliable or unreliable way of transmitting data. A user joins or leaves a session by sending a query to the Server.

The open/close function of the remote applications is not supported by InVerse.

There is no automatic sending of update information about the state of session to the users. It can be sent to a user after receiving a request. And InVerse does not save the state or the definition of a session.

5.3.2.6   DOE2000 Real-Time Collaboration Management Project

General Description

DOE2000 (U.S. Department of Energy) is a new initiative to develop and explore new computational tools and libraries that advance the concept of "national collaboratories" and Advanced Computational Testing and Simulation (ACTS) (http://www-unix.mcs.anl.gov/DOE2000/). The DOE2000 Collaboration Management (CM) project [21], begun in 1997, focuses on the definition and development of a sophisticated Collaboration Management environment, which will be integrated with problem solving environments and other workflow based tools. This work proposal covers the development of a Collaboration Manager that will handle management and integration of different tools into a common real-time collaborative environment. The Manager provides support for developing alternate environment interfaces, such that users might join a collaborative session by choosing one from a list of active collaborations, or connecting to a shared instrument, or logging into a shared notebook, etc.

PNNL (Pacific Northwest National Laboratory) is collaborating with the NCSA (National Center for Supercomputing Applications) on the development of a Java-based collaboration Management Engine, which is based on Habanero environment. PNNL has obtained source and distribution licenses to Habanero and is developing CORE, a hybrid system with advanced capabilities.

The CORE prototype [58] provides a wide range of communication tools to which remote instruments and other resources can be added. To start or join a collaborative session using CORE, users simply click the appropriate buttons on the WWW page, and all required software is launched on their machines. The central session manager and a desktop executive, that coordinate communication between participants, are hidden from the users' view. The desktop executive sends IP addresses and port numbers between computer, and configures the various components.

Available Functionality

CORE provides the following tools:

- Audio/video Conferencing
- Shared Whiteboard
- WWW Browser Synchronization (communication peer-to-peer)
- TeleViewer (Shared Screen Viewer)
- Shared Electronic Notebook that provides users with a shared version of the traditional paper notebook
- File Sharing
- Chat

The functionality of CORE is available through two standardized APIs:

- Collaboration Management API: provides access to collaboration management capabilities and allows development of alternate users interfaces
- Collaborative Tool API: allows the integration of new collaborative applications

Future Evolutions

The latest release (9/14/98) of the CORE2000 Session-based Collaboration Management and Real-Time Collaboration Engine (C2K_3.0) provides the following features:

- Based on Java 1.1.5 and NCSA's Habanero 2.0b
- COTS installation package creates Start menu items (Windows) or scripts (UNIX) to configure the tools and launch the client and server
- Improved cleanup of session tools
- Client query of current session information
- New tools:
    - Video (vic – video option for Multicast Backbone users)
    - Audio (vat – audio option for Multicast Backbone users)
    - CU-SeeMe (video and audio option for PC and Mac users
    - Voting Tool
    - Molecule Modeler (PDB file viewer)
    - 3D XYZ (XYZ file viewer)
    - Camera Controller
- EMSL TeleViewer tool now supported on NT
- Fully operational CORE2000 NT platform release

EMSL TeleViewer supports shared display, but not remote control (whit less security risk). The integration of AT&T Cambridge Laboratories' Virtual Network Computing collaborative application into CORE2000 will allow remote users to interact within the shared desktop with other users, providing full access to the applications residing on remote machines. Thus, remote users may collaborate in a more balanced way by sharing the control and operations of applications. The Web-Session Directory will allow users to monitor and join active sessions over the Internet.

Although this project continues developing more advanced systems, it proposes to continue in three specific areas:

1. Analysis of real-time Scientific Collaboration. The following two efforts are planned:
    - CORE2000 Usage Questionnaire: The purpose is to verify and validate the design decisions in developing CORE2000 tools and environment.
    - Automated Capture of Session Activity and Tool Usage: Capture usage data with respect to session activity and tool execution. They will develop collection utilities that will capture and save session and tool events.
2. Advanced Collaborative Research Environments:
    - Automated monitoring and logging capabilities will increase the amount and quality of information gathered.
    - Workflow tools that allow scientists to define and share the scientific process they are carrying out.
    - Task management tools for defining and organizing individual tasks among collaborators

3. Advanced Collaboration Management:
  - Develop an extensible Collaboration Manager (CM) engine that can support the use of multiple metaphors, the dynamic addition of new collaborative tools by third party developers.
  - Provide Capabilities for monitoring, logging and inter-tool communicating.
  - Allow the use of external Java/CORBA based services for authorization, authentication, encryption, resource discovery, etc.
  - Floor Control Mechanisms: to give collaborators the flexibility to choose the floor control policies that best match their collaboration needs and style. The floor control policy (e.g., free-for-all, turn-taking, owner-moderator, baton-passing) is established by how the arbitrator propagates events and controls among collaborating applications.
  - Multi-Session Bridge is a network conferencing tool that establishes a point-to-point unicast connection for the sharing of audio, video, and data. If more than two remote users are involved, it provides a means to combine IP Multicast and unicast connections to match and support the sparse distribution of participants and network performance.
  - Inter-tool communications for permitting users to easily define connections between collaborative tools, allowing data acquisition, analysis, simulation, and visualization tools to interact within a collaborative environment.

Platform
This prototype runs under Windows (3.1 and 95) and a variety of UNIX's systems (SunOS, Solaris, Irix, etc.).

Chapter 6. Communications

B. Baurens, L. Costa, A. Dracinschi, S. Fdida, V. Roca, and R. Vida

6.1 Multicast Technology

This section gives an overview of most of the directions taken by research in the multicast area. We first introduce the basic concepts. The following sections deal with high level services that can (or must) be provided on top of the underlying multicast routing infrastructure. Then we consider new evolutions in multicast routing: new protocols, their large scale deployment, and future trends. Finally we discuss multicast tools and applications.

6.1.1 Basic Concepts

Multicast communications, i.e. the ability to send efficiently information to one or more receivers at the same time, in such a way that packets are not sent several times on a given link, tend to be more and more used. This is an efficient way:
- to distribute information to a set of receivers (e.g. for cooperative work applications like audio-conferences, white board, etc.), or
- to discover resources (e.g. at boot time an IPv6 host looks for a configuration router by sending a request to the "all routers" multicast address).

In this section we introduce the fundamentals of Internet multicast transmissions.

6.1.1.1 The Two Levels of Multicast Transmissions
First of all we need to distinguish two levels of multicast transmissions: local and wide area. The reason is that these two situations are completely different as well as the solutions that are required.

Local-Area Multicast Transmissions
The local level takes advantage of the possible multicast transmission capabilities of the physical layer. Let's consider Ethernet: Ethernet supports point-to-point, broadcast and also multicast transmissions. This is made possible by the diffusion nature of the Ethernet technology (at least in the 10Base5, 10Base2, and non-switched 10BaseT versions). A block of MAC addresses has been reserved to multicast. They are identified by the Least Significant Bit of the Most Significant Byte of the address, which is set to 1. The Ethernet multicast address is then created by copying the low 23 bits of the IP multicast address in 01.00.5E.00.00.00. E.g. 224.0.2.2 leads to 01.00.5E.00.02.02.

As a consequence, several IP multicast addresses that are only distinguished by the 9 Most Significant Bits lead to the same Ethernet address. It means that each time a

K. Drira, A. Martelli, T. Villemur (Eds.): Cooperative Environments, LNCS 2236, pp. 153-175, 2001.

multicast Ethernet frame is received, the receiver must check that the IP multicast address was the one expected.

It is also possible to emulate multicast transmissions using Ethernet broadcast and an incoming IP-level filtering. This is the solution used in old generation Ethernet cards that do not support the multicast mode.

Using multicast on a physical network that does not rely on diffusion (like ATM) is both more complex and less efficient. It often requires going through a server which performs distribution to each receiver either in many one-to-one connections, or in a one-to-many connection (if available, like in ATM).

Wide-Area Multicast Transmissions

Wide area multicast transmission is completely different. It requires the use of multicast routers, i.e. hosts that are capable of building and managing the multicast distribution tree. According to whether this multicast router is on a leaf network (i.e. with end-hosts connected) or not (i.e. on a transit network), it will have different functionality:

• on a leaf network, the multicast router must discover the presence of local receivers (i.e. hosts willing to receive traffic destined to a multicast group). This is the purpose of IGMP (section 6.1.1.4).

• on a transit network, the multicast router participates in the distribution tree management and multicast packet forwarding (section 6.1.1.6).

6.1.1.2 The Group Model

The IP multicast model (or group model) is an open model where:

• anybody can belong to a multicast group, no authorization is required
• a host can belong to many different groups, there is no restriction
• a source can generate traffic to a multicast group no matter whether it belongs or not to the group
• the group is dynamic and one can subscribe to or leave a multicast group at any time
• the number and identity of group members is known neither to the source nor to the receivers

Each group is identified by an IPv (4 or 6) "multicast address" (section 6.1.1.3). Some addresses are also reserved for dedicated purposes (e.g. to identify all hosts, or all routers, etc.).

6.1.1.3 Multicast Addressing

Multicast IPv4 addresses are class D addresses that range from 224.0.0.0 to 239.255.255.255. A multicast address, unlike other unicast addresses, does not identify a given host, but identifies a multicast group for its whole duration. A multicast address, unlike unicast addresses, is not assigned statically by an authority, but is dynamically assigned (in fact chosen by the source). Because there is no allocation scheme yet (but it will change, see section 6.1.4.4), there is a risk that several disjoint sources chose the same address. According to the scope of traffic (i.e. TTL value), packets may be interleaved and applications may be corrupted.

6.1.1.4   The IGMP Protocol (Internet Group Management Protocol)

IGMP (Internet Group Management Protocol) is a level 3 protocol (like ICMP). Therefore an IGMP message is always encapsulated in an IP datagram. Its goal is to inform the local multicast router of the presence of hosts interested to receive traffic sent to a group. In that purpose the local multicast router periodically sends "QUERY" messages on the LAN, asking if anyone is currently listening some multicast group. Each receiver having subscribed to a group answers and informs the router of the group(s) identity. A feedback cancellation scheme (a receiver does not answers immediately but after some random time, listening to other announcements in the meantime) avoids an implosion of the router.

Several versions of IGMP exist:

- IGMP version 1: described in RFC_1112.
- IGMP version 2: described in RFC_2236. The major difference compared to IGMPv1 is the addition of the "fast leave detection" mechanism. It also enables a host to inform the local multicast router that it has left a group. It enables this router to update the multicast tree, dropping this branch immediately, if nobody else is interested by the group anymore.
- IGMP version 3: described in an Internet draft [83]. This version essentially adds the possibility to do per-source filtering.

IGMP is a protocol, which is restricted to the local dialog between receivers and their first-hop multicast router (local scope). This is completely different from the creation of the multicast distribution tree, which is of the responsibility of the multicast routers (wide-area scope) and the multicast routing protocols.

6.1.1.5   The Various Classes of Multicast Routing Algorithms

Several classes of algorithms for the creation of a multicast distribution tree exist. We can mention:

- flooding
- spanning tree
- Reverse Path Forwarding (RPF)
- Core-Based Tree (CBT)

Before introducing these approaches, we first focus on the underlying problem.

The Multicast Routing Problem

The multicast routing problem is the following. The interconnection network can be modelled as a directed graph, consisting of a set of nodes (vertices): V and a set of links (edges): E [74], [89]. Let G=(V, E) be that directed graph. A directed link of G from node u to node v is represented by the ordered tuple (u, v). Let M be the multicast group including the sources. M is therefore a subset of set V.

The multicast routing problem consists in finding one or more interconnection topologies, subset of G, that span all nodes included in M. If a single topology is sufficient, no matter what the source is, this solution will be called a "shared interconnection topology" (e.g. see the CBT algorithm, in this section). If several topologies are required, one per source, this solution will be called a "source directed interconnection topology" (e.g. see the RPF algorithm, in this section).

Note that the above definition does not assume the presence of symmetric links. In practice links (u, v) and (v, u) will often be the same and have similar transmission features (bandwidth, propagation time, length, etc.). The directed graph G will often be composed of many undirected links.

In the general case, M is a subset of V, making the finding of an optimized solution complex. For instance the "Steiner tree problem" is a NP-complete problem [74]. In some cases (e.g. with host-based multicast, section 6.1.6.4), M is equal to V and the "Steiner tree problem" reduces to the "minimum spanning tree problem" for which polynomial-time algorithms exist.

The Flooding Approach

A node receiving a packet checks if it is the first reception of this packet. If this is the case the packet is forwarded on each outgoing interface except the one where it has been received. Otherwise the packet is dropped.

The difficulty relies in the "first reception" test. One solution is for a node to remember all the packets received so far. Another solution is that each packet contains the list of all the nodes crossed. For instance, OSPF, which relies on a flooding algorithm, compares the date of the (database update) packet received with the modification date of its own database.

If this algorithm is both simple and robust, it is also very memory and network resource consuming.

The Spanning Tree Approach

In this algorithm we select a subset of the physical links to create a loopless tree of minimal cost, including all the nodes. This problem is known as the "Steiner tree problem in networks (SPN)" and is known in the general case a NP-complete problem. Besides the cost c_uv of each link (u, v) must be known.

If finding the minimum cost tree is not a requirement, then a simple algorithm exist: (1) select a core, and (2) keep only the links that are on the shortest path from this core and the other nodes (see the RPF algorithm, in this section).

Unlike the flooding algorithm, here some links may remain unused. This algorithm is simple, robust, requires little memory (a flag that indicates if a link belongs to the tree or not is sufficient). On the other hand, all the traffic is concentrated on a fixed subset of the physical layers, no matter the spreading of the receivers.

Reverse Path Forwarding (RPF)

This is the algorithm used by the DVMRP protocol (this section). The principle is the following:

```
let P be the packet received from source S on the
interface I;

if (I is on the shortest path to S)

forward P on all the interfaces except I;

else

drop P;
```

Checking, before forwarding the packet to a neighbour can increase the algorithm efficiency, if the current node is on the shortest path between the source and this neighbour.

This algorithm has several advantages:

- it only relies on the point-to-point routing database (to know if I is on the shortest path to S),
- the multicast distribution trees of different sources are also different, which enables a better load balance on the various links,
- it guarantees the fastest possible delivery of packets as each step only keeps the shortest paths.

The "Flood and Prune" Variant

The RPF algorithm has the advantage of simplicity. A major drawback yet is the fact that it leads to distributing packets to all the possible nodes. A variation has been designed to enable the pruning of useless branches that are not on the path to a receiver. This is the "flood and prune" algorithm.

During the first step ("flood"), all the possible nodes receive all the packets. A leaf multicast router that receives a packet but has no local host interested by this multicast group sends upwards a "prune" request. This is the second step ("prune"). Slowly, the intermediate routers are informed that some sub-trees do not lead to receivers and thus prevent themselves from forwarding the packets on these links.

This variant of RPF has the advantage of limiting the distribution tree only to the useful branches. But on the other hand it requires going through periodical flooding steps (to discover new receivers), and requires that each multicast router, no matter whether it is or not on a path to a receiver, keep state information for each multicast group.

Core Based Multicast

Here a core is first chosen for the multicast group. The receivers (in practice the last-hop multicast router) must send their subscribe request to this core. Each intermediate router remembers the interface from which this request has been received in order to include it into the distribution tree.

The created tree (called a "shared tree" for that reason) is the same for each source. This is both an advantage (less memory is required) and a drawback (the traffic is more concentrated). Another major asset of CBT is that transmissions are strictly limited to the routers that are on the path to a receiver.

6.1.1.6 The First Internet-Wide Multicast Deployment

Multicast has been deployed in the early 90s as an experimental world-wide service. The key protocol that forms the basis of this infrastructure is DVMRP. This section outlines its features and describes rapidly the MBONE multicast backbone.

The DVMRP Protocol

DVMRP (Distance Vector Multicast Routing Protocol) [88] is the multicast routing protocol in use in the MBONE (Multicast BackBone). DVMRP relies on the exchange of "distance vector updates" like its unicast analogue RIP. Each vector entry contains the destination (in this case a source), and a distance expressed in number of hops. These updates are sent on each multicast capable interface and on each multicast tunnel (see below). The multicast distribution tree is then created using the RPF algorithm and the distance database of DVMRP.

During the first DVMRP deployment, there was no pruning and transmissions were only limited by the TTL field (section 6.1.1.8). Since 1993, all the versions of DVMRP use the pruning version of RPF. Yet some packets regularly flood the whole MBONE, as far as made possible by the TTL value and the various thresholds (section 6.1.1.8). This periodic flooding is required in order to update the distribution tree, including new receivers and dropping those who left in the meantime.

The MBONE Infrastructure
The MBONE must be seen as an overlay of the Internet. As only a subset of the Internet routers can perform multicast packet forwarding, the MBONE consists in the interconnection of multicast-aware areas through tunnels. A tunnel is composed of two multicast routers, one per each extremity. Each multicast packet that needs to go through this tunnel is first encapsulated in a point-to-point packet (IP in IP encapsulation) addressed to the other side of the tunnel. This unicast packet is sent and can now be forwarded by unicast routers. When it reaches the other end of the tunnel, it is decapsulated and sent using native multicast in the second area.

If the presence of tunnels enabled a fast deployment of a world-wide multicast infrastructure, it also led to much inefficiency. For instance, a packet will cross several times the same physical link if it goes successively through two tunnels that share this link.

6.1.1.7   Creating and Deleting a Multicast Group
Creating a multicast group consists, for the source, in choosing a new multicast address and sending packets to that address. Upon receiving packets to a new address, multicast routers create new forwarding state and set up the distribution tree. Of course if there is no known receiver, this distribution tree is limited by the first-hop router (in case of DVMRP). But even in that case the tree exists and state is kept by multicast routers (e.g. to say that this group has been "pruned").

Deleting a multicast group consists, for the source, in avoiding sending packets to a multicast address. As the distribution tree consists of soft state kept by multicast routers, this tree will slowly disappear (for instance mrouted uses a default 5-minute timer).

6.1.1.8   Limiting the Scope with the TTL Field
Controlling the scope of multicast packets relies on the TTL (Time To Live) field of the IP header. As with unicast transmissions, the TTL is decremented each time the packet is forwarded by a router, and dropped when it reaches zero.

IP multicast with the notion of threshold generalizes this. These thresholds enable the creation of areas that a multicast packet can only cross if its TTL is superior to the threshold value. By convention:
- 32: defines the "organization boundary"
- 64: defines the "region boundary"
- 128: defines the "continent boundary"

Note that the notions of (organization, region, and continent) are not strictly defined.

6.1.2 Providing a Reliable Transmission Service

6.1.2.1 Introduction
We have seen so far the routing aspects, i.e. how to send information to any number of receivers in a flexible and dynamic way. But this is a (little) part of the problem and most applications ask for additional services. The possibility of doing reliable transmissions is the most common requirement. This is the goal of this section.

6.1.2.2 Classification of the Solutions
Two major tasks are required for a reliable transmission service: error detection and error recovery. In the following sections we describe the two principal solutions (FEC and ARQ) that are used by different reliable multicast protocols, as well as some hybrid solutions those have recently emerged.

ARQ Solutions (ACK and NAK-Based)
The basic idea of the ARQ (Automatic Repeat reQuest) approach [67] is to retransmit a packet only if it is lost by at least a receiver.

Depending on whether error detection is done by the sender or the receivers, reliable multicast protocols could use positive (ACK) or negative (NACK) acknowledgements.

When using positive acknowledgements (ACKs), the sender retransmits messages until ACKs from all destinations are received. This approach does not scale well because ACKs sent by each receiver for each received packet may lead to serious network congestion (ACK implosion). In addition the source has to know the exact composition of the multicast group.

Using negative acknowledgements (NACKs) shifts the error detection load from the source to the destination. Receivers transmit negative acknowledgements only when a packet loss is detected. In order to reduce the implosion problem, different NACK suppression mechanisms could be applied, since the sender only needs to know that at least one receiver is missing data.

FEC-Based Solutions
Forward error correction (FEC) based recovery [67] consists in sending redundant packets (also called parity packets) together with regular data packets. Reed-Solomon Erasure correcting code [52], [72] can be used to construct the parity packets. For every k data packets, n-k parity packets are constructed. All k the data packets can be reconstructed if at least k (original or parity) packets out of n are correctly received. This code has two drawbacks: there are a limited number of parity packets per data packet, and in practice the k parameter is limited to 30 or 60 for computational reasons. There exist other more powerful codes [46]: the Tornado code, Turbo code, LT code, etc. Some of them are patented.

The FEC-based approach reduces the end-to-end latency compared to the ARQ approach (a receiver does not have to wait for the retransmission of lost packets any more). But this is at the cost of bandwidth since additional packets are systematically sent.

Hybrid Solutions

In practice, using only FEC cannot guaranty a totally reliable service. Hybrid methods combining FEC with ARQ were thus proposed. There are two approaches to combine FEC and ARQ [67]: The layered approach considers FEC as an independent layer below the ARQ-based protocol [37]. The key advantage of such a solution is that FEC is transparent to the ARQ protocols and transparently improves ARQ performance. Besides, if an application does not require a complete reliability, the ARQ protocol may be skipped to only use the FEC layer.

The second approach proposes to integrate FEC and ARQ in the same layer, as part of the same protocol [29], [60]. The source uses the feedback from the receivers to learn how many packets were lost by the worst-case receiver. Only that number of FEC packets are then sent. This integrated solution outperforms the layered FEC-based approach, the benefits being more significant for large group sizes.

6.1.2.3 Examples of Reliable Multicast Transmission Protocols

The XTP Approach

XTP (eXpress Transport Protocol), presented for history, relies on the bucket algorithm to provide statistically reliable transmissions. Time is divided into periods and to each period a bucket is associated. A bucket collects reception information sent regularly by receivers. There are a limited number of buckets. This number is a trade-off between the response time and the reliability level. If some information still misses from the oldest bucket at some receiver, the information contained is nonetheless sent to the application and the bucket reused.

XTP also introduced the "slotting and damping" techniques. Slotting consists in forcing receivers to multicast their repair requests in order to avoid NACK implosion. Receivers also apply damping, which means that they use timers to delay their NACKs. If in the meantime they receive a request for the same packet from another receiver, they cancel their NACK. This scheme is now used in many other protocols.

The SRM Approach

SRM (Scalable Reliable Multicast) [26] is a NACK-based multicast protocol that guarantees out-of-order reliable delivery. The basic idea in SRM is that the original sender need not retransmit a lost packet. Retransmissions are performed by the nearest receiver who has the segment. SRM uses the damping and slotting techniques of XTP, reducing the response time by estimating the delay from senders to hosts. Closer hosts will choose a smaller randomization interval than distant hosts, both for NACK and retransmission timers. If the timers cannot be estimated with reasonable accuracy, many of the apparent benefits of SRM may not be realized in practice. SRM is used in a well-known MBONE application, the wb (section 7.5.3.1).

The Asynchronous Layered Coding (ALC/LCT) Approach

Asynchronous Layered Coding (ALC) [45], based in particular on the Layered Coding Transport (LCT) building block, is a scalable reliable multicast protocol using several data streams in a layered fashion. These streams will often be sent to different multicast addresses. Therefore the number of streams delivered to each receiver is dictated by the local bandwidth availability and network conditions. In order to provide a good reliability level, ALC relies on a FEC codec. No feedback mechanism is used so as to promote a good scalability.

According to the application, several delivery modes are considered:

• On demand mode

Receivers may join the ongoing object transmission session at their discretion, obtain the necessary encoding symbols to reproduce the object, and then leave the session. A typical example is a tool for the continuous transmission of popular files (e.g. a video-clip).

• Streaming mode

In streaming mode a receiver typically remains joined for a long period, receiving many objects. A typical example is a streaming of real-time MPEG video.

• Push mode

In push mode, all the receivers must be ready before the transmission starts. This mode is well suited to the plannified distribution of files (e.g. a database between the headquarter and various agencies).

6.1.2.4 Other Approaches

As most of the reliable multicast protocols evolved out of the necessity for solving specific problems, their basic design criteria were different. We will present in the following some of the approaches.

Cycle Based Protocols

Cycle-based protocols divide a file into a sequence of fixed-size packets and transmit the entire file to all the receivers. After the transmission is terminated, the protocol gets into a series of retransmission cycles, receivers sending a list of missing packets. Senders retransmit lost packets until everything is received correctly. Starbust MFTP, RMTP and MDP are examples of protocols that use this approach.

Group Communication Protocols

Group-communication protocols provide different ordering and delivery semantics to the application. In Reliable Broadcast Protocol (RBP) [67] a token site broadcasts ACKs to the entire group, and answers the NACKs of other members by retransmitting the missing packets. The responsibility of the token-site rotates among group members. The Multicast Transport Protocol Version 2 (MTP2) uses the notion of a master node, responsible for message ordering and rate control. A sender has to obtain a token from the master in order to transmit. The Uniform Reliable Group Communication (URGC) protocol uses a co-ordinator for ordering, but the responsibility of the co-ordinator rotates among all the group members.

Finally, a special approach is used by the Reliable Adaptive Multicast Protocol (RAMP) that provides different modes of reliability to different receivers depending on their requirements. Senders and receivers can switch between reliable and unreliable modes.

Building ACK Aggregation Trees for Improved Scalability

Tree-based protocols group the receivers in local domains or subgroups, each with a representative (Designated Router or Group Controller). Local regions are organized in a tree hierarchy. NACKs are sent to the local representatives, who retransmit the missing packets, or if they do not have them, the request is sent to an upper level in the tree. Protocols such as RMTP, TMTP, LBRM, LGMP, or LORAX [67] fall in this category.

To be simple to deploy, protocols that use ACK aggregation must be self-organizing; the receivers must be able to form the tree themselves using the local information in a scalable manner. Such mechanisms are possible, but are not trivial. The main scaling limitations come therefore from the tree formation and maintenance rather than from the use of ACKs.

6.1.3 Adding Congestion Control to Multicast Transmissions

6.1.3.1 Introduction
Multicast communication is by definition greedier in bandwidth than unicast communications within the same number of receivers. The design of a multicast congestion control algorithm is then an important and useful task. There are two potential approaches for congestion control: within the network (it involves routers and distribution trees rather than simple paths as in the unicast case), and end-to-end.

A key unsolved problem for congestion control schemes that operate within the network for multicast traffic is how to retain the capability for heterogeneity. Other problems include defining fairness, the timescale for congestion control, scalability.

6.1.3.2 The Various Models
There are two main models:
- sender oriented, and
- receiver oriented

Sender Oriented Congestion Control
In this model, the sender is in charge of analysing the feedback information (usually losses experienced) generated by the receivers. Based on this information, the sender adapts its sending rate in order to be TCP friendly (i.e. to behave as closely as possible to the TCP congestion control scheme). Yet this is not an easy task and it raises in particular many problems. The message implosion problem in case of large groups is avoided by combining probabilistic query / reply schemes, random delay responses and expanding scope search. The TCP-like approach has been proposed by [76], [48], [56], [11], [90] proposes a loss rate threshold at the sender to decide whether a receiver is congested or not. If the number of congested receivers is above a second threshold, it reduces the sending rate. If the second threshold is equal to one, this scheme is equivalent to adapting to the slowest receiver.

Multiple multicast groups based on data loss correlation are used by [48]. The former provides local recovery and loss feedback suppression. The latter uses SMACK messages (Selective Multicast ACKnowledgement) sent by receivers to compute the loss statistics at the sender side.

The previous two proposals react only to the most congested paths and ignore other loss information. This solution greatly improves scalability [56], [11]. On the opposite, the bounded fairness is achieved by reacting randomly to receivers congestion signals when losses occur [90].

Multicast transport protocols like RMP and RMTP are sender oriented and concentrate on organizing an explicit topology to provide repairs. These algorithms could eventually be used for congestion and flow control. PGM (Cisco) proposes experimental congestion avoidance strategies based on received NAKs at the source host.

Receiver Oriented Congestion Control
This class includes those proposals using hierarchical coding for continuous streams as [85] and exponential layering

```
bandwidth_for_N_layers = bandwidth_first_layer * 2^(N-
1)
```

for continuous streams and bulk data [86]. A receiver belonging to more/less layer groups of the same session receives more/less data or at a faster/slower rate. The receivers compute the rate using packet loss rate and RTT with [25], [66] equation:

```
Bandwidth = 1.3 * MTU / (RTT * sqrt(Loss_Freq))
```

This rate is compared with the current rate at which they are receiving the data and the receivers will join/leave layers to efficiently adapt to this TCP-like computed bandwidth. The TCP behaviour is mimicked by special exponential layering (the receiver leaving a layer halves the bandwidth - as TCP does) and by use of synchronization points for receivers in order to react in a coordinated way [86]. A small number of video streams is used in [42] with the same data at different rates and combines both approaches: (1) receivers feedback their rate requirements to the source which adapts within defined limits the corresponding groups rate and (2) receivers may move among groups using for this decision packet loss rates. These congestion control approaches are more appropriate within multicast communications, especially for large groups.

6.1.3.3   Congestion Control for Layered Schemes (RLM, RLC, FLID)
These receiver-oriented mechanisms can be used along with the ALC/LCT approaches [54]. They all assume that the data stream is sent into multiple layers, each of them being assigned to a different multicast group. A receiver subscribes to as many layers as made possible by the network quality. On detecting losses (through gaps in the sending sequence space), a receiver dynamically adjusts the number of groups subscribed, leaving some of them.

6.1.4   Other Associated Services

6.1.4.1   Introduction
The reliability and congestion control aspects have been seen in the previous two sections. If they are the main two requirements of multicast enabled applications, additional services will often be useful. This section introduces some of them (not exhaustive list).

6.1.4.2 Heterogeneity Support

Addressing the problem of multicast transmissions to a set of heterogeneous sources and receivers is of the utmost importance. Indeed a multicast group may be composed of high-end receivers (workstations) attached to a high performance network (high-speed LAN), whereas other ones have limited processing power (Personal Data Assistant) or network access (low-speed modem, GSM modem). Three solutions are possible to address this heterogeneity:

- router-based filtering techniques
- packet scheduling techniques
- transcoding techniques

The first class of solutions relies on filtering [16], [47]. These techniques discard packets from flows whose bandwidth exceed their fair share. The TUF proposal [16] adds a tag to each packet sent to identify the "priority level" (or drop precedence). Adding information within the packet enables the sender to keep some control on the discard process. Therefore it is preferable to bind discard techniques like RED, RIO, etc. Besides no state is kept in routers, which warrants a good scalability. [47] also advocates the use of filtering within routers but without any involvement by the source and the receivers. Here, per-flow state must be kept in each router. Although promising, both approaches require extensions to multicast routers (or at least some key routers) for congestion reports ([47] only) and filtering. Therefore they cannot be deployed immediately and other solutions must be used in the meantime.

The second class of solutions relies on packet scheduling within several transmission layers (see references below). Each layer can be associated to a different multicast group and the filtering is performed by the join/leave mechanism of multicast IP [54]. This approach is thus receiver oriented and has the advantage of being immediately deployed.

Finally, transcoding within some routers or proxy to dynamically adapt the data flow to the receiver features (e.g. to reduce an image complexity) can also be used. But these solutions are CPU intensive, can only be used with a limited number of data flows and require the availability of adequate routers or proxies.

6.1.4.3 Group Management

Multicast group management services deal with activities relating to group membership and group dynamics. They should provide the following functionality [51]:

- creation and deletion of groups with specific characteristics,
- membership administration (joining and leaving) according to the authentication policy specified at group creation time,
- queries on group membership and characteristics,
- group event notification (i.e. informing interested parties of changes in group state),
- group property management, allowing changes in membership policies, group visibility or members' roles,
- floor and integrity conditions control.

Integrity Conditions

Integrity Conditions are conditions on group membership and topology that have to be satisfied for group communication to take place. They are of two kinds:

- Active Group Integrity (AGI): conditions on active group membership
- Association Topology Integrity (ATI): conditions on the topology of the association

Integrity conditions can be classified as follows:

- minimal conditions: a minimal number of participants is required for group communication to take place
- maximal conditions: an upper bound is fixed on the number of participants
- quorum conditions: a given percentage of participants is required, for voting procedures for example
- conditions on mandatory participants: there are some special participants (i.e. the chairman of a video-conference) whose presence is mandatory for the communication
- atomic conditions: fixing the exact number and identity of members who should participate

If the integrity conditions are not satisfied, the group association can be released (hard AGI/ATI) or temporarily suspended until they will be satisfied again (soft AGI/ATI).

6.1.4.4 Multicast Address Allocation

The Multicast Address Allocation Architecture [82] elaborated by IETF's MALLOC Working Group is three layered, comprising a host-server protocol (MADCAP), an intra-domain protocol (Multicast AAP) and an inter-domain protocol (MASC).

The Multicast Address Dynamic Client Allocation Protocol (MADCAP) allows hosts to request multicast address allocation services from Multicast Address Allocation Servers (MAAS).

Multicast Address Allocation Protocol (Multicast AAP) is used by MAAS servers to co-ordinate allocations within a domain in order to ensure that they do not collide.

Multicast Address Set Claim (MASC) forms the top level of the hierarchical address allocation architecture. Routers use this protocol to claim address sets that satisfy the needs of MAAS servers within their allocation domain. Child domains listen to multicast address ranges acquired by their parents and select sub-ranges that will be used for their proper needs. When a MASC router discovers that there is not enough multicast address available, it claims a larger address set.

6.1.4.5 Administrative Scoping

Because the TTL (Time To Live) header field has limitations, an administrative scoping has been proposed. The MZAP (Multicast-Scope Zone Announcement Protocol) enables the definition of (hierarchical) multicast scope zones of any size to better control the dissemination of multicast traffic, which is another way to improve IP multicast scalability.

6.1.4.6 Session Announcement
Three session protocols are used for multimedia session management:
- Session Description Protocol (SDP): Request For Comments (RFC) 2327 describes multimedia sessions and gives scheduling information
- Session Announcement Protocol (SAP): periodically multicasts to a well known address announcement packets containing the SDP description of the session
- Session Initiation Protocol (SIP): RFC2543 is used to invite users to a session. It does not allocate multicast addresses, this is done by SAP

They are the underlying protocols used by the sdr session management tool (section 7.5.3.1).

6.1.4.7 The Building Block Approach
Since 1999 an activity has begun within the "Reliable Multicast Transport" group of the IETF in order to identify and standardize various "building blocks" [93]. These building blocks are in fact the components that are common to many different multicast protocols. Examples are Forward Error Correction (FEC) codecs, Congestion Control, Generic Router Support, etc. A protocol instantiation is thus composed of one or more building blocks linked together with highly protocol specific, tightly intertwined functions.

The building blocks of Table 1 are under progress (May 2001):

Table 1. Building Blocks description

Block name	Block draft
Design Space / Building Blocks	rmt-design-space: informational RFC 2887 rmt-buildingblocks: informational RFC 3048
FEC (section 6.1.2.2)	draft-ietf-rmt-bb-fec-02.txt draft-ietf-rmt-info-fec-00.txt
ALC/LCT Protocol Instantiation (section 6.1.2.3)	draft-ietf-rmt-pi-alc-02.txt draft-ietf-rmt-bb-lct-01.txt
Layered Congestion Control	draft-ietf-rmt-bb-lcc-00.txt
Congestion Control	draft-ietf-rmt-bb-pgmcc-00.txt
Track Architecture	draft-ietf-rmt-bb-track-01.txt draft-ietf-rmt-pi-track-security-01.txt
Tree Building (section 6.1.6.4)	draft-ietf-rmt-bb-tree-config-02.txt
NACK-Oriented Reliable multicast Building Block (section 6.1.2.2)	draft-ietf-rmt-pi-norm-01.txt

6.1.5 New Multicast Routing Protocols and Their Large Scale Deployment

6.1.5.1 Introduction
DVMRP, used in the first world-wide MBONE initiative, has too many limitations to be considered a viable solution. Therefore new multicast routing protocols appeared during the past few years: MOSPF, PIM-DM, PIM-SM, MSDP, MBGP, BGMP, etc. The trend is to create a hierarchical multicast routing infrastructure, as with unicast

routing, with domains connected by inter-domain routing protocols. Some of the above protocols are limited to intra-domain multicast communications (MOSPF, PIM-DM, and PIM-SM), while others are for inter-domain multicast (MSDP, MBGP, and BGMP).

6.1.5.2 The Multicast Open Shortest Path First Routing Protocol

Multicast Open Shortest Path First (MOSPF) [57] is a multicast extension to the OSPF unicast link-state routing protocol. In OSPF each router periodically sends link-states to all other routers in the networks, so each router builds up a complete network map. With this information each router is able to compute the shortest-path to every destination in the network using the Dijkstra's algorithm. MOSPF extends these link-states to also carry information about group membership. Each router advertises the presence of multicast group receivers attached to it. Therefore MOSPF can construct a shortest-path multicast tree, i.e. the path from the source to each receiver in the multicast tree is the unicast shortest-path. Instead of relying on flooding/pruning information like DVMRP, in MOSPF each router keeps a database with the group members at all routers in the network. Yet a limitation is that this feature avoids MOSPF from scaling to large networks.

6.1.5.3 CBT Multicast Routing

Core Based Trees (CBT) is the early multicast routing protocol relying on center-based trees. CBT trees are bi-directional and shared by all the sources of the same group. It means that routers store per-group information instead of per-(source, group) information as in DVMRP and MOSPF. When a member wants to join the group, it sends a join message for the group towards the core router. This message instantiates forwarding state in the way to the core router, constructing the multicast tree. When a sender sends data to the group, the packet reaches a first on-tree router that then replicates this packet on all the on-tree interfaces except the one the packet came from. The good core placement is a difficult problem. Without it, multicast trees can be quite inefficient.

6.1.5.4 The PIM-DM/SM Routing Protocols

Protocol Independent Multicast (PIM) consists of two multicast routing protocols:

Dense-Mode (DM) PIM

PIM-DM [23] is intended for intra-domain routing and assumes that group members are densely distributed in the network. PIM-DM is functionally very similar to DVMRP (i.e. relies on a RPF with flood-and-prune algorithm), but it differs on some details and on the fact that PIM assumes no specific unicast routing protocol.

Sparse-Mode (SM) PIM

PIM-SM [91] was firstly intended to wide-area multicast routing. It assumes that group members are sparsely distributed in the network, in which case source-based trees (i.e. trees built by dense-mode protocols) turn inadequate. PIM-SM constructs shared trees similarly to CBT, the difference being that PIM-SM trees are unidirectional. Rather than "core", PIM-SM uses the notion of "rendez-vous point"

(RP). To each group is associated one (or more) RP. New group receivers send "join" messages to the RP. Like CBT, each intermediate router takes advantage of these "join" messages to update the distribution tree. Data issued by a source is first encapsulated in unicast and sent to the RP before being distributed in the multicast tree (the tree is unidirectional). For those very active sources, and because going through a RP before joining a receiver is moderately efficient, PIM-SM enables the creation of a Reverse Path Forwarding tree rooted at this source. It is thus less dependent on the center location than CBT.

6.1.5.5 Intra versus Inter-domain Routing: MSDP/MBGP

The operation of PIM-SM is difficult in the inter-domain level because routers are not all multicast capable. Since PIM-SM relies on the unicast routing protocol to construct multicast trees (assuming that the reverse unicast path is good to forward multicast traffic), join messages may reach non-multicast routers complicating PIM's operation. The use of PIM-SM in the inter-domain level still has two problems: designing a scalable mechanism for mapping multicast groups to RPs and the fact that Internet Service Providers (ISPs) do not desire to depend on other ISP's facilities - the RP location in other ISP will not be acceptable in many cases.

The near-term solution to these problems resides in the use of the Multiprotocol Extensions for BGP-4 (MBGP [8]), PIM-SM, and the Multicast Source Discovery Protocol (MSDP [24]). MBGP allows multiple routing tables to be maintained for different protocols. This way, routers may construct one routing table with unicast-capable routes and another with multicast-capable routes. PIM can then send join messages detouring non-multicast routes. MSDP provides a solution to the ISP interdependence problem. ISPs run PIM-SM within their own domain with their own set of RPs. RPs within one domain are interconnected and connected to RPs in other domains using MSDP to form a loose mesh. MSDP sets up a group-shared tree within each domain. When a source in a specific domain starts sending, the RP in this domain sends a Source Active message to RPs in other domains. Joining members in other domains send source-specific join messages following the MBGP routes in the inter-domain level. This solution solves PIM-SM's problems only in the near-term because every RP in every domain must be told about every source, so MSDP does not scale with the number of senders.

6.1.5.6 Intra versus Inter-domain Routing: BGMP

The Border Gateway Multicast Protocol (BGMP [81]) is another solution proposed to inter-domain multicast routing. BGMP builds shared trees for active multicast groups and allows receiver domains to build source-specific inter-domain branches where needed. The default behaviour of BGMP is to have shared trees in the inter-domain level because it assumes that intra-domain connectivity is richer than inter-domain, so inter-domain shared trees are likely to be efficient. Multicast trees are bi-directional to minimize third-party dependence.

6.1.5.7 The Internet2 Multicast Initiative

The MBONE (section 6.1.1.6) was the first experimental Internet-wide multicast deployment. The experience gained with the MBONE led to reconsidering the deployment of multicast services within the new Internet2 infrastructure. The guidelines require using sparse-mode protocols and native multicast. Therefore no tunnel is allowed and all routers must support MSDP/MBGP for inter-domain multicast routing.

Internet2 is in fact composed of two high-speed backbones: vBNS and Abilene. The vBNS initiative started in 1995 and supports inter-domain multicast since mid-1999. The Abilene backbone is newer and only recently (early 1999) become operational. The multicast service is therefore not as advanced as in vBNS. A link is provided to other multicast backbones (e.g. TEN-155).

More information can be found at URL: http://www.internet2.edu/multicast/

6.1.5.8 Multicast Deployment in Europe

A native multicast service has been deployed in Europe using the TEN-155 pan-European research network. IP Multicast routing/forwarding within the TEN-155 backbone and towards the European National Research Networks (NRNs) connected to it, make use of the PIM-SM/MBGP/MSDP protocols. It now completely replaces the DVRMP cloud of the previous MBONE.

More information can be found at URL: http://www.dante.net/mbone/

6.1.6 Future Trends in Multicast Routing

As we saw before, multicast routing protocols for wide area networks have limitations. Recently, several new proposals appeared that questions the traditional multicast approach. Some of them propose a simpler service, others remove the need for inter-domain multicast routing, or introduce Quality of Service aspects in the routing decision.

6.1.6.1 Simple Multicast

The Simple Multicast proposal [7], [8] tries to reduce or eliminate some of the complexity and overhead of traditional IP Multicast approaches. The basic idea is identifying the group by the pair (C, M), where C is the core router, while M is the multicast address. By routing on the destination and source address, there can be 2^{32} addresses per route/core/source, thus solving the address allocation problem.

Simple Multicast is scalable to the global Internet, this scalability being achieved by using a trivial multicast address allocation scheme, un-coupling core selection and discovery from the multicast protocol and using bi-directional trees. Carrying the core IP address in the join message solves the inter-domain routing problem. Unicast forwarding tables can thus be used to deliver the join.

6.1.6.2 Express Multicast

Express (EXPlicitly REquested Single Source multicast) [36] is a recently proposed single-source protocol extending IP Multicast to support the channel model. A multicast channel is a datagram delivery service identified by a tuple (S, E), where S is the sender's source address and E is a channel destination address. Only the source host S may send to (S, E). When joining a channel, a new member receives only the packets sent by S to E. Two channels (S, E) and (S', E) are unrelated, despite the common destination address. Express is implemented using ECMP (Express Count

Management Protocol), a management protocol that maintains the distribution tree and supports source-directed counting and voting.

The Express protocol is specifically designed for subscriber-based systems that use logical channels. Even if elaborated for single-source applications such as Internet TV or file distribution, multiple-source systems can also be built on top of it by using multiple channels (one per source) or by allowing several sources to share a channel, using higher level relaying through the channel's source host. Several references (section 6.1.6.3) explain how to implement the single-source model of EXPRESS using current protocols.

6.1.6.3 Using Single Source Variants of PIM-SM

The current trend is to use the "Source Specific Multicast" (SSM) [35] to set up a simplified multicast distribution service. The Channel model of Express has largely motivated this trend. The expected benefits are:

- a simplified addressing model (in particular that avoids cross-delivery of traffic when different sources send to the same multicast address),
- a simplified routing architecture.

PIM-SM and IGMPv3 enable the deployment of this service [75], [10]. Only minor changes in the PIM-SM protocol are required and IGMPv3 already offers a per-source filtering capability. This SSM model could well become the general multicast routing service since it is then straightforward to build a multi-source service on it.

6.1.6.4 Host-Based Multicast

Host-based multicast is a new hybrid scheme to offer a group communication service. In this approach end-hosts (or well-identified hosts, for instance an edge router) auto-configure themselves to create a multi-node distribution topology, mixing multicast and unicast routing. For instance, where multicast is the most efficient technique (e.g. in case of several hosts on the same Ethernet segment), a multicast area is kept. In other situations, when unicast routing is the most efficient technique (e.g. in case of inter-domain connection), then a unicast tunnel is created. Several motivations exist:

- it offers a total control of the distribution tree created,
- additional properties can easily be offered (e.g. to offer reliable communications over a lossy link, in case of a path through frequently congested routers, etc.)
- to include mobile nodes that are not suited to standard multicast routing,
- to include very specific areas (e.g. an "ad-hoc" network where nodes communicate without the help of any fixed infrastructure) that rely on dedicated multicast routing protocols,
- to include nodes those do not have access to a multicast distribution service.

[44] and [12] introduce a host-based approach, AMRoute, for the particular case of ad hoc networks. Even if this may not be the most efficient scheme they introduce new ideas (mesh and trees) that may be of interest even in the Internet case.

[27] introduces a host-based approach, Yoid, for the case of (non-mobile) hosts connected to the Internet. It introduces a rendez-vous point to provide information about the session and initiate several management signalizations and describes the tree management protocol (YTMP). The architecture is rather ambitious and other services (like adding reliability) are also considered.

REUNITE describes a recursive approach to build multicast distribution tree. Unlike the AMRoute and Yoid schemes, REUNITE is not an end-host scheme as it consists in building a tree among routers consisting in unicast tunnels.

6.1.6.5 Multicast Routing for Mobile Hosts

Multicast routing for mobile host is still a hot research topic. Several situations must be identified:

- so-called ad hoc networks, where a set of mobile hosts and routers are connected by wireless links, without the help of any fixed infrastructure or any central administration. These routers/hosts are free to move randomly and to organize themselves arbitrarily. The network's wireless topology may thus change rapidly and unpredictably. This situation is addressed by the Mobile Ad-hoc Networks (manet) IETF working group:

    http://www.ietf.org/html.charters/manet-charter.html

- (wireless or wired) mobile hosts. This (more or less important) mobility can be hidden by the "mobile IP" protocol. More information can be found in the associated mobile IP IETF working group:

    http://www.ietf.org/html.charters/mobileip-charter.html

Doing multicast transmissions is a challenge in these two situations. The protocols required to support this mobility are totally different to that used in case of fixed hosts and routers.

Several proposals have been made in case of ad hoc networks: AMRoute [44], ODMRP, and AMRIS. The most efficient ones are mesh-based and are more or less based on a flooding scheme [42].

The case of mobile hosts is completely different, as the goal is to enable a seamless and transparent connection to the standard multicast infrastructure [41]. Several inefficiencies exist with the classic triangular routing scheme of mobile-IP (traffic sent by a remote host is first captured by the mobile's home agent, and then tunnelled to it's current location). With tunnelling, the routing path may be far from optimal as all the traffic goes through the mobile's home agent. Besides, when several mobile hosts having subscribed to the same multicast group are visiting the same foreign network, a copy of each packet is sent to this foreign network! To improve the situation [43] introduces a new "multicast home agent" (MHA). This MHA remains the same as long as the mobile roams in the MHA's service range. If out of range, the MHA is moved to a location closer to the mobile's current position. This is a good solution to find a balance between efficiency and multicast tree updates.

6.1.7 Tools to Help and Monitor the Multicast Deployment

Using multicast services often means debugging problems as this service turns out to be complex and therefore unstable. In this section we introduce some tools that can help this task, as well as a world-wide infrastructure to evaluate the performance of various multicast connections.

6.1.7.1 Tools for Multicast Configuration Debug
The tools of Table 2 are currently used to debug multicast problems [4]:

Table 2. Multicast Debug Tools

Tool name	Role
Mrinfo	shows the multicast tunnels and routes for a router/mrouted
Mtrace	traces the multicast paths between two hosts
RTPmon	displays receiver loss collected from RTCP messages
Mhealth	monitors tree topology and loss statistics
Multimon	monitors multicast traffic on a local area network
Mlisten	captures multicast group membership information

A presentation of these tools can be found in [5] and at URL: http://www.cs.ucsb.edu/~almeroth/.

6.1.7.2 Performance Measurement Tools
National Internet Measurement Infrastructure's goal (NIMI) is to measure the global Internet. It was designed to be scalable and dynamic. NIMI is scalable in that NIMI probes can be delegated to administration managers for configuration information and measurement coordination. It is dynamic in that the measurement tools are external to NIMI as third party packages that can be added as needed.

More information can be found at URL: http://www.ncne.nlanr.net/nimi/

6.1.8 Multicast-Enabled Applications and Libraries

6.1.8.1 Introduction
This section introduces already existing multicast-capable applications especially in the cooperative work area. It also covers some prototype/products offering advanced multicast services that enable the easy development of new applications.

6.1.8.2 RTP/RTCP for End-to-End Feedbacks
RTP (real-time transport protocol) [78] provides end-to-end network transport functions suitable for applications transmitting real-time data, such as audio, video or simulation data, over multicast or unicast network services. These services include payload type identification, sequence numbering, timestamping and delivery monitoring. Yet RTP does not guarantee quality-of-service! This latter function, if required, must be provided by some external means (e.g. using diffserv or intserv architectures).

RTP comes along with a control protocol (RTCP) to allow monitoring of the data delivery in a scalable manner, and to provide minimal control and identification functionality. For instance, RTCP enables a source to be aware of the losses experienced by (a subset of) the receivers. This information can then be used to adapt the flow to the current network conditions.

Most of the current MBONE tools (see below section 7.5.3.1) are using RTP/RTCP.

6.1.8.3 The Various Multicast Libraries (Free and Commercial)

Here is a list of multicast libraries and multicast file transfer tools. Some are research prototypes, others are commercial products:

MCL (MultiCast Library)
- Generic multicast library, very easily used and well suited to layered multicast transmissions schemes.
- Free, source code, in C, available for various architectures.
- http://www.inrialpes.fr/planete/people/roca/mcl/mcl.html

MDPv2 (Multicast Dissemination Protocol)
- Protocol framework and software toolkit for reliable multicasting of data objects.
- Free, source code, in C, available for various architectures.
- http://manimac.itd.nrl.navy.mil/MDP/

OmniCast
- OmniCast (Starburst Software) is one-to-many content distribution software for guaranteed, reliable, multicast distribution.
- Commercial Product.
- http://www.starburstcom.com/index.html

PGM for FreeBSD
- L. Rizzo's PGM implementation of PGM This is a PGM Host implementation for FreeBSD. Its use requires that multicast routers support PGM features (in other words use CISCO routers everywhere ;-)
- Free, source code, in C.
- http://www.iet.unipi.it/~luigi/pgm.html.

WhiteBarn's PGM
- The WhiteBarn PGM implementation (WhiteBarn, Inc.)
- Source code free for non-commercial use only.
- http://www.whitebarn.com

RMDP (Reliable Multicast Transport Protocol)
- RMDP is a library providing a reliable layered multicast service for service for bulk-data transfers (e.g. a file). Based on Forward Error Correction and a layered congestion control scheme.
- Free, source code, in C and Java versions.
- http://www.cs.ucl.ac.uk/external/L.Vicisano/rmdp/

RMF (Reliable Multicast Framework)
- RMF is a (more or less) generic framework to ease the implementation of various reliable multicast styles of protocols.
- Free, source code, in C++ and Java versions.
- http://www.tascnets.com/mist/RMF/

RMTP-II (Reliable Multicast Transport Protocol)
- Reliable multicast protocol. Product distributed by Talarian Corporation.
- Commercial Product.
- http://www.talarian.com/rmtp-ii/

JRMS (Java Reliable Multicast Service)
- Reliable multicast library and services from Sun Microsystems
- uses the TRAM protocol (tree-based reliable multicast)
- Free, source code, in Java
- http://www.experimentalstuff.com/Technologies/JRMS/

Swarmcast
- An implementation of LCT
- Free, source code, Java
- http://sourceforge.net/projects/swarmcast/

6.2 Network Quality of Service Management

6.2.1 Introduction to Differentiated Services

There is a clear need for relatively simple and coarse methods of providing differentiated classes of service for Internet traffic, to support various types of applications, and specific business requirements. The differentiated services approach to provide quality of service in networks employs a small, well-defined set of building blocks from which a variety of aggregate behaviors may be built. A small bit-pattern in each packet, in the IPv4 Type of Service (TOS) octet or the IPv6 Traffic Class octet, is used to mark a packet to receive a particular forwarding treatment, or per-hop behavior, at each network node. A common understanding about the use and interpretation of this bit-pattern is required for inter-domain use, multi-vendor interoperability, and consistent reasoning about expected aggregate behaviors in a network. Thus, the Working Group has standardized a common layout for a six-bit field of both octets, called the 'DS field'. RFC 2474 and RFC 2475 [6] define the architecture, and the general use of bits within the DS field (superseding the IPv4 TOS octet definitions of RFC 1349).

The diffserv Working Group (WG) [20] has standardized a small number of specific per-hop behaviors (PHBs), and recommended a particular bit pattern or 'code-point' of the DS field for each one (RFC 2474, RFC 2597, and RFC 2598).

Additional components required to support differentiated services include such traffic conditioners as traffic shapers and packet markers that could be used at the boundaries of networks.

The diffserv WG defines a general conceptual model for boundary devices, including traffic conditioning parameters, and configuration and monitoring data. It is expected that a subset of this will apply to all diffserv nodes. The group also defines a Management Information Base (MIB) and a Protocol management Information Base (PIB) for diffserv nodes, and an encoding to identify Per Hop Behaviours (PHBs) in protocol messages. Diffserv through tunnels are also considered.

The diffserv WG will develop a format for precisely describing various Behavior Aggregates (BAs), which were initially defined in RFC 2474 and 2475. A BA is a collection of packets with the same codepoint, thus receiving the same PHB, from edge to edge of a single diffserv network or domain. Associated with each BA are measurable, quantifiable characteristics which can be used to describe what happens to packets of that BA as they cross the network, thus providing an external description of the edge-to-edge quality of service that can be expected by packets of that BA within that network. A BA is formed at the edge of a network by selecting certain packets through use of classifiers and by imposing rules on those packets via traffic conditioners. The description of a BA contains the specific edge rules and PHB type(s) and configurations that should be used in order to achieve specified externally visible characteristics.

Such security threats as theft of service or denial of service attacks, and suggest counter-measures, are also considered.

6.2.2 Availability of Differentiated Services

Recent Linux kernels offer a wide variety of traffic control functions, which can be combined in a modulare way. They are included in all development kernels, starting from version 2.3.41, and will be natively included in the 2.4.x future standard kernel distributions.

More information on the current status, source code, configuration examples are available at: http://icawww1.epfl.ch/linux-diffserv/

Cisco IOS[tm] (release 11.3 and above) quality of service features offer a variety of queuing, traffic shaping and filtering technologies for implementing traffic priority and controlling congestion end-to-end across the network.

More information can be found at: http://icawww1.epfl.ch/linux-diffserv/

Chapter 7. Groupware

B. Baurens

7.1 Introduction

GroupWare is technology designed to facilitate the work of groups. This technology may be used to communicate, cooperate, coordinate, solve problems, compete, or negotiate. While traditional technologies such as the telephone is qualified as GroupWare, the term is ordinarily used to refer to a specific class of technologies relying on modern computer networks, such as email, newsgroups, videophones, or chat.

GroupWare technologies are typically categorised along two primary dimensions:
- whether users of the groupware are working together at the same time ("real-time" or "synchronous" groupware) or different times ("asynchronous" groupware), and
- whether users are working together in the same place ("co-located" or "face-to-face") or in different places ("non-co-located" or "distance").

In this chapter, we mainly focus on real-time technologies where application-sharing in general and multimedia conferencing are typical and main applications.

7.2 Some Research Activities and Case Studies

A non-exhaustive list of interesting source of information for research topics and case studies about groupware:

The OLC group (Outils et Logiciels pour la Communication/ Software and Tools for Communicating Systems) at LAAS, has been working for long on design of software and tools to be used for developing advanced time constrained network co-operative applications   (http://www.laas.fr/laasve/index.htm).

Computer Supported Cooperative Work (CSCW) is the main research topic of the University of Calgary's GroupLab with wide coverage projects, from asynchronous to real time conferencing, and from same-place to geographically distributed meetings. Human Computer Interface (HCI) projects have concerned usability of World Wide Web browsers, personal information management and evaluation methodologies
    (http://www.cpsc.ucalgary.ca/projects/grouplab/index.html).

The Argonne Futures Lab performs basic and applied research in advanced communications, collaboration, and visualization technologies (e.g. teleimmersion) to enable the development of wide-area collaborative computational science
    (http://www-fp.mcs.anl.gov/fl).

German's GMD Research Topic about Communication and Cooperation Systems led to the participation of the organisation to well-known projects such as CESAR or BSCW (http://orgwis.gmd.de/projects/BSCW).

K. Drira, A. Martelli, T. Villemur (Eds.): Cooperative Environments, LNCS 2236, pp. 177-262, 2001.
© Springer-Verlag Berlin Heidelberg 2001

The RODEO group at INRIA with projects such as ivs or Rendez-Vous has tackled videoconference on IP   (http://www.inria.fr/rodeo/rv).

The UCL (University College London) Networked Multimedia Research Group is developing IP multicast conferencing technologies and applications to support collaborative research, technical development and distance education. Some of its developed tools are "rat", "vic"... (http://www-mice.cs.ucl.ac.uk/multimedia)

An initiative of several University departments (SURA organisation: Georgia Institute of Technology, University of Tennessee...), in the US lead to the development of case studies and "cookbooks" on the videoconferencing and Distance Learning themes (http://sunsite.utk.edu/vide). See also the CANARIE ANA Multipoint Videoconferencing Project
(http://www.gait.bcit.bc.ca/Projects/videoconferencing/index.html).

7.3 Application Sharing

Application sharing is a feature of many collaborative applications that enables the conference participants to simultaneously run the same application [1]. The application itself resides on only one of the machines connected to the conference. A lot of software is bundled with conferencing solutions as detailed in section 7.4 below (Conferencing) like Microsoft NetMeeting, Sun SunForum, PictureTel LiveShare etc. Some systems offer more CAD-oriented features and services such as Magics Communicator or Catia Conferencing.

The T.128 ITU standard, covered by the T.120 umbrella standard (see section 7.4.5 below) is usually used to manage application-sharing sessions.

With the availability and the leverage of prices for network resources, especially linked to the development of the Internet, application sharing and collaborative information sharing are more and more proposed as run time collaboration services on the Web (see also section 7.4.2.2 below) via dedicated portals or ASP (Application Service Provider). Examples of such ASPs are EAI's e-vis.com or MSC, Collabware sites.

7.4 Multimedia Conferencing

7.4.1 Operative Aspects of Conferences

The deployment of a multimedia conference solution necessitates a careful study of the planned usage. It includes considerations about the technological environment, user skills, and application domains in order to select the most adequate system(s).

Technical and human requirements can be better recognised when considering the three main following human factors: task of session (meeting, education, work-group, face-to-face conference...), media (audio, video, application sharing...) and mode (interactive or not, formal or informal).

- Session

Differences between the nature of a conference (meetings, collaborative work, distance education, and entertainment) may influence how the conference will take place. Needed tools, considerations about roles and interaction modes (see below) will be defined for each of these kinds of sessions.

- Media

This factor allows making a distinction between the video, audio and shared workspace components. For particular sessions, it may appear that the video is of less importance whereas the sound synchronisation and the availability of tools for sharing applications could be key factors of success of the conference.

- Modes

Different modes of communications can be distinguished. This is important for understanding the use and the success of videoconferencing. For example, one can consider two main modes of interactions between the conference users: "lecture" (typically in a teaching session) and "collaborative" (typically for working groups of engineers). In the same way, communication can be quite formal (e.g. business meeting or classroom/teacher configuration) or informal (working groups…).

7.4.2 History

Most real time collaboration tools used in the industry are based on the adequate deployment of network resources and tools such as:

- leased lines,
- routers, switches, gatekeepers, firewalls,
- terminals: desktop stations equipped with dedicated communication facilities (cards, client software, LAN interfaces, modems, etc.), conference rooms (with electronic whiteboards, several cameras, video/audio control equipment, etc.

The emergence and wide-spread adoption of the World Wide Web offers a great deal of potential for the developers of collaborative technologies, both as an enabling infrastructure and a platform for integration with existing end-users environments. For instance, data and voice networks continue to converge on IP.

The offer palette is expanding everyday on the WWW providing virtual conference rooms, shared workspaces, and delocalised "intranets". Everyone's "browser" is then used as a kind of universal access tool, allowing the use of new services, work areas, and publication means.

7.4.2.1 Traditional Solutions

Multimedia (tele-)conferencing is gaining maturity through the definition and the implementation of two key standards, namely H.320 and H.323 promoted by the ITU.

At the beginning of the nineties, H.320 proposed a set of recommendations for multipoint and point-to-point conferences over circuit-switched networks (ISDN and leased lines). The standard defines parameters and rules for enabling processing, formatting, synchronisation of audio and video signals over the communication links. It included as well the T.120 standards for data conferencing thus providing a complete multimedia conference set of standards. H.320 is the most established and most popular solution for quite big organisations (because of cost constraints) providing high-quality conferences and improvements for inter- and intra-enterprise communication. ISDN line growth is still quite strong, as service providers increase availability and drastically reduce the cost of basic rate services.

The industry is nevertheless going through a major change. Standards are becoming more and more mature and the generalisation and success of the Internet leads to a move towards IP-based solutions. Low-cost solutions to be deployed on a LAN or over the internet are now possible. It allows in particular to bring conferencing capabilities right on users desktops without the necessity of using dedicated rooms and equipment. Standards related to videoconferencing on IP are grouped under the H.323 standards family.

Main problems related to the use of IP instead of circuit-switched solutions are:

- lack of quality of service (limited bandwidth, audio/video synchronisation problems...)
- lack of control with regards to the network management: bandwidth allocation, traffic management, and dynamic configuration of the network. Network congestion problems can handicap dramatically videoconference session.

In the other hand, circuit-switched solutions mainly suffer from:

- necessity of dedicated rooms with extensive use of hardware resources: cameras, wide-screen televisions,
- costs (material and leased lines),
- versatility limitations (connection possibilities, no or limited access to user's workspaces, pre-planning of sessions...).

H.323 allows a mass deployment of multimedia conferencing throughout organisations with direct benefits for collaborative work, distance learning, Tele-medicine, etc.

Additionally, the ITU-T defined the H.324 standard for addressing video and audio communications over low bit rate connections such as Plain Old Telephone Services (POTS) modem connections.

The challenge is to create H.323 products that integrate into established networks and use resources that are already present, for example, interfacing to a wide variety of products on the IP network side, such as TCP/IP hubs, switches, and routers. In addition, networked conferencing companies must present a seamless integration with the existing H.320 standard of ISDN products.

7.4.2.2 Real-Time Collaboration Using the Web

Real Time Collaboration benefits from the extensive use of the Internet in business and industrial organisations and is undoubtedly a major trend. Services offered start from marketing and sales presentation up to real time discussions, eventually with audio and application sharing.

Some solutions do not even require any change in Information Technology configuration of end-user organisations, other require the installation of light-weighted client software.

Examples of "new" collaboration service providers and portals on the Web are:

- Virtual Room Videoconferencing System (VRVS), a joint project between the California Institute of Technology and CERN,
- ActiveTouch WebEx Meeting Center,
- Sneaker'sLabs iMeet,

- PlaceWare,
- ICQ Tools,
- e-vis.com
- GMD's BSCW/CESAR projects,

Within the service model there is more than one method of payment and delivery. Some vendors charge per minute per connection, some by a series of hosted events, and others rent by the month or year per concurrent server connection. A few have combination approaches.

7.4.3 Standards Organisations

Using industry standards, a product from one vendor can provide a guaranteed level of compatibility with products from other vendors. Companies can continue to build compatible add-on products that will successfully inter-operate with different real-time communication and conferencing products. Depending on the standards that these products support, users can potentially share programs and information, see each other on video, talk to one another, or perform all of these functions simultaneously.

The main organisations taking an active part in the standardisation effort for multimedia conferencing are:

- International Telecommunications Union (ITU)
- Internet Engineering Task Force (IETF)
- International Multimedia Teleconferencing Consortium (IMTC)

International Telecommunications Union
It has its headquarter in Geneva, Switzerland. This organisation co-ordinates, develops, regulates, and standardises global telecommunications and organises regional and world events.

For more information about ITU, see the ITU Web site: http://www.itu.int/.

Only paying members can access the majority of the ITU standards information from the ITU Web site.

Internet Engineering Task Force
The Internet Engineering Task Force (IETF) engineers and develops protocols for the Internet. This organisation is a large, open, international community of network designers, operators, vendors, and researchers concerned with the evolution of the Internet architecture, as well as the smooth operation of the Internet. The IETF maintains working groups for research and technical study.

For more information about IETF, see the IETF Web site: http://www.ietf.org/.

International Multimedia Teleconferencing Consortium
The International Multimedia Teleconferencing Consortium (IMTC) is a non-profit corporation founded to promote the creation and adoption of international standards for multipoint document and video conferencing. This organisation provides a forum for its world-wide members to develop product specifications and educate others on standards-based development. The IMTC and its members promote a "Standards

First" initiative to guarantee interoperability for all aspects of multimedia teleconferencing.

For more information on IMTC, see the IMTC Web site: http://www.imtc.org/

The IMTC Web site provides informative documents on the T.120 and H.323 standards. These documents are particularly helpful for people who are not paying members of the ITU. The IMTC also sponsors mailing lists and activity groups that foster standards-based product development and interoperability.

7.4.4 Multimedia Communication Standards

This section introduces the main ITU "Recommendations" concerning multimedia communication and conferencing. They are mostly called standards but, being only recommendations, are in fact open and subject to interpretations by the various equipment providers leading to interoperability problems. The following Table 1 gives an overview of the standards tackled in this section.

Table 1. Overview of ITU "Umbrella" Recommendations

Standard Name	H.320	H.321	H.322	H.323 V1 / V2	H.324
Approval Date	1990	1995	1995	1996/1998	1996
Type of Network	Narrowband ISDN	Broadband ISDN ATM LAN	Guaranteed bandwidth packet-sw networks	Non-guaranteed bandwidth packet-sw networks	PSTN or POTS
Video	H.261 H.263	H.261 H.263	H.261 H.263	H.261 H.263	H.261 H.263
Audio	G.711 G.722 G.728	G.711 G.722 G.728	G.711 G.722 G.728	G.711 G.722 G.728 G.723 G.729	G.723
Multiplexing	H.221	H.221	H.221	H.225.0	H.223
Control	H.230 H.242	H.242	H.242 H.230	H.245	H.245
Multipoint	H.231 H.243	H.231 H.243	H.231 H.243	H.323	
Data	T.120	T.120	T.120	T.120	T.120
Com. Interface	I.400	AAL, I.363, AJM I.361, PHY I.400	I.400 & TCP/IP	TCP/IP	V.34 Modem

Next section (section 7.4.4.1) gives a rough overview of the standards used for supporting multimedia conferencing. Emphasis is put on video and audio codecs.

Exploitation costs of ISDN-based solutions, the development of LAN conferencing requirements, the growing popularity of the Internet and, more generally, of packet-switched communication mediums helped in promoting the H.323 suite of standards. H.323 can be viewed as an evolution of the H.320 series towards packet switched networks. The two standards have overlapping video and audio codecs, both propose to use T.120 for data conferencing and have similar methods for conference establishment and controls.

Section 7.4.4.3 will present a summary of the H.320 standard suite. Section 7.4.4.5 will present with more details the components of packet-switched conferencing solutions.

7.4.4.1 Overview of Enabling Standards

H.22x and H.24x Series: Multiplexing, Multipoint, and Control
- H.221: Frame multiplexing for a 64 to 1920 Kbps ISDN channel.
- H.223: Multiplexing protocol for low-bit rate multimedia terminals (such as Public Switched Telephone Lines (PSTN)).
- H.225: Media Stream Packetisation and synchronisation on non-guaranteed quality-of-service LANs.
- H.230: Frame-synchronous control and indication signals for Multipoint Control Units (MCU) systems.
- H.242: System for establishing audio-visual ISDN terminals using digital channels up to 2 Mbps
- H.243: Procedures for establishing communication between three or more audio-visual terminals using digital channels up to 2 Mbps.
- H.245: Control of communications between visual telephone systems and terminal equipment on non-guaranteed bandwidth LANs.

Audio and Video Codecs
In order to face the problems of bandwidth limitations, multimedia communication requires the use of so-called audio and video codecs. The goal is to compress (respectively de-compress on the other side) the different streams of data at their source (resp. destination).

A codec can either be provided as a piece of hardware or supported by dedicated software. Hybrid solutions are also used in order to meet cost requirements, hardware solutions being much more expensive than software ones. The processing power available in a modern workstation or a PC is largely up to the task. Since most compression algorithms require more computations to do compression than decompression, some vendors make a slightly more expensive compromise and provide some special hardware for compression and perform decompression in software.

There are many compression algorithms. For instance, for video, the ITU has created an international standard called H.261. H.261 is a good compression algorithm for video conferencing and it performs very well. Unfortunately it is also very computationally intensive and as such generally requires special purpose hardware in order to use it. Because of this many companies have created their own proprietary algorithms. These are too numerous to mention. Inter-operability is still a big issue in industry and each company is striving to make their method standard.

Video Compression Algorithms

The two following standards are detailed:

- H.261: Supports 352x288 (CIF or FCIF) and 176x144 (QCIF). DCT-based algorithm tuned for 2B to 6B ISDN communication. Required for H.320, H.323 and H.324.
- H.263: Much-improved derivative of H.261, tuned for POTS data rates. Mostly aimed at QCIF and Sub-QCIF (128x96 -- SQCIF). Optional for H.323 and H.324, although industry is focusing on it for POTS. Being added as an option to H.261.

The H.261 Video Codec

H.261 is a video compression standard designed for communication bandwidths between 64 kbps and 2 Mbps, measured in 64 kbps intervals. Two picture formats, 352-by-288 CIF (Common Intermediate Format) and 176-by-144 QCIF (Quarter CIF) are defined. QCIF operation is mandatory, while CIF operation is optional, but much more commonly used for high quality conferencing installations, such as videoconferencing room systems.

H.261 utilises both intra-frame spatial and inter-frame temporal encoding. In intra-frame encoding mode, DCT-based spatial compression is used (Discrete Cosine Transform). 8x8 blocks are DCT transformed, quantified and run-length/entropy encoded. In inter-frame encoding mode, a prediction for blocks in the current frame is made based on the previous frame. If the difference between the current block and the predicted block is below a certain threshold then no data is sent. Otherwise the difference is calculated and DCT transformed, quantified and run-length/entropy encoded. All H.261 based systems are required to decode motion compensation signals, however the encoding of motion compensation is optional and will greatly enhance the video signal.

Another optional feature in H.261 is the ability to do pre- and post-processing of the video signal. Pre-processing acts as a noise filter, to reduce the amount of data being sent due to poor lighting or non-moving backgrounds. Post-processing reduces the blocking and noise artefacts in the video signal, and can be used to increase apparent frame rates and reduce jerky motion caused by irregular frame rates.

The H.263 Video Codec

H.263 is a relatively new video codec, designed especially for low-bitrate connections, but scalable for data rates ranging from 28.8 modem connections to high speed LANs. The coding algorithm of H.263 is similar to H.261, but with substantial improvements and changes which yield higher frame rates, better clarity, and improved error recovery. Half pixel precision is used for motion compensation, while H.261 used full pixel precision and a loop filter.

H.263 supports five resolutions, however due to the emphasis on low-bitrate connections, 128-by-96 SQCIF and 176-by-144 QCIF formats are most commonly displayed and are required for H.324 based applications. The 352-by-288 CIF format is used with H.320 and H.323 on some desktop and room systems, and two higher resolution formats are defined but not commonly found in commercial equipment.

The H.263 codec includes four optional encoding features that can be implemented to further improve video performance. These include Unrestricted Motion Vectors, Syntax-based arithmetic coding, Advance prediction, and forward and backward frame prediction (also known as P-B framing). On Intel-based systems which support

MMX technology, the advance prediction and P-B framing features can be coded to use the MMX instruction set for optimal performance.

The following Table 2 depicts the various image formats supported by each recommendation:

Table 2. ITU image formats for videoconferencing

Videoconferencing Picture Format	Image Size (in pixels)	H.261	H.263
sub-QCIF	128 x 96	Optional	Required
QCIF	176 x 144	Required	Required
CIF	352 x 288	Optional	Optional
4CIF	702 x 576	N/A	Optional
16CIF	1408 x 1152	N/A	Optional

Audio Compression Algorithms

- G.711: 64 Kbps as 8K samples/sec, 8-bit compounded PCM (A-law or μ-law), high quality, low complexity. Required for H.320 and H.323.
- G.722: Low-level audio codec supporting 7 KHz speech at 48, 56, and 64 Kbps.
- G.723: Speech codec at 6.3 and 5.3 Kbps data rate. Medium complexity. Required for H.324; Optional for H.323.
- G.728: Low-level audio codec supporting 3.4 KHz speech at 16 Kbps; high quality speech coder, very high complexity. Optional for H.320 and H.323.
- G.729 G.729A: Low-level audio codec supporting 3.4 KHz speech at 8 Kbps. high quality speech coder, medium complexity.

Audio quality is at least as important to a video conference experience as the video quality, and in fact the two are closely related since a high bit rate audio solution will reduce the amount of communications bandwidth which is available for the video signal.

Frequency response is an important concern with audio codecs, which are generally tuned to the frequency spectrum of the human voice. For example, G.711 is a 3 Khz narrow-band audio codec that is a required minimum for H.320 calls. It uses only 16 Kbps of communications bandwidth, but the audio quality will be comparable to a typical telephone call.

At higher connection rates, G.722 might be preferred, which is a wide-band, 7 Khz audio codec. The sound is comparable to a FM radio, but it requires up to 64 Kbps of communications bandwidth for the audio signal. A good compromise might be G.728, which consumes only 16 Kbps of communications bandwidth, but produces 'toll quality' telephone audio by using a technique called Code Excited Linear Prediction (CELP). CELP produces higher quality speech, but are more complicated and requires more signal processing to encode.

7.4.4.2   System and Network Architecture of Multimedia Conferences

The picture of Figure 1 shows an example of all elements possibly incorporated in a multimedia conferencing global system.

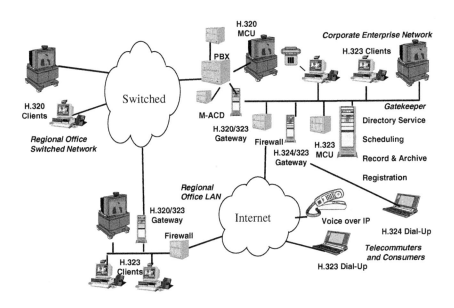

Fig. 1. System and network architecture of a multimedia conferencing network

7.4.4.3   H.320 – Synchronous Circuit-Switched Networks

Most videoconferencing systems in commercial use today use ISDN telephone lines to transmit the audio/video and data signals between endpoints. ISDN (Integrated Services Digital Network) is a point-to-point circuit switched connection consisting of two bearer channels ('B' Channels) for a total of 112 to 128 Kbps available bandwidth. Typically, the two 'B' channels are aggregated together to create a single high bandwidth 'virtual' connection. This connection can then be subdivided for use by the audio, video, and data subsystems.

The H.320 specification, ratified by the ITU (International Telecommunications Union) in 1990, is actually a collection of standards defining the organisation of data into packets, the control and framing of these packets, the encoding of the data, and the format of the information contained as data. These sub-specifications can broadly be divided into three categories:

- Video compression standards (including H.261 and H.263),
- Audio codecs (including G.711, G.722, and G.728),

- Transmission and Control standards (such as H.221 framing and H.231 multipoint control)

ISDN solutions require the rental of dedicated lines to the telecom operators leading to relative high exploitation costs.

7.4.4.4 H.324 – Public Service Telephone Networks

The H.324 specification (Figure 2) defines a standard for video and audio compression over V.34 modem connections using low bandwidth (28.8 Kbps) analogue telephone lines. Ratified by the ITU in 1996, H.324 will be an important factor in bringing videoconferencing services into the home and small office. With numerous 'Videophone' products now appearing in the consumer market, several H.324 interoperability test sessions have been hosted by the ITU during 1997.

H.263/H.261 video codecs and G.733 audio codec are used. Additionally, main components of the standards are H.223 and V.34 modem controls.

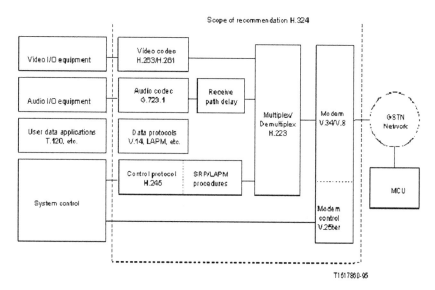

Fig. 2. H.324 Terminal Equipment

H.223

The purpose of H.223 is to provide a mechanism to combine together and send various media data across a phone connection. Various media data include control, audio, video, and data streams. By using H.223, the higher level entities of one side of a phone connection can transmit data to the equivalent entity on the other side of the phone connection.

Modem (V.34) Control

The V.34 modem can do video call first. If modem supports V.8/V.8bis, we can do voice call first. The V.34 modem uses about 20% bandwidth for control signal. If modem support V.80 synchronized transmission mode, it can use 100% bandwidth to transfer data.

7.4.4.5 H.323 - Packet-Switched Networks

The H.323 standard, ratified by the ITU in 1996, covers the technical requirements for audio, video and data communications services over LANs not providing QoS (Quality of Service) and, more commonly, across IP-based networks, including the Internet. Multimedia applications possibly from different vendors can inter-operate by complying with H.323. It is the dominant standard to be supported by Internet phones, audio conferencing and video conferencing terminals.

Some components of the recommendation are optional, other are mandatory. For example, video facilities and T.120 data conferencing are optional. If present, data conferencing applications must comply with the T.120 standard, video capabilities must comply with H.261 in QCIF mode. On the other hand, voice communication is mandatory and all H.323 terminals must be capable of encoding and decoding audio according to the G.711 algorithm. Note that this is the same codec that is specified for H.320 compliance.

H.323 (as H.320) defines the four major components:

- terminals,
- gatekeepers,
- gateways,
- Multipoint Control Units (MCUs).

H.323 Terminals

Terminals are the client endpoints (this term is used as a synonym in the following). The architectural view of a terminal equipment in the H.323 recommendation is represented by the Figure 3 below.

H.323 includes three sub-specifications related to control, connection, and bandwidth allocation on the network. They are:

- the H.245 Call Control Channel,
- the Q.931 Call Signalling and Call setup,
- optionally the RAS Channel, which performs registration and bandwidth administration functions (see gatekeeper functions below).

H.323 uses reliable (TCP) end-to-end services for these important control functions, but uses UDP (User Datagram Protocol) for the actual audio and video data streams to provide 'best effort' delivery of packets in an unreliable network environment. Some systems may also use IP Multicast (for multipoint conferencing).

The RTP real-time protocol on top of UDP handles audio and video streams (timing and synchronisation issues in particular).

Version 2 of H.323 (issued in 1996) foresees endpoints to possibly request a certain quality of service using the Resource Reservation Protocol (RSVP). It is up to the underlying network and its equipment to deliver it.

H.323 Gatekeepers

Gatekeepers perform management services for H.323 conferencing zones. A gatekeeper is an optional element in H.323. When a gatekeeper is enabled in an IP network, all H.323 endpoints contacting that network must make use of it. The gatekeeper helps to preserve the operational quality of the LAN by performing following functions for all components declared in its zone (terminals, gateways, MCUs):

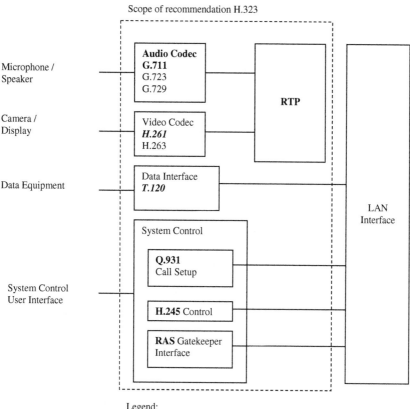

Fig. 3. H.323 terminal equipment

- Admissions control

By authorising access to the LAN for H.323 endpoints including gateways and MCUs, the gatekeeper not only limits the amount of bandwidth these entities use on the network, but guarantees access only to recognised entities. The gatekeeper grants permission for both placing and accepting calls from H.323 endpoints. For a connection to be successful, an H.323 endpoint must be recognized by the gatekeeper and must also be registered in the gatekeeper's zone, i.e. the collection of endpoints, gateways, and MCUs, independent of IP subnet boundaries that the gatekeeper manages.

A zone can have only one gatekeeper. When multiple endpoints on a LAN contain a gatekeeper, all but one should be disabled. However, the H.323 Recommendation also states that admissions control may be set to admit all requests from recognised entities.

- Bandwidth Control

As designated in the Registration Admission Status (RAS) specification, the gatekeeper, through admissions control ensures that bandwidth is available within its

H.323 zone for email, file transfers, and other designated applications. While the gatekeeper can modify the bandwidth usage during a call, the criteria doing so is not specified in H.323.

- Address translation

As defined in the RAS specification, the gatekeeper accepts both external E.164 telephone number addresses received from endpoints outside the LAN and alias (names) addresses from LAN endpoints. It then translates the numbers and names to network-recognisable addresses, for example, IP addresses. The initiating endpoint can then complete the connection. Gatekeepers may also pass the H.245 signalling (used to negotiate channel usage and capabilities) between two endpoints or between each of several endpoints and the MCU.

Gatekeepers can thus be considered as kind of routers in a H.323 conference. Additional optional functionalities are:

- call management: list of on-going calls with main characteristics which can be forwarded to another device (for example for billing purposes)
- PBX functions: the gatekeeper can forward calls to another endpoint if the user does not answer a call (used for instance for "video voicemail or receptionist" functionality,
- bandwidth management (e.g. rejection of calls if insufficient remaining bandwidth).

H.323 Gateways
Gateways are access points that allow LAN users to connect to a wide area network (most commonly using ISDN lines) or local area networks at other sites. Gateways provide many services. A main function is the translation between H.323 endpoints and other types of terminals, including address translation, and conversions between transmission formats (i.e. H.225.0 to H.221) and communications procedures (for example H.245 to H.242). In addition, the Gateway also performs call setup and clearing services to both the LAN and the switched-circuit network sides.

H.323 MCUs
The Multipoint Control Unit (MCU) supports conferences between three or more endpoints. Under H.323, an MCU consists of a Multipoint Controller (MC), which is required, and zero or more Multipoint Processors (MP). The MC handles H.245 negotiations between all terminals to determine common capabilities for audio and video processing. The MC also controls conference resources by determining which, if any, of the audio and video streams will be multicast.

The MC does not deal directly with any of the media streams. This is left to the MP, which mixes, switches, and processes audio, video, and/or data bits. MC and MP capabilities can exist in a dedicated component or be part of other H.323 components.

More about Multipoint Conferences
The H.323 recommendation defines different methods and configurations for the support of multipoint conferencing (i.e. conferences with at least three endpoints). Architectures include centralised, decentralised (both can be mixed) and hybrid conferences. This is determined by the fact that multicast is used or not.

In a centralised multipoint conference, audio, video and data streams are sent by all terminals to the MCU in a point-to-point way. The MC centrally manages the conference using H.245 control functions. The MP is in charge of data distribution, audio and video switching and mixing and sends the resulting streams back to the terminals (unicast or multicast).

A typical MCU that supports a centralised conference consists of an MC and an audio/video/data MP.

In a decentralised architecture, H.323 terminals multicast audio and video to other participating terminals without sending the data to an MCU. Nevertheless, control functions are still centralised in the MCU and H.245 control channel information is transmitted in a point-to-point mode to an MC. There is no MP.

Receiving terminals are responsible for processing the multiple incoming audio and video streams.

In mixed multipoint conferences, some endpoints are operating in a centralised multipoint conference and some in a decentralised multipoint conference. A single MCU controls the whole conference.

Hybrid multipoint conferences allow endpoints to transfer H.245 signals and either an audio or video stream to the MCU in a point-to-point mode. The remaining type of signal is further distributed to other terminals through multicast.

Network bandwidth is better preserved in a centralised architecture with an MCU supporting the reception of multiple unicast transmissions, mixing audio and switching video and output a multicast stream. Another solution is to output multiple unicasts from the MCU to the participants.

Multicast makes more efficient use of the bandwidth but emphasises higher computational loads on the participant endpoints.

Additionally, network routers and switches of the network infrastructure must support multicast features.

7.4.5 T.120 Data Conferencing Standards

The T.120 family of specifications defines a series of communications and applications protocols for real-time, multipoint data communications. T.120 provides real time data conferencing standards that allow people at multiple locations to conduct a voice conference call and create and manipulate still images such as documents, spreadsheets, color graphics, and photographs. T.120 data conferencing services can be supported on top of all transports (ISDN, LAN, POTS, and Internet). Although the driving market force behind T.120 was teleconferencing, it can satisfy a much broader range of applications including interactive gaming, virtual reality on the Internet, real-time news feeds, and process control applications.

In 1996, Microsoft introduced NetMeeting, a collection of T.120 data conferencing applications for use on Windows platforms. This product is available from Microsoft for free and highly participated in the gain of popularity of this kind of applications.

7.4.5.1 T.120 Architecture

The illustration of Figure 4 shows the T.120 architecture. This architecture follows the Open Systems Interconnection (OSI) model, which specifies a series of layers, including lower level networking protocols for connecting and transmitting data, and interaction with higher level application protocols.

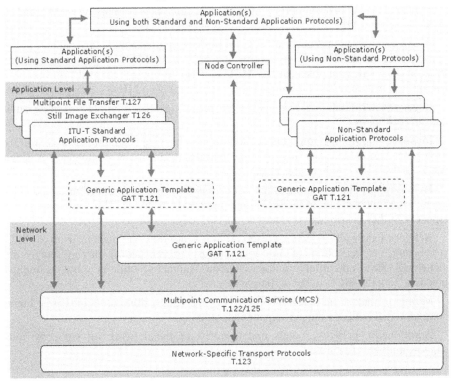

Fig. 4. T.120 Architecture

T.120 is an umbrella standard that encompasses the following communication and application standards and components:

T.121

This standard provides a generic application template (GAT), which specifies a common set of guidelines for building application protocols and the management facility that controls the resources used by the application. T.121 also describes how an application protocol, such as T.127 for file transfer, performs the following functions:
– Registers itself with the conference.
– Applies its capabilities locally and remotely.
– Interoperates and negotiates capabilities with other applications.
To ensure application consistency, T.121 is a required standard for products developed under T.120. The ITU also recommends that non-standard applications incorporate T.121 to provide product interoperability.

T.122

This standard defines the multipoint services, which allow one or more participants to send data as part of a conference. These multipoint services are implemented by T.125, which provides the mechanism for transporting the data. Together, the T.122 and T.125 standards make up the T.120 multipoint communication services (MCS). T.122 supports various conference topologies.

T.123

This standard is responsible for transporting and sequencing data, and for controlling the flow of data across networks, including connect, disconnect, send, and receive functions. For data transport, T.123 defines a series of network interface profiles. Also, T.123 provides an error-correcting mechanism that ensures accurate and reliable data delivery.

T.123 Annex B, an addition to the T.123 data conferencing standard, also defines the protocol for secure data conferencing.

T.124

This standard provides the generic conference control (GCC) for initiating and administering multipoint data conferences. The GCC performs the following functions:

− Serves as the information center, directing users and data in and out of conferences and monitoring progress so that the latest conference information is always available.
− Maintains lists of conference participants and their applications; the GCC identifies compatible applications and features so that products can interoperate.
− Tracks MCS resources so that conflicts do not occur when conference participants use multiple application protocols, such as T.127 for file transfer and T.128 for application sharing.

T.125

This standard specifies how data is transmitted within a conference. T.125 defines the private and broadcast channels that transport the data, and ensures accurate and efficient communication among multiple users. T.125 also implements the multipoint services defined by T.122.

T.126

This standard specifies how an application sends and receives whiteboard information, in either compressed or uncompressed form, for viewing and updating among multiple conference participants. The role of T.126 is to manage the multi-user workspace provided by the whiteboard.

T.127

This standard defines how files are transferred simultaneously among conference participants. T.127 enables one or more files to be selected and transmitted in compressed or uncompressed form to all or selected participants during a conference.

T.128
This standard was proposed by Microsoft as an addition to the T.120 standard and is accepted by the ITU-T. T.128 specifies the program sharing protocol, defining how participants in a T.120 conference can share local programs. Specifically, T.128 enables multiple conference participants to view and collaborate on shared programs.

Node Controller
The node controller is the command and control entity for T.120 and is responsible for administering network-level events, including the management of conference connections, participants, and conference data. This controller takes command of the other T.120 layers, particularly the transport layer, and uses the GCC, MCS, and other protocol services to manage the entire conference. The node controller acts as the translator, ensuring that events are interpreted and ordered correctly.

7.4.5.2 Collaborative Meeting Tools[1]
Desktop conferencing with or without video lets collaborators hold virtual work sessions and meetings. These meetings can be desk-to-desk, floor-to-floor, building-to-building, city-to-city, country-to-country, and even space to Earth through the use of satellite technology. Desktop conferencing software includes virtual meeting and collaborative tools. These tools replace--and in many cases enhance--aspects of in-person meetings and post-meeting follow-up.

Application and File Sharing
Application sharing allows two or more desktop videoconferencing users to collaborate on PowerPoint presentations, spreadsheets, graphic design programs, and other software in real time. The application runs on only one computer, but appears to run on all the PCs involved in the session. All the participants can use keyboard and mouse controls in sharing the application.

Document Conferencing
Document conferencing lets two or more desktop videoconferencing users simultaneously write and edit a legal brief, X-ray, news release, annual report, or any other document. This is similar to distributing a document at a meeting and letting each person review and mark up their own copy. Usually document conferencing is achieved when one collaborator cuts and pastes the document from an application onto the shared whiteboard.

Whiteboarding
Whiteboarding lets desktop videoconferencing users create a shared workspace similar to a white board on the wall of a meeting room. Collaborators can use electronic highlighters, pens, and other markers as visual aids to the virtual meeting. As one collaborator highlights a portion of text, for example, the same highlighted image appears on the other person's computer screen. Xerox has brought whiteboarding to group conferencing through its LiveBoard product. LiveBoard's 67-inch screen lets participants share a workspace using infrared pens. Desktop PCs running MeetingBoard software can connect with LiveBoard.

---

[1] This section was extracted from [73]

7.4.6 Web Conferencing

Web conferencing is an entirely new medium offering a way for businesses to effectively communicate time-critical information while still meeting the demands of today's business climate. With Web conferencing you can now conduct live interactive meetings or presentations with anyone, located anywhere, using only a Web browser and a phone.

A Web conference is simply the combination of a phone call with live web-based visuals and interaction. To present simply select a PowerPoint presentation from your computer, upload it into the application, and then point the audience to the URL where the meeting is scheduled to occur.

Everyone who logs on can share in the visual presentation, and interact with each other from the comfort of their office, home, or wherever they may be at the time.

Web conferencing enables you to communicate effectively, decreasing the amount of time spent travelling and ultimately leading audience to understanding, so you can get results fast.

Business professionals can use a wide variety of rich visual contents to get their message across while actively engaging their audience and receiving real-time feedback with live interaction. Types of rich content you can present include, PowerPoint slides delivered in real-time, annotation tools, live software demonstrations, polling, web tours and streaming audio and video. The presenter is given full control of the meeting to ensure that they can deliver their message in a compelling manner.

Presenters can control content but can also control the level of interactivity during a presentation including the participant's ability to ask text-based questions, review slides, chat and indicate their "mood" through the seating chart. In smaller collaborative meetings oriented towards workgroups who need to closely collaborate over a document or idea, even more interactivity is possible, such as creating new content on the fly and illustrating points collaborative on whiteboards.

7.5   Products

7.5.1 Application Sharing

7.5.1.1   VNC

General Description
VNC (Vitual Network Computing) has been originally designed in ATT laboratories to allow remote use of a computer over the Internet. This provides its potential use in a wide number of heterogeneous environments (networks, systems). Sources are available for free. VNC is composed of a server program located to the machine to which access is wished and a client program (viewer) where the user actually works.

Available Functionality
VNC is able to distribute on TCP/IP connections the whole Windows 95/NT office screen running on a server towards one or several clients. For X11-based applications, it is possible to select precisely which application will be shared by the program. In this case, the VNC server acts like an actual X-Window server: the client is able to launch selected applications from the client machine.

• Visualisation possibilities
On client screen, the distant pointer of the server, on the server the local pointer. On X applications, both server and local client(s) pointers can be also visualised.
Some option allows to control also remote or local pointer and/or keyboard according to the needs.
Cut&Paste operations between server and client machines are possible.
• Application Sharing
Functionality depends on the type of VNC server. For Unix machine with X11 window applications, application running on the server machine AND application running on client machines can be shared among the different clients. For Microsoft Windows VNC servers, only the machine running the VNC server can share its desktop. The VNC server might nevertheless be replicated on several "client" machines.
No state is stored at the viewer. This means you can leave your desk, go to another machine, whether next door or several hundred miles away, reconnect to your desktop from there and finish the sentence you were typing. Even the cursor will be in the same place. With a PC X server, if your PC crashes or is restarted, all the remote applications will die. With VNC they go on running.
Two types of users are available: a "native" viewer (for instance in Visual C++ on PCs) and a "universal" one based on Java. This last solution can suffer from performance problems in particular when important display updates are necessary. In particular, problems may arise with some video sequences/formats.
The VNC servers also contain a small web server. If you connect to this with a web browser, you can download the Java version of the viewer, and use this to view the server. You can then see your desktop from any Java-capable browser.
VNC provides also some authentication mechanisms between the server and the client in order to manage authorisation accesses. SSH, a secure shell may be also coupled with VNC for improving security levels.
VNC does not offer annotation facilities on the shared applications.

Reliability, Maintainability
The different software appears to run without major crashes. The VNC user community is quite important and dynamic. Source code, FAQs and major resources are available on-line from ATT research Web site under
        http://www.uk.research.att.com/vnc.

Platform
Linux 2.x for x86, Solaris, MacOS, Windows 95/98/NT 4.0/2000/CE 2.x
Some limited solutions also available for almost all platforms (including SGI Irix 6.2, HP-UX, FreeBSD...).

Price
For free under the terms of the GNU Public Licence

7.5.1.2 RealPresenter G2

General Description

RealPresenter G2, developed by Intel and Real, is a business communications application for the web. With RealPresenter G2, one can broadcast presentations that include Microsoft PowerPoint slides or Web pages with audio and video narration to anyone on an Intranet or on the Internet. It is not an application-sharing tool per se, but fulfills the same needs than the sharing of both Power Point and Web client applications.

Already, many companies use the Internet to Webcast important announcements, such as earning reports, and include slide presentations. RealPresenter simplifies the process of broadcasting slides by automating the task in an application. Real's streaming media technology allows Web surfers to watch video or listen to audio in real time rather than making them download the media to their hard drive and play it back.

Available Functionality

- PowerPoint 97 & PowerPoint 2000 Integration: Record, broadcast and publish Internet presentations directly from PowerPoint 97 or 2000,
- Platform Support: RealPresenter G2 runs on Windows 9x and Win NT 4.0. Playback any 4.0 or higher browser with RealPlayer 7 or RealPlayer G2.
- Live Broadcast Capability: broadcast a presentation live to up to 15 people directly from a computer,
- RealAudio and RealVideo Narrations: broadcast and record a narration using the quality streaming media including RealAudio and RealAudio plus RealVideo,
- Audience Interaction: receive questions and comments from an audience via RealPresenter G2 direct email link,
- Index information: index a presentation with author, title and a description,
- Presentation Dashboard: create a broadcast using navigation buttons (start, stop, pause, help and exit),
- Integrated RealServer: Integrated basic server provides streaming right from the desktop,
- Audience notification: notify an audience about upcoming broadcast events happening now and archived presentations,
- SureStream Support: use RealSystem G2 SureStream support to simultaneously create streams, scaling from modem users to LAN users,
- RealVideo Codec Control: RealVideo codec control allows you to tailor your video to your audience,
- A/V Equipment Check: ensure audio and video equipment is optimized before broadcast,
- Presentation tips: learn the ropes of Internet presentations.
- Free microphone,
- Live broadcast capability: broadcast a presentation live to up to 25 people directly from a computer,
- Multicast Support: manage the network load by using multicasting,

- Network Server Connection: reach thousands of desktops through a company's RealServer and RealProxy network,
- Web Tour: record, broadcast and publish live and on-demand a web site or Intranet.

Reliability, Maintainability
Network usage: RealPresenter G2 tries to be a network-friendly application. To do that, it captures slides as JPEG (i.e. it doesn't keep the PowerPoint format). These are converted in a streaming format that is RealPix. RealPix compresses up to 60 percent of the JPEG. The Audio/Video feed is compressed into Real audio/video in real time. See Intel developer's site for more information about RealPresenter G2:

http://developer.intel.com/ial/iips/index.htm

Platform
Windows 95/98/NT 4.0/NT 5.0.

Price
A basic free version can be downloaded from Real's site and a deluxe version of the plug-in can be purchased for about 70 Euros.

7.5.1.3 XTVision /XMX
General Description
XTVision (formerly X/TeleScreen) application-sharing software from VisualTek Solutions, Inc., turns your workstation into a powerful conferencing tool. XTVision lets you share unmodified, off-the-shelf X-Windows applications across multiple displays on your Intranet or across the Internet. Additional information can be found at: ftp://ftp.visualtek.com/pub/XTVISION20/

Available Functionality
XTVision gives the conference initiator two methods for granting chalk control to conference participants. In the Anarchy mode, chalk control passes dynamically to the user who is currently typing input. The initiator specifies how long each user retains control of the chalk when typing pauses. When a user pauses longer than the specified time (from 1 to 60 seconds), control reverts to the group and any other user can pick up the chalk by simply starting to type.

The Polite mode requires each user to request the chalk by clicking his or her face icon in the Conference Control Window (the area displaying the X/TeleScreen options). All the displays then show that user's icon with a raised hand. The current user can pass the chalk by clicking on the requester's icon.

In the Master mode, the initiator of XTVision has the input control; she can provide control to other participants as requested. This is similar to a presentation system where one person is the master and the rest are observers.

XTVision ships with NetBook, a spreadsheet-like conference manager. NetBook maintains the list of shared applications and invocation details, and keeps track of conference participants, their TCP/IP addresses, email addresses, and any other information you choose to include. NetBook's database structure simplifies setting up, organizing, and maintaining a variety of conference and userdata. Once in place, NetBook makes conference and application invocation both quick and easy.

Reliability, Maintainability
In its 2.0 version. Online support through FAQs and detailed documentation on the Web.

Platform
- Hewlett Packard 9000 series 700 and series 800 running HP-UX
- Intel X86-based PCs running Solaris 2.x
- IBM Workstations running AIX 4.x
- Silicon Graphics Workstations running IRIX 5.x, 6.x
- Sun Microsystems Workstations running SunOS 5.x, Solaris 2.5.x or later.

Note: Another product developed as freeware at Brown University for use in our electronic classroom, XMX, is a standalone utility for sharing an X Window System session on multiple X displays.

The shared client applications appear to each participant in a virtual root window, which is subject to local window management. In this way, the shared X session coexists with each user's private X session. Available in its 2.1 Version for Solaris 2.6, AIX 4.2, Intel Linux 2.0 and HP-UX.

Price
- XTVision Single Workstation License: 1500 Euros for one WS license - Includes license for 2 simultaneous connections.
- Additional License: 250 Euros for each additional connection (user).
XMX is free under Brown University copyright notice.

7.5.1.4 Magics Communicator
General Description
This tool allows users to initiate an engineering conference on 3D CAD models in real-time via Internet or LAN. Developed by a Belgian company called Materialise:
      http://www.materialise.be

Available Functionality
- Conference - Visualise - Measure – Annotate: start an online conference and discuss your model in real time via Internet, LAN or modem.
- Support various formats such as: STL, IGES, VDA and DXF 3d faces, with fast rotation, zooming and cross sectioning.
- Annotate: allow adding 2D and 3D annotations, shapes, text and bitmaps.
- Measure: easily create 2D drawings from 3D files. Extensive feature recognition allows measuring of distances, radii and angles in 3D. Add tolerances and additional info.

- Presentation: Make a 3D slide show with adjustable colours, shading and transparency.
- Ease of use: Communicator's straightforward interface ensures that even non-CAD users will be comfortable with the program in no time.

Magics Communicator conferencing is limited to sharing Communicator presentations and chatting, it is not a general application sharing tool.

Compared to general Internet sharing applications, it is a lot faster. Because both parties have the same software installed, proprietary protocol for sending small commands over the Internet is used, instead of sending the entire screen contents over the Internet.

Magics Communicator does not include video conferencing nor require any special hardware; both partners in a conference only have to have simple windows PC, no cad station or graphic cards or video cards are needed.

At the moment, conferencing is restricted to a face to face construction. You can conference with only one other user at a time.

Type of Application
Client server. The server can either be hosted by Materialise or installed at end-user premises.

Reliability, Maintainability
- Encryption and password protection for secure data transfer are supported.
- No support/help/documentation on-line yet.
- Platform
- Intel-based PC under Windows NT, 95 or 98.

Price
Magics Communicator licenses come in two varieties: Basic License and Pro License. They can be fixed licenses, restricted to use on one PC. Or they can be floating licenses, restricted to use within a local network.

- Fixed basic license: includes all basic functionality of Magics Communicator (visualization, measuring, annotation, conferencing etc.) Prices: 299 Euros for the first license, and 249 Euros for following licenses.
- Fixed Pro License includes all basic functionality, with the addition of IGES, VDA and DXF 3D Faces import, DXF 3D faces and VRML export, password encryption of files and conferences: 999 Euros

It is also possible to get a Server License which includes the installation of server software on the clients network, enabling clients to conference via their own communication server instead of via the communication server at Materialise. Price on request.

7.5.1.5 CATIA Conferencing Groupware
General Description
Developed using technology from InSoft/Netscape, CATIA Conferencing Groupware gives people located at different places around the word the ability to work together to review CATIA designs:

http://www-3.ibm.com/solutions/engineering/escatia.nsf/Public/ds_cgw

The product provides conference management tools to start, invite, join, and quit a conference. Chat tools allows communication through text, audio and video. Images can be captured from the screen, windows or video and then shared between the participants. 2D whiteboards permit users to work simultaneously viewing and annotating 2D images such as views of CATIA models. When used in conjunction with the CATIA 4D Navigator product, users can simultaneously view, annotate and manipulate 3D models.

Available Functionality
- Networked Collaborative Work
Conferencing Groupware allows users located around the world to interactively work together on the same CATIA model in real time. Multiple users are able to work at the same time on the model to make modifications.

The system automatically replicates the CATIA model, viewpoint and annotations to all participants in the conference. To save time, the system redisplays only modified elements. In addition to optional audio and video conferencing, users can communicate through text-driven conference "chats" while editing and manipulating the CATIA model.

Conferencing Groupware is said to provide the highest quality audio and video synchronization through an adaptive, fully scalable algorithm that transparently balances frame speeds and sampling rates in response to varying CPU and network loads. Users can preset their video bandwidth throughput to work within their network limits while still achieving the highest productive and effective quality.

- 2D or 3D Annotation
When used in conjunction with the CATIA 4D Navigator product, users can work in a 2D or 3D space with each participant represented by a different color. Users can hand draw, employ primitive markups or use text to annotate the model. When working in 3D, participants are able to simultaneously manipulate the model in walk or fly mode to change the viewpoint. Participants can use telepointers to identify a specific location for discussion on the model.

- Reliance on accepted standards
Network standards such as TCP/IP and UDP, image standards such as TIFF and GIF, video standards such as JPEG and Indeo- H320 audio and video multisite conferencing standards (said to be partial: may mean interoperability problems).

- Multiple Network Offerings
Conferencing Groupware offers users a full range of network support to meet a mixed need and budget requirement. The system basically works on any line that

supports Internet protocol: Public phone lines, LAN (local area networks) that support TCP/IP including Ethernet, ISDN (Integrated Services Digital Network), ATM (Asynchronous Transfer Mode), etc.

In a mixed network environment, the system supports both multipoint and point-to-point data transmission in the same conference.

Type of Application
Integrated in CATIA environment.

Reliability, Maintainability
See global CATIA information

Platform
UNIX platforms: IBM, HP, Sun, and Silicon Graphics

Price
Price on request.

7.5.1.6 Timbuktu Pro 2000

General Description
A remote control software for Windows and MacOS environments:
http://www.netopia.com/ebusiness/

Available Functionality
Timbuktu Pro 2000 makes it easy for anyone to quickly find users on the Internet or LAN, especially those Timbuktu Pro 2000 users with dynamic IP addresses-like the ones handed to you from your Internet Service Provider. The Timbuktu Pro Internet Locator server is hosted by Netopia 24 hours a day; it matches your email address with your TCP/IP address in real-time, whenever you are online. Any Timbuktu user can take advantage of the Internet Locator service and connect to any other Timbuktu Pro 2000 user simply by knowing their email address.

Timbuktu Pro now supports the Lightweight Directory Access Protocol (LDAP) for scalable Timbuktu Pro directory services. Simply browse the LDAP directory for the target machine and you're connected with one click ease.

Timbuktu Pro's ironclad security provides state-of-the-art secure screen blanking, password encryption, user level defined privileges, password ageing, event logging, master password protection, and more. The attended access feature prompts users to ask for permission before attempting to control your computer or being admitted as a temporary guest.

Multiple Access Mode Technology over Internet, Network, DSL, Dial-up, and from Dial Direct connections provides a choice of connectivity options for virtually any environment insuring that any mobile worker, telecommuter, or collaborator can connect and communicate without fail.

Reliability, Maintainability
This is a mature version of the product. Widely spread solution together with pcAnywhere product.

Platform
Windows NT 4.0/NT 5.0 (2000), MacOS 8.1 or above.

Price
About 170 Euros; 10-pack at 650 Euros; 30-pack at about 1700 Euros

7.5.1.7 Symantec pcAnywhere
General Description
pcAnywhere is a leading solution for remote control requirements like remote troubleshooting and helpdesk support, and for providing connectivity for remote and mobile users. This proven, comprehensive solution allows helpdesk personnel to more quickly resolve user problems, and allows remote employees to easily access office-based files and applications: http://www.symantec.com/pcanywhere

Available Functionality

- Connect to your office PC at home or on the road.
- Control your office PC remotely over the Internet.
- Connect to servers from your office or home to remotely administer your network-anytime.
- Use pcAnywhere on multiple operating system platforms
- Use pcAnywhere with a broad range of protocol support, including modem, ISDN, infrared, TCP/IP, IPX, SPX, and Internet.
- Optimize pcAnywhere 's performance with features, including SpeedSend, ColorScale, and AutoColorscale that provide the best performance when operating over low-bandwidth connections.
- Control a remote computer while transferring files in the background.
- Transfer a file in seconds with the parallel cable that's included with pcAnywhere for direct file transfers.
- Switch between voice and remote control sessions during a single phone call using standard data/fax modems with Voice First/Data Switching support.
- Change from a remote control session to video conferencing with a single click.
- Simplifies remote-control connections across the Internet. Displays available hosts and gateways on selected Internet or Intranet subnets using Internet Smart List host list.
- Lets you create a list of files that are automatically updated or synchronized upon connection to a host with AutoXfer.
- Synchronizes screen resolutions of host and remote PCs.
- Change from a remote control session to video conferencing.

Security aspects are in particular highlighted:

- provides restricted drive access, file-transfer rights restrictions, host callback, host screen and keyboard locks, and more.
- Supports Microsoft Cryptography API to implement low level encryption services-securing session initiation, remote control, file transfer, chat, logs and pcAnywhere objects
- Scans for viruses automatically during file transfer using Symantec Norton AntiVirus technology.
- Maintains Windows NT security by establishing a remote connection before logging in.
- Leverages Windows NT user and group security to authenticate remote users.
- Allows administrators to remotely start, stop, and check status on hosts on Windows NT workstations and servers in a Microsoft network with the Remote Host Service Administration Utility file.

Type of Applications
Remote control software

Maintainability and Support
Symantec pcAnywhere has management console and SNMP support
Graphical utility lets an administrator enforce network policies and distribute and maintain applications.
Symantec provides consulting, education, and support services. Very complete online documentation on the Web with FAQ, white papers, documentation. Additional information is available at http://www.symantec.com/pcanywhere

Impact of Utilization
Step-by-step "wizards" to walk you through setup and configuration.
The system is in its 9.2 version. Leading product with numerous technologies awards from specialised press.

Platform
- Windows 95, 98, or NT 4.0/NT 5.0 (2000), MacOS 8.1 or above.
- 486sx 25MHz or higher processor
- 16 MB of RAM (20 MB recommended)
- 32 MB of hard disk space
- VGA video (minimum)

Price
About $179.95

7.5.2 Web Conferencing

7.5.2.1 Mirabilis ICQ

General Description
ICQ is an Internet application that let people to interact simultaneously by means of chat sessions, messages and e-mail exchange integrated functions. An external server (some privacy issue may be risen) supports all the operations made by the clients. In order to use the tool users have to register themselves in order to get a personal number with a password: http://www.icq.com

Available Functionality
At Societa Ialiana Avionica some practical experiments (using no more than 4 simultaneous users) were performed (both with internal working group and in IST projects context, like OCCAMM). Experiments gave results about usability, performance and human factor relevance. We found a good usability (GUI and service provided), some performance problems (some time it's difficult to connect to the server) and a good reaction in terms of human factor. In fact, interaction among partners is faster, and important issues can be discussed better than using e-mail because a "chat session" is really a virtual meeting. Since data and messages pass through an external server it is strongly recommended to not use ICQ for Mission Critical projects.

This paragraph will list all the relevant available functionality of the tool. It should be considered that the tool (and the connected services infrastructure) is used to "connect people", this means that it is a very general tool, not a virtual enterprise focused one. For this reason most of the features listed by the manufacturer are not to be considered. Relevant features are:

- Contact list;
- Personal discussion list
- File transfer capability;
- Integrated mail client;
- External application support (Microsoft NetMeeting, Netscape conference, internet telephony tools);
- Voice message;
- Chat rooms (basic virtual meeting capability);
- Reminder and notes;

Type of Applications
ICQ is a client-server application running on TCP/IP networks.

Reliability
No software problems were encountered during the trial activities.

Maintainability
Automatic update from Mirabilis ICQ web server.

Learnability
Due to the wide target it was built to be very user friendly.

Impacts of Utilisation
Major impact of utilisation concerns the availability of chat rooms and integration with external groupware application.

Platforms
Here all the available platforms are listed:
- Windows 95/98/NT4 - 99b Beta v.3.19 Build #2569
- Windows CE - v0.97 Preview
- Windows 3.1x - v1.111 Beta
- PowerPC - v.2.0 Beta
- 68K Mac - v1.7.2 Beta
- JAVA - v0.981a Preview
- Windows NT 3.5x - v1.113 Beta
- Palm Computing ® Platform - 1.0.2 Beta version

Price
ICQ is totally free.

7.5.2.2   SneakerLabs iMeet
General Description
iMeet is a solution for holding live, Web-based conferences over the Internet. A cost-effective and innovative solution. iMeet offers features including real-time PowerPoint presentations, whiteboarding, polling, Questions and Answers, and more. iShow is the unique application-sharing feature of iMeet that enable live demonstrations of any software application to anyone, anywhere on the Web. In addition, LIVE help is available directly from within each conference through SneakerLabs' iServe technology: http://www.sneakerlabs.com

Available Functionality
Key features include:
- a shared Web browsing (a user can surf the Web and share the view and operations he performs),
- PowerPoint presentations
- Application sharing with iShow, another product of Sneaker's Lab. Whiteboard collaboration is also supported.
- LIVE tech support during the conference
- Streaming audio/video support - Use iMeet with any of Web-based streaming media.
- Polling and transcript capabilities - Discover your audience's preferences on the fly.

- Multiple presenter support - Easily transfer control to anyone in the conference.
- Proxy and firewall friendly - The majority of today's Internet business is conducted through a firewall and iMeet can handle it: iMeet identifies firewalls and proxy servers automatically and tunnels through them without affecting your company's network security.
- This kind of service is naturally platform and necessitates no software or hardware installation being a 100% Web-based service.

Type of Applications
100% Web-based service, based on so-called Bersama client/server infrastructure. Bersama supports message passing among clients who are registered with a central server. Conversations are grouped by "channels" or "rooms", allowing for public, private, and moderated interactions. Many channels may exist on a single Bersama server, and many Bersama processes may run on a single machine.

The Bersama client is a lightweight Java class that abstracts away the complexities of low-level socket programming, while remaining a high-performance interface for sending data to the Bersama server and other Bersama clients.

Reliability
Users receive accounts with login and password for connections to "privatised" areas. Reliability depends on the service provider.

Maintainability
Not applicable

Learnability
Seems to be quite user friendly and intuitive.

Platforms
All with recent Netscape or Internet Explorer navigator versions.

Price
$500 set-up fee (one-time charge), $250/month per each block of 10 simultaneous users.

A pay-per-use option is also available.

7.5.2.3 ActiveTouch WebEx Meeting Center
General Description
WebEx Meeting Center is a hosted service, eliminating the need for investment in hardware, software installation, training, and maintenance. Concurrent user licensing in Meeting Center gives you the flexibility for anyone in your organisation to hold web meetings. Your WebEx Meeting Center can be tailored to your needs, with configurable features, customised look-and-feel branding and a rich set of interactive, multimedia meeting features.

Available Functionality
Key features are listed below:
- Customised Branded Service
  Customised branding lets you seamlessly add interactive meeting capabilities to your company's web site.
- Presentation Sharing
  Allows any meeting participant to spontaneously share any presentation without uploading the file to a server, where the security of the file could be compromised. Allows very high resolution with full screen viewing capability.
- Document Sharing
  Allows meeting attendees to jointly view ANY document or graphic with high resolution, multi-level zooming and annotation capabilities. The owner of the document can optionally allow other participants to save a copy of the annotated document for later offline viewing. Any saved document can be viewed later without the need for the original application that created the document.
- Application Sharing
  Run any software application for effective live demos and training.
- Application Share Control
  The presenter can even share control of any software application with others in a meeting, for unmatched interactive meetings on the web.
- Web Co-browsing
  Allows easy sharing of web-based information. Any participant can navigate the web and synchronise the browsers of other participants. Co-browsing is fully interactive and control can be passed to any participant, thus enabling users to complete web forms together, and to annotate any web pages.
- File Transfer
  Users can conveniently upload and download files as desired (but do not need to transfer files for sharing).
- Polling
  Permits presenters solicit feedback from attendees online.
- Desktop Sharing
  Presenters can share anything on their PC system, including any application, for unmatched live demos and training that involve more than just one application.
- Desktop Share Control
  Customer support personnel can take control of a user's PC system (with the user's approval) to instantly provide live assistance and resolve problems immediately.
- Browser-based
  No software installation, configuration or updating is required, for rapid setup and deployment. All WebEx Meetings run in a standard browser. New functionality is added to the browser automatically when new releases occur.
- Scalable
  Supports hundreds of concurrent meetings with thousands of participants.
- Telephony Integration
  Integrates with any Public Switched Telephone Networks or PBX system and all phones, including wireless. Use Voice over IP telephony integrated with the meeting.

- Security

WebEx Meeting Center works with existing firewall technology, offers unlisted meetings, password protection and encryption to protect sensitive data. Additional security is available with optional SSL and VPN.

- Video Integration

With a simple desktop video camera, videoconferencing is enabled without the need for any special equipment, software or set-up. Participants can see live video within the browser, including users that are behind firewalls.

Type of Applications
100% Web-based service.

Reliability
Users receive accounts with login and password for connections to "privatised" areas. Reliability depends on the service provider. WebEx Meeting Center runs on the WIN (WebEx Interactive Network), a globally distributed, fully-meshed, fault-tolerant, carrier-grade network that provides scalable, reliable and secure interactive communication and collaboration services world-wide.

Maintainability
Not applicable.

Learnability
Seems to be quite user friendly and intuitive. Help pages and FAQs available. Comprehensive Support information.

Platforms
All with recent Netscape or Internet Explorer navigator versions. A Java Client enables platform-independent meeting participation on Windows, Mac OS and UNIX.

Price
Good and numerous customers references.

The free meetings offered at WebEx.com are limited to 4 people per meeting. The application-sharing feature is limited to 10 minutes.

Per-pay-use: Pricing starts at 20¢ per minute.

Monthly rates: tbc.

More info: http://www.webex.com/

7.5.2.4 e-vis.com

Supports two kinds of online conferences:

- application conference to view and share the documents placed in the server side Documents folder;
- 2D or 3D conference to share CAD and graphics files.

The product capabilities lie beyond the scope of Web Conferencing. Detailed information is available in section 5.1.3.5.

7.5.2.5 PlaceWare
General Description
A Web conference place.

To ensure a successful meeting, PlaceWare lets you select the best type of virtual conference room (whether for a large presentation or a smaller collaborative meeting). You can share all types of graphical content with the audience, broadcast applications from your desktop, stream audio and video, take your audience on Web tours, collaborate using whiteboards, conduct instant audience polls, create on-the-fly content etc.

Available Functionality
To address security, PlaceWare offers multilevel access options in our product to prevent unauthorised parties from accessing content and viewing private material. PlaceWare comes automatically with Personal Identification Number-based passwords and security, which defines access for the audience and presenters. To increase security, Access Control Lists can be set-up to define who has access on a per meeting basis. HTTP security is additionally supported for an additional level of protection where necessary. And the service now offers authentication tools that can integrate with existing internal authentication system providing a single authorisation interface to your users.

24 hours to have a secure hosted server up and running with user's own virtual conference center, ready to hold Web conferences.

Type of Applications
100% Web-based service.

Reliability
PlaceWare is said to have an unparalleled track record for reliability. Robust server technology, developed from years of research at Xerox PARC, offers unmatched uptime for all participants in a meeting or presentation. In general, industry-leading 99.9% percent success rate in enabling meeting participants to connect and join in a Web conference.

Additionally, all Web conferencing E-services are also backed by our iVault™ Hosting Infrastructure, giving the confidence that all your mission-critical meetings will come off flawlessly. Our iVault infrastructure is located at Exodus Communication's world-wide Internet Data Centers to ensure maximum Internet bandwidth, dedicated and guaranteed uptime, and 24-hour support.

Maintainability
Not applicable.

Learnability
Seems to be quite user friendly and intuitive. Help pages and FAQs available. Comprehensive Support information.

Platforms
All with recent Netscape or Internet Explorer navigator versions. A Java Client enables platform-independent meeting participation on Windows, Mac OS and UNIX.

Price
Good and numerous customers reference.
  The annual hosted service price is $400 per seat (U.S.)
  End-user support packages are available on a per-event or on a monthly subscription basis and are priced as low as $600.
  More info: http://www.placeware.com/

7.5.3 H.323 Terminals and T.120 Software Tools

Most products available on the market provide T.120 functionality, which are considered a key aspect of the conferencing features. User needs are not limited to the possibility of seeing and hearing each other but also include additional features like data sharing, whiteboard, chat, application sharing and remote control, etc.

Hardware vs. Software:
Different types of solutions for H.323/H.320 conferencing can be found on the market. Depending on the audio and video codec solutions we have to consider:
• Software-only (SW) based solutions. These solutions necessitate a powerful machine as most of the CPU power is lasted by compression/decompression treatments. Moreover, this solution is not viable in multipoint conferencing configurations. Such a configuration is mainly encountered in H.323 (over IP) conferences from single desktop terminals.
• mixed Hardware-Software (HW-SW) solutions usually composed of a codec-card to be plugged on the computer (PCI board in most cases) and associated software enabling basic videoconferencing features (call setting, session controlling and closing…). Some cards do not provide 100% hardware-based codecs for video AND audio. Hybrid solutions may for example supports full hardware video coding/decoding but a software-based audio coding/decoding. This may also vary according to the video/audio standard supported (one video standard may be supported with a pure HW solution coding/decoding and the other through a software solution). In the same way, compression can be hardware-based whether decompression is done by a piece of software.
We consider mainly products offering video/audio codec features complying with H.32x standards series. Video capture-only cards are not in the scope of this survey since multimedia conferencing standard video codecs are mostly not provided: some are mentioned in section 7.5.4.13 for information purpose only.

7.5.3.1 Mbone Project Tools
General Description
Mbone tools support multipoint (up to 8) multimedia conferencing via the Mbone. The set consists of vic (Video Conferencing tool), vat (Audio Tool), rat (Robust

Audio Tool), nte (Network Text Editor), wb (WhiteBoard) and sdr (Session DiRectory):

- LBNL Audio Conferencing Tool, vic
  Developed by the Network Research Group at the Lawrence Berkeley National Laboratory in collaboration with the University of California. The LBNL very popular video conferencing tool.
      ftp://ftp.ee.lbl.gov/conferencing/vic/
  An improved version is available at URL:
      http://www-mice.cs.ucl.ac.uk/multimedia/software/vic//
  See also [53].
  Most flavors of UNIX and Windows are supported.
  Vic can be used either for point to point video conferencing or for multipoint conferencing via the Mbone. vic is based on the draft Internet standard Real-time Transport Protocol (RTP) developed by the IETF Audio/Video Transport working group. RTP is an application-level protocol implemented entirely within vic -- you need no special system enhancements to run RTP.

- LBNL Audio Conferencing Tool, vat
  The LBNL audio tool, vat, is a real-time, multi-party, multimedia application for audio conferencing over the Internet. Based on RTP.
      http://www-nrg.ee.lbl.gov/vat/

- Robust Audio Tool, rat
  Another open-source audio conferencing and streaming application. Includes many real-time error recovery mechanisms.
      http://www-mice.cs.ucl.ac.uk/multimedia/software/rat/
  Most flavors of UNIX and Windows supported.

- WhiteBoard, wb
  The most popular whiteboard tool. Available (in binary format only) at URL:
      http://www-nrg.ee.lbl.gov/wb/

- Network Text Editor, nte
  A whiteboard working only in text mode. Most flavors of UNIX and Windows are supported.

- Session Directory, sdr
  A popular tool for announcing and being informed of MBONE sessions. Enables the automatic launching of MBONE tools with proper parameter configuration. The latest release of most of the above tools is available at URL:
      http://www-mice.cs.ucl.ac.uk/multimedia/software/

Type of Applications
Features unique to vic include: an "Intra-H.261" video encoder, voice switched viewing windows, multiple dithering algorithms, interactive "title generation", and routing of decoded video to external video ports.

Reliability, Maintainability, Learnability
These tools are widely spread in the internet community, in particular in the UNIX world. Deployment and use are quite trivial. Regular contributions of developers and of users ensure the development of improved versions over the time. Comprehensive information, FAQs, source codes, etc can be found from: http://www-mice.cs.ucl.ac.uk/multimedia/projects/shrimp

Platform
Available for PC, Sun Solaris and Linux.

Price
Freeware.

7.5.3.2   The Mash Project
General Description
This research project (http://www-mash.cs.berkeley.edu/mash/) seeks to define a comprehensive architecture for multimedia communication and collaboration over the Internet using IP multicast (see Figure 5). It can be seen as an experimental follow-up to some of the MBONE tools.

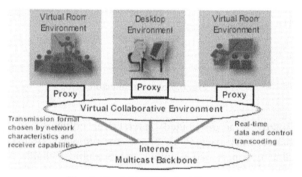

Fig. 5. The MASH Project Concept

The MASH project includes following parts:
- libsrm (Scalable, Reliable Multicast framework) is a multicast toolkit that can be customized by applications with different reliability semantics. In addition to serving as a generic toolkit to enable new and interesting Reliable Multicast (RM) applications, the toolkit is also intended as a vehicle for research into protocol issues in RM such as data naming, loss recovery, local recovery, congestion control, and data consistency.

libsrm software architecture (see Figure 6) includes:
  - The core Scalable Reliable Multicast (SRM) engine, that implements a distributed and randomized loss recovery protocol based on "slotting and damping" with NxN delay estimation,
  - Hierarchical namespaces,

- Scalable namespace announcements using Standard Network Access Protocol (SNAP)
- Rate-controller for data transmission
- 2-step local recovery.

libsrm is implemented as an event-based library and plugs into any event system (e.g., Tcl/Tk) via a simple API that allows handlers for timer and I/O events to be registered. The toolkit has C and Tcl APIs.

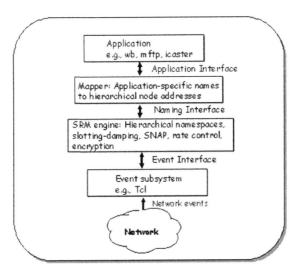

Fig. 6. libsrm architecture

- mb (MediaBoard) is a distributed, interactive, collaboration application that provides a shared workspace (whiteboard) for remote participants. MediaBoard requires reliable transport and employs the Scalable Reliable Multicast (SRM) (www-nrg.ee.lbl.gov/floyd/srm.html) protocol machinery for data delivery. Developers are currently generalizing SRM into a protocol framework that can suit the diverse needs of a variety of reliable-multicast applications through specialization and MediaBoard has served as the chief application for this design.
- SCUBA (Scalable, ConsensUs-based Bandwidth Allocation) is a mechanism for real-time multimedia bandwidth sharing that exploits receiver interest. The scheme uses a distributed algorithm to establish consensus among all participants in the conference on the sharing of the session bandwidth. The scheme uses a voting mechanism to establish consensus. It achieves scalability through voter sampling that results in a low convergence time to consensus with high confidence bounds.
- Media Archival and Playback. The archive portion of the MASH project is divided into two areas: exploring formats for new datatypes, and developing collaboration archive architecture.
- Coordination and Control Architecture. A coordination framework centered on the "Coordination Bus" glues together sub-components of the MASH system to create new applications. A developer can mix and match components from the MASH toolkit by composing them across the Coordination Bus to build an arbitrary

application. As part of the MASH project, developers continue to evolve and elaborate the rudimentary Coordination Bus technology that was previously developed in the MBone tools: vic, vat, and wb.

- MeGa: An Agent Architecture for Multimedia Transmission in Heterogeneous Networks. It is a comprehensive architecture for deployment of Media Gateways. The architecture relies on a completely soft state protocol, which facilitates robustness and flexibility. Bandwidth control of the gateways is through the use of the SCUBA protocol. The architecture has been implemented and deployed and is in regular use on the Berkeley campus.

The following Figure 7 presents an image of a user's screen showing the MBone video tool vic, the MBone audio tool vat, and the MASH shared whiteboard tool mb.

Fig. 7. MASH user's screen example

An overview of mb user interface is presented on the picture Figure 8:

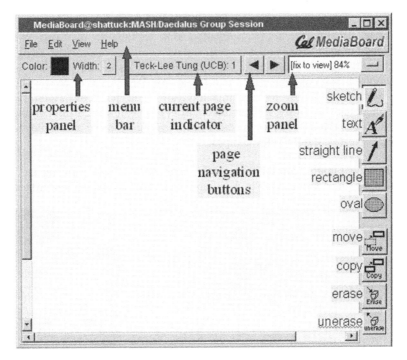

Fig. 8. Overview of MASH mb user interface

Type of Applications

The principal research vehicle for the MASH project is a multimedia networking toolkit called the "MASH shell'" or simply MASH (developers refer to the MASH shell in lower case and the MASH project in upper case). MASH employs a "split programming model", where complex multimedia programming tasks are decomposed into an arrangement of simple objects that are linked together and configured by a scripting language like Tcl (http://sunscript.sun.com/TclTkCore/).

The MASH shell is the backbone of a number of new applications for multimedia networking and collaboration. In addition to subsuming existing tools like vic and vat, MASH supports a number of new tools that serve as vehicles to explore scalable multicast protocols and to exercise our design framework. These tools include a floor control application, a next-generation whiteboard called MediaBoard, an archive system and supporting tools, new applications for webcasting, and so forth. In the MASH framework, each of these new tools is simply a script that is executed by the MASH shell. For example, vic is now a Tcl script that is interpreted by the MASH Tcl interpreter, rather than a stand-alone, monolithic executable. This model assumes that the MASH interpreter and the tool you want to run are both in your command path.

There are two possible approaches to build new applications on top of MASH that differ in terms of complexity. The easier but less flexible path is to build new applications or applets entirely with the existing set of mash objects. Documentation on scripting mash applets (www-mash.cs.berkeley.edu/mash/software/scripting-api.html) defines the APIs to the built-in object classes without covering too many details of the C++ implementation. A large set of built-in multimedia and networking objects should provide a rich set of primitives to build interesting and arbitrary applications.

If an existing object set is inadequate (e.g., doesn't support compression hardware), user can extend the mash shell with his own C++ compiled-in objects by simply conforming to the Tcl programming model.

The MASH programming model is based on an architecture where multimedia data are generated by one or more source objects, piped through one or more filter objects, and eventually, consumed by one or more sink objects. A source, for example, might be a video capture device, a filter might be a color space converter, a compressor, a packetizer, etc, while a sink might be a network transmission protocol.

Reliability
All products are under construction. But there exist alpha and beta experimental releases.

Availability of Localised Versions
It is possibly to download and install pre-compiled binaries, but one can also build MASH from source code.

The tools resulting from this continuing work, even if recent and rather elaborated are not widely used compared to the MBONE ones. Mash should more be seen as a framework for research in the collaborative work and multicast transmission environment.

Platform
MASH system runs on most Unix platforms as well as Windows NT/95 and supports the Netscape plug-in API.

Price
Freeware.

7.5.3.3 SunForum
General Description
The SunForum application is a suite of data collaboration tools based on ITU T.120 and H.323. The application suite is said T.120 and Microsoft NetMeeting compliant and runs only on Sun Ultra stations with Solaris 2.6 or 7.

Available Functionality
• Audio/Video Conferencing: Standards-based (H.323) audio and video conferencing allow SunForum to conduct desktop video conferencing across standard TCP/IP networks. SunForum supports NetMeeting style point-to-point video conferencing that allows SunForum to connect to a Windows user running Microsoft NetMeeting.

- ability to conduct multipoint (multicast) videoconferences.
- Full-duplex Audio with Echo Suppression. In conferencing applications without echo suppression, conference members will usually use an operator style headset.
- Enterprise Configuration Support: SunForum 3.0 has improved support for enterprise installations. Network administrators to limit audio and/or video capabilities in SunForum may use a global configuration file. Additionally, SunForum 3.0 works with network management tools like gateways and gatekeepers.
- 24-bits-per-pixel Application Sharing: Support for true-color application sharing has been added to SunForum 3.0.
- Run-in-background Feature: the Run in Background command allows SunForum to run silently in the background. The user interface does not clutter the display, but SunForum monitors the network and notifies the users about incoming conference calls.
- Supports NetMeeting Style SpeedDials: SpeedDials are small text files that contain the conference address of a machine. By e-mailing a SpeedDial, it makes it easy for team members to connect together for a conference.

In addition to the new Audio/Video features, SunForum 3.0 provides:

- whiteboard with PCs running NetMeeting compatible products like Microsoft NetMeeting and PictureTel LiveShare Plus 4.0, or work with products based on the T.126 standard like Lotus (DataBeam) MeetingTools or the Polycom (3M/Lucent) ShowStation.
- Sharing of X-based applications with users of PCs, Macs, and workstations that are T.128 compliant. Users on Ultra workstations or non-Sun hardware can work on an application resident on another person's machine and make changes in real-time.
- Control of Windows applications running on PCs using NetMeeting, PictureTel LiveShare Plus, or any other T.128 based shared application.
- Transfer of files with other T.127 compliant systems.
- shared clipboard (for cut-and-paste operations), to make text and graphics instantly available to your workgroup.
- LDAP and NetMeeting ILS directory access
- Chat in an interactive text window.

Type of Applications
Client (T.120) application.

Reliability, Maintainability, Learnability
This software is now published in its 3.0 version (approximately one major version a year) and benefits from the support of Sun as the conferencing solution for Sun Workstations (as pendant to NetMeeting on PCs). User Manuals, FAQs and patches are available on-line through Sun's Web site:

More information on:
http://www.sun.com/desktop/products/software/sunfrum/sunforumjtf.html

SunForum is based on Data Connection technology DC-Share, T.120 and H.323 data, audio and video conferencing product for UNIX. Data Connection is a British software company, specialising in the development of core systems technology for the major players in the computer industry. They developed core components of Microsoft NetMeeting and, additionally to SunForum included their DC-Share technology in:

- SGI's SGImeeting
- HP's VISUALIZE Conference for HP-UX.

Price
Distributed for free by Sun, binaries and documentation. It seems that no possibility of customization is provided.

7.5.3.4 Lotus Sametime
General Description
Sametime is a server application supporting multicast conferences of clients such as NetMeeting or CuSeeMe. The T.120 standard is adopted for all applications such as the chat, whiteboard, and application sharing.

Available Functionality
Based on server architecture for managing multicast, Sametime provides significant bandwidth saving and an improved awareness level for the users.

The three foundations of real-time collaboration pointed out by Lotus for its product are awareness, conversation, and shared objects:

- Awareness: Awareness means here that a member of a team is aware of when other members are online. Sametime Connect is an easy-to-use desktop application that provides complete awareness and conversation features. It lets people find other team members online and creates personalized lists of team members and colleagues. Features for managing user privacy are also included so a member can control their own online presence. Users can also list their presence as "active", "away", or "do not disturb".
- Conversation: once a team member is aware of who's online, immediate communications is easy. A single mouse-click lets them send an instant message to anyone, or start a chat session with several people or launch an instant, online meeting.
- Shared Objects: for richer communications, an user can take advantages of Sametime's shared objects capabilities by quickly moving to an application-sharing or whiteboard session. With application sharing, a user can share any application from his desktop word processing, spreadsheets, project management software without requiring anyone else to have that software installed.

Moreover, Sametime allows users to have spontaneous or scheduled collaboration. Meetings can be launched on-the-fly or can be scheduled in the Meeting Center. Sametime's scheduled meeting option lets a user plan projects updates, seminars, or other meetings. Agendas and preparatory materials anytime before, during or after the meeting.

At last, Sametime supports a wide range of clients to meet the unique needs of everyone on the team:

- The Sametime 1.5 Connect Client interoperates with AOL's Instant Messenger (AIM) service to allow users to send instant messages to AIM users world-wide as well as to colleagues on the Sametime Server.
- With a browser, anyone can join an online meeting at any time without having to install additional client software, removing any client installation and cross platform obstacles. Lotus Notes users can also access all of the Sametime features directly from the Notes client.
- Other options include using a T.120 client such as NetMeeting.

Sametime keeps a central address book on the server, and in Lotus Domino environments, it shares the public Notes address book. From the Connect Client, users can add addresses and sort them by online status, send instant messages, and drag invitees into a group chat. Sametime is interoperable with AIM, as well as with Microsoft Outlook and Netscape Messenger. Meetings and discussions are accessed from the client or a Web browser.

LDAP seems not to be supported. IMPP (Instant Messaging and Presence Protocol), a joint standardisation effort of Lotus and Microsoft should be supported in a short term perspective.

Notes users can access these collaboration features directly from the Notes client.

The Meeting Center lets you schedule and monitor online meetings and even share applications with other Sametime users via a browser, the Notes Client, or Microsoft NetMeeting. When sharing applications, all invitees view the host's screen in a window, and the host designates which users can "drive" the applications being shared.

Sametime includes some advanced repository functions for the management of users. For example, it is possible to contact persons using criteria such as the web page they are consulting for example (and not only limited to the fact whether they are on-line or not). A particularity of the system is to provide more advanced security management features than NetMeeting:

- Three levels of security are provided for secured conferences and allows proxy parameterisation.
- Certification of people joining a conference through the server is also provided.
- In terms of reliability, the conference can go on even when a client is out of service (which is not the case with NetMeeting for example). The system is based on a true Client/Server implementation (server and client application are distinct).

A programming interface and a development toolkit based on C++ and Java is provided with two types of services: those relative to the User Interface, and those related to the server semantics (connection, registration, sending of instant messages, WhoIsOnLine or WhoIsHere functions...) thus providing a complete set of meeting management functions.

For example, two types of services are provided by the Java API:

- Basic community services as chat services or GUI services
- Meeting Services allowing client Java applets and applications to create and join meetings, manipulate parameters to automate some actions, choose which viewers will be used in a meeting, and control whether the viewers will be docked in the browser window or floated in their own window.

Type of Applications
Client/server (T.120) application.

Reliability, Maintainability, Learnability
Lotus provides Sametime as a key solution of its portfolio. Commercial references of big companies are provided too.

Sametime installs easily on a Windows NT server, especially when coupled with Domino. If installed in a non-Domino environment, Sametime, installs its own server back-end to store the address book, meeting centre, and threaded discussion data.

Different types of services are provided by Lotus (with pricing) but the Web Sites provide reasonable set of FAQs, technical tips and white papers.

More information on:

http://www.lotus.com/home.nsf/welcome/sametime

Platforms
Windows 95, 98, or NT

Price
Starts at 5000 Euros 20 Euros per user. Server requires: Pentium/166, 128MB RAM, 300MB disk space, Microsoft Windows NT 4.0 with Service Pack 3.

7.5.3.5 Cu-SeeMe (Pro)

General Description
This software is a pioneer in the world of videoconferences. CU-SeeMe (now v1.0) is originally a freeware, issued from a project of Cornell University for audio and video conferencing over the Internet. Users can either connect directly to each other or they can enter a conference at a so-called "reflector". It offers colour video (M-JPEG codec is used) and now, view up to 24 participant windows simultaneously. It is available for PC, Mac, Linux and Amiga. This "product" is very popular and started to be used in universities and research context. It benefits from a very large user community and developers community. The rights to the product were subsequently purchased by White Pine who made it a commercial product by moving, among others, towards H.323 standards.

Good start page at: http://cu-seeme.net/

• White Pine CU-SeeMe Pro

White Pine Software has taken over the commercialization of CU-SeeMe and has developed enhanced CU-SeeMe, which supports full-color video, a whiteboard and H.323 standards. It provides directory service, contact list, multipoint video conferencing (up to 12), IP or email call, phone book, H.323 interoperability (when connected to a MeetingPoint conference server). CU-SeeMe is available for PC and Mac. Its code is not open (unlike its university's counterpart).

Maintainability
Technical support seems to be allright with direct connection on WhitePine's Web. Regular evolutions of the product are made during the 3 past years (since buy by WhitePine).

Platforms
Windows 95/98 or Windows NT 4.0.

Price
About 80 Euros (without camera).

7.5.3.6 Microsoft NetMeeting
General Description
NetMeeting is the Microsoft product for virtual meetings and cooperative work. To get the full performance from this tool audio (sound card, microphone and speakers) and video (video card and digital camera) supports are needed. It is well integrated with the Microsoft Office suite and Outlook.

Microsoft NetMeeting includes support for the H.323 audio and video conferencing standard. NetMeeting can be used to place calls to and receive calls from products that are H.323-compatible, including the Intel Internet Video Phone. With appropriate equipment and services, NetMeeting can place a call to a telephone using an H.323 gateway.

Support for multi-user conferences: Many people can join a NetMeeting data conference for communication and collaboration. The top provider in NetMeeting provides the node controller that manages participants and their applications.

This application uses external directory servers to provide all the operational functions. Directory servers may be purchased if necessary (Mission Critical projects).

Available Functionality
In NetMeeting, we find these different applications:

- Share Program: Only one computer needs to have the program, and all participants can work on the document simultaneously,
- Video and Audio Conference: NetMeeting's audio and video let a user see and hear other people. Even if he is unable to transmit video, he can still receive video calls in the NetMeeting video window,
- Chat: end users can talk with multiple people. In addition, Chat calls can be encrypted, ensuring that their meetings are private,
- Whiteboard: a user can explain concepts by diagramming information, using a sketch, or displaying graphics. He can also copy areas of his desktop or windows and paste them to the Whiteboard,
- File Transfer: end users can send and receive files to work on.

NetMeeting is both a client program and a platform. The NetMeeting client provides users the benefits of real-time audio, video, and multipoint data conferencing. The

NetMeeting platform also provides software application programming interface (API) support so that software developers can integrate these conferencing features into their own products and services.

- Audio/Video codecs

For optimal performance over the Internet, NetMeeting specifies H.263 and G.723 as the default codecs. NetMeeting can negotiate other codecs, such as H.261 or G.711, depending on the requirements of other H.323-compatible products. Also, NetMeeting creates appropriate payload formats and handlers.

- LDAP

The IETF LDAP (Lightweight Directory Access Protocol) standard provides the directory services support for NetMeeting. The Microsoft Internet Locator Service (ILS) servers utilise the LDAP interface to create directories of current NetMeeting users that people can call and communicate with over TCP/IP connections.

- User Interface

The NetMeeting user interface (UI) provides an easy-to-use format with icons and buttons. This UI is flexible, allowing users to view the full NetMeeting window, or a compact window that shows either the data conferencing features only or the audio and video conferencing features only.

- SDK

The NetMeeting SDK provides software developers with software application programming interface (API) support and information to build solutions using the NetMeeting platform. They can incorporate NetMeeting features, such as program sharing, Chat, and Whiteboard, into their programs and Web pages.

The NetMeeting 3 SDK provides a scripting guide for Web developers and other scripting application developers, a low-level T.120 application guide, and a COM guide. Because most of the components are implemented using the Component Object Model (COM), they can be called from any COM-supporting languages, such as C/C++, Microsoft Visual Basic, and Java.

The following APIs can be used:

- COM API: a programmable access to NetMeeting features through C/C++ and other languages supporting COM.
  This API includes, for example, objects such as:
    - Conference Manager Object: Manager of the overall conferencing system. Only one conference may be active at a time, all others are idle.
    - Local System Object : Information about the local user and local computer
    - Call Object: Monitors and controls an incoming or outgoing calls to a remote conference.
    - Conference Object : Manages a local active conference,
- scripting API that includes the NetMeeting UI ActiveX control and a NetMeeting scripting object model. The API allows including NetMeeting functionality in a Web page or other scripting environment using the underlying installed NetMeeting 3 software. By using the ActiveX control in any control container including a Web page, it's possible to manage the NetMeeting user interface (UI) viewed by an end user.

- COM T.120 Application API: This API lets NetMeeting client applications do the following:
    - Join and leave a conference at will.
    - Access remote system resources such as the registry, channels, and tokens after joining a conference.
    - Query applet rosters.
    - Launch an applet remotely.
    - Replace the underlying transport.
    - In addition, this transport API provides the following features:
        Compatibility with earlier versions of NetMeeting that used Public Switched Telephone Network (PSTN) framing.
        The ability to disable the Windows Socket connection while using the plug-in transport.
- Internet Locator Service (ILS) API defines the COM-based Internet Locator Service Objects, formally known as User Location Service (ULS) Objects. The objects let an application communicate with other applications over the Internet, similar to the Directory Service Support provided with NetMeeting.

Type of Applications
NetMeeting is a client-server application running on TCP/IP networks. Both components are included in the same application and can not be dissociated.

Reliability
No software problems were encountered during the trial activities. Some performance limitations with, for instance, application sharing.

Maintainability
Automatic update from MicroSoft Developer Network.

Learnability
Aligned with most of the common Microsoft end-user applications (very user friendly).

Impacts of Utilisation
Major impact of utilisation concerns the availability of chat rooms and integrated video and audio capability.

Platforms
Here all the available platforms are listed:
- Windows 95/98/NT4/2000

Note that with Windows2000, Microsoft now proposes Exchange 2000 Conferencing Server. It supports load balancing, fail-over, and control of attendee access conferences. By allocating bandwidth for each conference technology provider, Conferencing Server lets customers run any combination of conferencing services simultaneously. It also provides integrated scheduling and management services to help maximize network bandwidth and availability—what Microsoft calls meetings without walls.

Price

Not applicable for the client application. See also:

http://www.microsoft.com/windows/netmeeting/

Microsoft Site Server (Microsoft Back-Office suite), WinNT-4.0: $1200 (5 clients access) up to $2000 (25 clients access).

7.5.3.7 VDOPhone

General Description

Full-Duplex audio, color video, chat, quick note, photo album and business card. Web based on-line directory (clubVDO) and audio/video control panel. ITU standard H.323 compliant. Professional version supports PSTN (H.324 standard) call.

Available Functionality

Connect over any TCP/IP network: dial-up Internet connections using analogue phone lines, digital lines such as ISDN, or high speed connections such as LAN, Frame Relay, T1, etc.

Only provides one-to-one conferencing, not multiparty.

H.324 Modem Connections: VDOPhone Professional supports both IP connections and H.324 (POTS) modem to modem connections.

Provides good video resolution (H.263 codec) and up to 15 frames per second depending on your available bandwidth.

Echo Cancellation feature eliminates echoes and delivers hands free speakerphone quality audio.

You can create a virtual business card that includes your photo, your name, your email address and a brief description. These Virtual Business Cards will be displayed with each incoming call, for screening purposes. A photo album can be managed so that dialling is just as simple as clicking on their picture.

VDOPhone has an Optimized performance for a computer using a MMX Pentium Processor from either Intel or AMD. Support for Direct Draw enabled graphics display boards for full screen display.

Type of Application

Desktop application on PC.

Reliability, Maintainability, Learnability

The system is in its 3.2 version. Good ratings from specialised surveys in the press.

Test drive (IP calls only) available on Internet: http://www.vdo.net/

Support: quite extensive FAQ on the web with possibility of e-mail support. There is also a club of users, which seems quite active.

Evolutions: license rights, core technology, name and web site are currently for sale!

Platform
Windows 95/98

Price
About 70 Euros (professional version including H.324).

7.5.3.8 Smith Micro Software: Internet CommSuite
General Description
Full-Duplex audio, color video, text chat, file transfer, instant message, whiteboard. Internet Fax, video answering machine, photo album, video sentry and multimedia email. Directory service, public and private user room, phone book and buddy list. ITU standard H.323 compliant. Point-to-point communication only.

Evolutions: Smith Micro Software, headquartered in Aliso Viejo, CA, is a leading developer and marketer of e-Commerce and communication software products and services. They have several subsidiaries in the US and propose a quite large palette of products, mainly for PCs and Macs. They claim to have shipped over 40 million copies of products in communication software domain.

Web page: http://www.smithmicro.com/products/ICS/icsmain.htm

Reliability, Maintainability, Learnability
Very good FAQ on the Web and dedicated European support based in the UK. Limited and thus simple functionality.

Platform
Windows only. A similar product for MacOS (connex) does exist.

Price
About 50 Euros for the package.

7.5.3.9 VocalTec: Internet Phone
General Description
Full-Duplex audio, color video, PC-to-Phone communication, community browser, multiparty audio conferencing (up to 100 users), chat, voice mail, whiteboard, file transfer, on-line web directory, answering machine, statistics supervision for call performance. ITU standard H.323 compliant. Available for PC (all MS Windows versions) and Mac.

Support: quite extensive FAQ on the web with possibility of e-mail support. On line manuals on: http://www.vocaltec.com/

Reliability, Maintainability, Learnability
Well-settled company in the domain of voice over IP and coupling of IP with telephony. Quite numerous awards delivered from the press.

Price
About 50 Euros.

7.5.3.10 Acer's EasyAxess

General Description
Acer Softec Audio/video conference over PSTN (H.324 standard), LAN and the Internet.

Available Functionality
Text chat, text to speech email, video/audio mute. Directory service, video answering machine, zoom and snapshot. Integrates a rich telephony function with voice command control, Text to Speech email...

EasyAxess performs up to 15 frames per second for bi-directional real time video and audio conferencing through a standard V.34/V.80 modem (PPP) at 33.6/28.8 Kbps, Internet, Intranet, or any TCP/IP network.

Compliant with ITU standard H.324, H.261, H.263, H.223, H.245 and G.723.1.

Support for Microsoft's API, Video for Windows, DirectX, ActiveMovie and ActiveX.

Learnability
Simple graphical user interface.

Maintainability
Extensive FAQ on the web with possibility of e-mail support.

Acer Softech is active in the fields of system software development (BIOS...), network management and visual communication (chairman of the switched network conferencing activity group of the International Multimedia Telecommunications Consortium (IMTC)). More info under: http://www.acersoftech.com/home.htm. The product has its own dedicated entry on the Web: http://www.easyaxess.com/

Platforms
Windows95/98

Price
About 70 Euros.

7.5.3.11 NetSpeak's WebPhone

General Description
Other extended Web Phone system for point-to-point conferencing with H.323 compatibility for PC.

Available Functionality
Full-Duplex audio, color video, chat, personal directory, PC-to-Phone calling, caller ID, call conferencing, speed dial, video snapshot and online/offline voice mail. Four lines with call holding, muting, Direct Number Dial (DND) and blocking. ITU

standard H.323 v2 compliant (H.263 video codec, G.723 audio codec). Available for PC (all MS Windows versions).

Maintainability
FAQ, some on-line documentation and comprehensive technical support available at: http://www.webphone.com/. NetSpeak is a well-settled American company in the domain of advanced telephony solutions on IP networks. WebPhone comes also bundled with CreativeLabs products (Webcams but also video, audio cards...).

Platforms
Windows95/98/NT

Price
About 50 Euros.

7.5.3.12 Bull Jingle
General Description
Jingle supports multi-user audio and videoconferences without limit on the number of participants. Jingle can use either IP multicast or IP multi-unicast without requiring additional stuff (such as reflectors or Multipoint Control Units) to support multi-user conferences. It supports access to directory services compliant with LDAP version 2.

Support for multi-user data sharing through NetMeeting (chat, whiteboard, file transfer, application sharing).

Available Functionality
Jingle implements the following standards from IETF:
• RTP (will interoperate with any other RTP-compliant product such as vat, rat and vic)
• T.120 recommendation
• H.261 video codec
• ITU-T G.711 u-law (64 kbps, 72 kbps with RTP overhead)
• ITU-T G.711 A-law (64 kbps, 72 kbps with RTP overhead) - receive only
• GSM 6.10 (13 kbps, 21 kbps with RTP overhead)
There is also a Jingle navigator plug for incorporation of calls into Microsoft Internet Explorer and Netscape Navigator.

Support: It is a freeware provided by Bull. Some on-line documentation and technical support available at: http://www.dyade.fr/jingle/jingle.html.

Maintainability
The product seems not to be followed since end 1998 and is even not presented on official Bull's site.

Price, Platform
Available as freeware on Windows 95 and NT.

7.5.3.13 Other Systems

The systems listed below are relative cheap software PC solutions providing video/audio conferencing and some data conferencing tools. Most are not H.32x compliant and use rather particular codecs and/or Microsoft's Video for Windows API specifications. Nevertheless, they usually support any standard Video for Windows capture device.

- ScreenShare

ScreenShare, from Vizitel is an application independent, interactive, desktop and live image conferencing software product that provides real-time interactive working plus live motion video. Since ScreenShare's compression is specifically designed to give the maximum interactive functionality over digital cellular (GSM) and the standard (POTS) telephone network, it is extremely efficient over ISDN, the Internet and your LAN/WAN when using TCP/IP. An adaptive algorithm adjusts the time an image spends in compression to the actual data transmission rate. Any image of any Windows application, or the images from a TWAIN scanner or VFW camera can be captured and sent to the receiver's computer screen. As it is the image that is shared and not your actual data, 'what if' conversations can take place with ScreenShare's interactive 'whiteboard' drawing tools. Price around 150 Euros.

- Intel Video Phone (video phone application only)

Full-Duplex audio, color video, on-line web directory, speed dial, direct dial and H.323 proxy support. ITU standard H.323 compliant. Pack with USB camera: 100 Euros.

- HoneyCom v4.0

Full-Duplex audio, colour video, text chat, shared image, shared whiteboard, file transfer, business card. Meeting room server, public and private meeting rooms, instant message with video snapshot (MiniMe). A gateway for LAN users, multipoint video conferencing (up to 3) support. No H.32x compliance. Around 35 Euros. Available for PC (all MS Windows versions, except 2000).

- Dwyco video conferencing system

Full-Duplex audio, colour video, public & private chat, file transfer, call screening, zap message system (send and receive video/audio/text messages), public & private conference rooms. Directory services and multipoint video conferencing support. Freeware. No H.32x compliance. Available for PC (all MS Windows versions, except 2000).

- Buena Vista

Multipoint videoconferencing over ISDN, LAN and the Internet. Full-Duplex audio, color video, chat, whiteboard and directory service (active users/conferences). Available for PC, SGI Indy and SGI O2. Freeware developed by the Northeast Parallel Architectures Center (NPAC) of the Syracuse University (USA). It only uses standard codecs (H.263 and H.261 for video, GSM and ADPCM for audio), the codecs have been optimised to ensure frame rates as high as possible (may lead to inter-operability problems), conference participants can use different audio/video formats and switch between them as dictated by network conditions without affecting session setup. For LAN applications, it supports high bandwidth, high quality video formats (YUV9/PCM) and handles both half-duplex and full duplex operation with either manual or automatic switching. It offers session archiving and replay capabilities. It is extensible as it provides an API and a framework to create and integrate new applications. BuenaVista is also a part of a generalised Web-based collaborative system developed in NPAC, TANGO.

- IRIS Phone
Full-Duplex audio, colour video, searchable white page, phonebook, user photo and info display. Multi user conferencing (up to 5), multiple call handling, whiteboard, file transfer. Record conversations, answering machine, audio/video mail, black list and more. No H.32x compliance. Available for PC (all MS Windows versions, except 2000)

- Wintronix XtX Communications Suite
Full-Duplex audio, color video, chat, whiteboard, file transfer, snapshot, address book. Directory service, audio/video recording, speed dial and video mail. It supports multipoint video conferencing (up to 10). Available for PC (all MS Windows versions).. No H.32x compliance. Price around 70 Euros.

- iVisit
Freeware, iVisit is a video conferencing software similar to CU-SeeMe. Tim Dorcey, who created CU-SeeMe, has now created iVisit. It supports multipoint video conferencing without a reflector and you can make your own conference. Available for PC and Mac. It doesn't comply with the H.323 standard for videoconferencing. The authors claim they wanted to use unique characteristics of the Internet (thus trying to better use packet-switched characteristics) rather than transplanting telephony-based communication models to it. As an example, video is provided black-white only for bandwidth saving purposes. As a consequence, the system is reported to perform very well on low-bandwidth connections. See www.ivisit.com.

- ICUII
Full-Duplex audio, color video, real-time chat, quick message, welcome message. Directory services, watch pals, small text message in video screen, email/IP user lookup. Available for PC (Windows 95/98) and Mac. No H.32x compliance. Price around 140 Euros with capture card and camera.

- Rendez-Vous
A successor to the IVS (French INRIA Videoconferencing System): an integrated audio/video and schedule tool over multicast or unicast IP. It supports multipoint video conferencing via the Mbone. Available for PC, Sun Solaris, SunOS, SGI Irix, DEC OSF1, x86 Linux and x86 FreeBSD. Freeware.

- Isabel
Video/audio/data multipoint conferencing (up to 20) over ATM, ISDN, Internet, Mbone... Selectable events (tele-conference or tele-meeting), 3 modes (coordinator, client or participant), slides, screen capture, scanner presentation, whiteboard, shared display and shared editor. Based on Parallax Hardware. Designed by Technical University of Madrid (UPM) and used in European Broadband Programs, such as the RACE/ACTS Summer Schools or Global Events. Available for Sun Solaris, SGI O2, Linux - Quickcam & V4L. Freeware.

- Command Tech's MediaFone
Video: Net Command Tech MPEG4 Video Codec; Video Formats: RGB and YUV; Audio: MS GSM 6.10 Audio Codec Supplied with Windows 95/98; Window size: (160 X 120) - (720 X 540); Frame rate up to 15 frames/sec; Command Tech, based in Florida, develops and markets software and hardware products that allow users of personal computers and other electronic devices to send and receive video and data over the Internet and intranets.

7.5.4 Desktop Videoconferencing Systems

There is a continuing drop of price for group systems supporting both H.320 and H.323 standards as well as set-top devices.

Desktop conference is exploding, especially for PCs. Most products available on the market are available only on Windows platforms. For workstation targeted system, we consider in a first step Sun/Solaris systems which are likely to be the most popular platforms. A fundamental issue is the interoperability of the systems. In this fast evolving market, appliance to standards is the first choice criteria.

7.5.4.1 SunVideo Plus Multimedia Kit
General Description
SunVideo Plus is a real-time audio and video capture and compression card. This single-wide, fully compliant PCI card can capture, broadcast, and transmit raw audio and video. With this card, users of Sun's PCI-based systems can now videoconference, broadcast video over the Internet/intranet, capture video for authoring/content creating, create video mail, and so on.

Type of Application
This solution include SunVideo Plus 1.3 single slot (PCI) card for real-time audio and video capture and compression, a Sun camera II (PAL) and Sun Microphone II.

Available Functionality
Supports SunForum 3.0, the audio and video conferencing software of Sun as well as the Java Media Framework 2.0, allowing developers to access the card for audio/video applications in this environment.

Some other features:

- NTSC/PAL input video signals
- hardware H.261 video codec support
- direct (uncompressed) video capture
- JPEG support
- hardware MPEG1 codec support
- hardware support for Acoustic Echo Cancellation
- hardware G.728, G.722 and G.711 audio codec support
- support the standard video application interface of Solaris (XIL interface)

Table 3 gives the detailed characteristics of the card.

Reliability
No particular claim has been identified about this product in various groups of discussions neither surveys.

Maintainability
Sun's site provides a good level of information about this product including drivers, FAQs etc.
More information can found on:
http://www.sun.com/desktop/products/Graphics/sunvideoplusfeatures.html

Platform
Unix/Linux, supports Solaris 2.5.1, 2.6 and Solaris 7.

Price
About 1700 Euros.

Table 3. Overview of SunVideoPlus Card Features

Uncompressed Video	1/4-screen PAL (384x288)	25 fps
	Full-screen PAL (786x576)	12,5 fps
Compressed Video	JPEG 1/4 screen	30 fps
	MPEG-1 SIF (352x288) PAL	30 fps
	H.261 CIF (352x288)	15 fps
	H.261 QCIF (176x144)	30 fps
	H.263 QCIF 176x144)	15fps
	YUV 1/4 screen	30 fps
Acoustic Echo Suppression	G.728 delay >= 128 msec	ERLE >= 40 db
	G.723 delay >= 328 msec	ERLE >= 40 db
	G.722 delay >= 198 msec	ERLE >= 40 db
	G.711 delay >= 384 msec	ERLE >= 40 db
PCI Bus Speed	PCI 2.1 compliant, 33 MHz, ½ slot	
Network	Ethernet/Fast Ethernet, twisted pair standard	
Video	3 analogue video inputs; 2 RCA jacks (composite); 1 ini-DIN (S-Video)	
Audio	Line In, microphone in Line out, headphone out.	

7.5.4.2 Osprey 1x00 Cards
General Description
The Osprey-1500 offers virtually identical capabilities as the Osprey-1000 (for PCs), only it is designed to be compatible with the new Sun PCI based SPARC workstations running Solaris 2.5.1, 2.6 or 2.7. Video I/O, Audio I/O, and support for standard compression formats make a perfect multimedia platform to complement the power of Sun workstations. Developers can quickly create interoperable video communication systems on Suns using the Osprey-1500's standard XIL interface or its SunVideo binary compatibility mode.

The Osprey-1500 supports standard video and audio compression formats. A powerful processor called the VCP from 8x8 serves as the primary compression engine. Through different microcode modules, video standards such as H.261, H.263, CellB, JPEG, MPEG-1 and uncompressed formats can be supported with no change in the hardware. Complementing the VCP is a Digital Signal Processor from Analogue Devices that provides advanced audio processing including the G.728, G.722, G.711, and G.723 standards, as well as acoustic echo cancellation (AEC).

Type of Application
By providing Video and Audio input/output and support for standard compression formats, the card is well suited for advanced video multitask operation. This card belongs to a complete range of products for video capture, interface to TV and multimedia conferencing. The card is said to be compatible with the SunVideoPlus Card and to support SunForum.

Available Functionality
• Video compression: H.261, H.263, JPEG, MPEG-1 (I-frames), CellB
• Video decompression: H.261, H.263
• Video capture: YUYV, RGB555, RGB565, RGB-8bit
• Audio formats: G.728, G.723, G.722, G.711 (μ-law/A-law), PCM (8,16 bit)
Table 4 describes some performance figures provided by Viewcast (manufacturer).

Table 4. Overview of Osprey 1500 Card Features

	H.263	H.261	H.261	H.263	Uncompressed	JPEG-based encoder on board
image size	QCIF	CIF	QCIF	CIF	Sub QCIF to full-screen	QCIF/CIF
peak frame rate	30	22 (codec); 30 (encode or decode)	30	20	30	30
image depth	4:1:1 YUV	4:1:1 YUV	4:1:1 YUV	4:1:1 YUV	8/16/24 bit (YUV and RGB)	4:1:1, 4:2:2, 2:1:1
API	OPI, XIL	OPI, XIL	OPI	OPI	OPI, XIL	OPI, XIL
% CPU approx. (PII 400)	about 2%	about 2%	About 2%	about 2%	diskwrite limited	about 2%
Bitrate (Kbits)	64-768	64-768	8-192	8-192	up to 28 Mbytes/sec	.1 – 4 Mbits/sec
HW or SW	HW codec	HW codec	HW codec	HW codec	NA	HW compress

OPI (Osprey programming interface) is not required to be installed for general use of Osprey-1100/1500. This API is used when application are developed for both

Solaris and Windows platforms: the 1500 family is also available on PCs (see below, Osprey 1000 card) and support the same interface and software development tools. On the other hand, OPI-based applications will not work correctly with, for instance workstations equipped with the SunVideoPlus card. In that case, use of the Sun video Interface (XIL) is recommended.

Maintainability
Manufacturer is Viewcast, an US-based company. Osprey Technologies Inc. is a business unit of ViewCast.com and has a mission to provide video enabling products and technologies for the corporate desktop. These products are supported on the volume computing platforms and complement industry-leading video applications.
    Last drivers and documentation is always available from:
        ftp://ftp.mmac.com/pub/OSPREY1K/solaris/

Reliability
No particular problem has been reported in reviews/user group discussions.

Learnability
Well-documented product.

Platform
The 1500 model is compatible with Sun PCI-based workstations running Solaris 2.5.1, 2.6, or Solaris 7. Osprey-1000 cards are supported on Windows NT.

Price
About 1700 Euros for Solaris, 1250 Euros on Windows.

7.5.4.3 Winnov Videum Conference Pro
General Description
This package combines a PCI board (Videum AV, can also be purchased separately) with a color video camera and a Videum Software CD (see below).

Available Functionality
Main features include:

- full-duplex audio for videoconferencing (hands-free operation), compatible with existing sound card,
- CCD video camera with integrated, local and remote camera control (brightness, saturation, hue) via Videum Zoom applet (see below), separated microphone.
- hardware video compression (one format only, winnov specific), the rest is done by software
- digital pan, tilt and zoom (using any camera) via Videum Zoom applet,
- 2 audio input support for (existing) soundcard or headset
- up to 3 video sources: one composite video, one MXC, one S-Video,

- amplified Audio Out for use with non-amplified speakers or headsets,
- said to support all videoconferencing protocols (H.320, H.323, and H.324).

Videum Software 2.7:

- set of applets for basic controls (configuration of audio, video, audio and still image captures, hardware settings, status reporting, camera controls...)
- includes 3rd-party software such as: Microsoft NetMeeting, Microsoft NetShow Server and Toolkit (streaming internet video), RealNetworks RealProducer G2, Visual Basic sample applications for adding video to any application using Videum ActiveX Controls.
- Video e-mail: allows to capture a video from Videum Capture applets, save it in ASF format (Microsoft NetShow format) and send it through usual e-mail application.
- Windows 2000 Support: Multiple Board support in Windows NT4.0 and Windows 2000 (PCI only).
- "Full featured" SDK (Visual Basic and C++). Not so much details on it neither from Web sites nor from vendors (in France at least).

Do not provide audio nor video hardware-based H.26x, G.7xx codecs. Hence CPU is quite extensively solicited during conferencing with video.

Possibility of adjusting audio/video quality balance and image quality (fps).

Reliability

One of the references in terms of PC desktop systems.

Maintainability

Good access to support with extensive WEB interface for Software downloads, direct contact with the technical staff, FAQs. Newsgroup for developers.

More info: http://www.winnov.com/products/vidconfopropci.htm

Learnability

Very well rated in several dedicated reviews
        (e.g. see http://www.netmeeting-zone.com).

Platform

Windows 95/98/NT4 and 2000 (NT 5) compatibility. Linux drivers are available (pier-development) but are not supported by Winnov.

A laptop version is available with PCMIA connection.

Price

Attractive price: about 400 Euros (Pro version, with camera).

7.5.4.4 MAX i.c. Live

General Description

A multi-function card as it replaces the on-board video display card, capture card, audio card and modem.

The MAX i.c.Live Video Compression System (VCS) supports high-quality, two-way video communications and video streaming simultaneously with its patented MAX i.c.Live Internet Media Processor technology. The MAX i.c. VCS also offers an easy-to-use software browser for high-speed Internet access, state-of-the-art entertainment features like Dolby Digital (AC-3) audio coding and Digital Disc (DVD) output.

Available Functionality
Main video conferencing features provide H.323 and H.324 compatibility together with video compression/decompression and audio synchronization processed on board
- H.263/H.261 video compression
- G.723.1 speech compression at 6.3 or 5.3 kbps
- Acoustic echo cancellation
- Voice-first calling and receiving
- Remote and local video window viewing
- V.80 modem support for synchronous data over an asynchronous interface
- V.8 multifunction modem operation mode determination
- Cypress Research Megaphone videophone application

MAX i.c.Live Media Processor card also delivers:
- Integrated Video I/O: Fully Accelerated SVGA Video, hardware-based MPEG Video decoding for streaming or DVD video, MPEG-1 hardware-based Video encoding for video, complete DVD feature support
- Integrated Audio: 32-voice MAX Forte Wavetable Synthesizer, Dolby Digital SRS 3D positional sound, 8 simultaneous play and record, general MIDI support
- Integrated Communications Support: 33.3 Simultaneous Voice/Data Fax Modem, Full-duplex Speakerphone with Voice Mail

Reliability
Quite numerous press releases. Enthusiastic rating in DEV.X review (http://www.netmeeting-zone.com).

Maintainability
No particular help, on-line technical support available on the Web. Quite recent technology.

Platform
Windows 95 and 98 only.

Price
From 400 Euros.

7.5.4.5 ELSA Vision II
General Description
This well-rounded solution provides good 32-bit performance. Videoconferences can be realised via ISDN (H.320) IP networks (H.323) as required. ELSAvision II is distinguished by its tight conformity to standards, excellent compatibility and extensive conferencing functions. Web page: http://www.elsa.com

Available Functionality
- ISDN connection
  Basic Rate Interface (S0bus, I,430) and ISDN PBX systems with S0interface; D-channel protocols DSS1 (Euro-ISDN), 1TR6 (German national ISDN), AT&T 5ESS Custom, point-to-multipoint connection, point-to-point connection, National ISDN-1, DGT1 (Taiwan), CAPI Version 2.0 Software interface.
- Transfer protocols
  Level 2: X.75, V.120, bit transparent, HDLC transparent (64,000 bps) Level 3: T.70NL, Transparent, ISO 8208, T.90; simultaneous operation of two B channels possible.
- Video connection
  Two analogue video inputs (PAL or NTSC standard composite FBAS signal) or one S-Video-In and one Video-In.
  H.320 support: H.261, H.242, H.221, G.711, G.722, G.728, and T.120 data conference (NetMeeting bundled).
- Video resolution
  Up to 30 frames per sec., freely resizable window; high resolution (704 x 576 pixels) still picture transfer compliant to H.261, annex D. Screen display: Any resolution and colour depth of the PCI graphics board can be used.
- Audio connections
  Headset (Audio-In and Out), Line-In, Line-Out (speakers)
- Sound transmission
  Real-time or video-synchronised
- Camera control
  Via serial interface.
    - Hardware: Combined ISDN-video board, high-quality analogue colour camera with integrated microphone for speakerphone operation, comfortable headset.
    - Software: Microsoft NetMeeting conferencing software, ELSA-RVS-COM office communications software, ELSA-ZOC terminal program, LapLink for Windows remote-access software, the ELSA ISDN monitor utility for ISDN status monitoring.

Reliability, Maintainability
For over 15 years now, ELSA has been developing, producing and marketing PC peripheral equipment for computer graphics and data communications. ELSA's international sales and marketing subsidiaries will continue to expand along with origin German market.

Software is now in its 4.0 version.

Extensive list of compatibility tests with other videoconferencing systems, also through independent test laboratories (CSELT, Centro Studi E Laboratori Telecommunication S.P.A). Quite rarely provided by other manufacturers.

3 years Warranty.

Platform
Windows 95/98/NT 4.0

Price
About 1150 Euros.

7.5.4.6   Intel Proshare 500

General Description
It is one of the most popular products on the market. However, a recent agreement has been settled, shifting the distribution to PictureTel. It is thus questionable whether this product will be further supported since it can be considered as a concurrent of the home products (550 System).

The system includes:

- conferencing software with integrated NetMeeting (v2.1) and PhotoExchange (high resolution image capturing)
- Single PCI ISDN/audio/video capture card
- headset with microphone, composite color video camera

Available Functionality
For H.320 conferencing, it is worth noting that ISDN interface is provided on the card; thus single Basic Rate Interface (BRI) 2B+D, 112-128kbps phone line is then required for making ISDN calls. All Euro and US switching systems are supported, compatible with ISDN PBXs.

- Multipoint support
- Common ISDN API (CAPI) 2.0 support
- H320 B-channel connection status display and single B-channel H.320 call support
For H.323:
- LAN connections up to 800kbps (400kbps send + receive),
- Bandwidth and gateway selectable from 56kbps to 800kbps
- H.323 gatekeeper, proxy/firewall support
- ILS support
No H.324 support.

Dynamic bandwidth allocation but without neither visualisation tool nor possibility of adjusting it (audio/video quality balance) during communication.

- No possibility of change of audio/video codec during communication
- 17kbps required for audio-only conferences (G.723 codec).

- about 392kbps used on a LAN for videoconferencing; about 70% of the CPU is used in videoconference mode; on WAN, when explicitly limited to 128 kbps, 117kbps are actually used with 12fps video image [18].

Well rated in several comparative tests both for Intranet and Internet conferencing.

- Video:
  Video Inputs: composite video and S-Video, Video up to 30 fps in CIF and QCIF.
  Snapshot of local or remote video window
  Brightness, sharpness, focus and white balance camera controls
  H.261 and H.263 codecs both in CIF and QCIF, software only and requires Intel MMX processor,
  No video capture.
- Audio:
  G.711, G.723 (default codec) and G.728 audio codecs (hardware for G.723).
  Acoustic echo cancellation built-in.
  No Audio/Video adjustment controls.

Reliability, Maintainability
Support accessible upon http://support.intel.com/support/proshare/, which leads indirectly to the site of PictureTel (see above). It seems that the PDK (Product Development Kit) which was proposed as an option to the Proshare 500 system is no more supported: it does not appear anymore in the catalogue thus making the system quite "closed".
  Warranty: Hardware: 1 year, Software: 90 days.

Platform
Version 5.1 supports Microsoft Windows 98 in addition to Windows 95 and Windows NT 4.0.

Price
About 730 Euros.

7.5.4.7 PictureTel 550 System
General Description
It is one of the most popular products on the market benefiting from a long experience of the company: http://www.picturetel.com/
  The system includes:

- conferencing software with integrated NetMeeting (v2.1)
- Single PCI ISDN/audio/video capture card (manufactured by Zydacron)
- headset with microphone, composite or S-video color video camera.

Available Functionality
For H.320 conferencing, it is worth noting that ISDN interface is provided on the card; thus single BRI 2B+D, 112-128kbps phone line is then required for making

ISDN calls. All Euro and US switching systems are supported, compatible with ISDN PBXs.

- Multipoint support: 56kbps up to 384kbps call size
- For H.323 conferencing:
  - LAN connections up to 800kbps (400kbps send + receive),
  - Bandwidth and gateway selectable from 56kbps up to 384kbps call size
- No H.324 support.
- Dynamic bandwidth allocation with visualisation tool and possibility of adjusting it during communication.
  - Possibility of change of audio/video codec during communication
  - 47kbps required for audio-only conferences (G.728 codec).
  - about 442kbps used on a LAN for videoconferencing; about 40% of the CPU is used in videoconference mode; on WAN, when explicitly limited to 128 kbps, 131kbps actually used with 7fps video image.
- Video:
  Video Inputs: two S-Video or composite inputs, Video up to 30 fps in CIF and QCIF, Snapshot of local or remote video window, Contrast/brightness/colour/hue control on camera control, H.261 hardware and H.263 software codecs both in CIF and QCIF,
  No video capture.
  Possibility of adjusting video quality (fps) but no adjustment of audio/video balance.
- Audio:
  G.711 Alaw and uLaw, G.722, G.723 and G.728 (default codec) audio codecs (hardware for G.728), Full-duplex acoustic echo cancellation built-in, graphical audio level display of near and far-end.
- Openness:
  Developers tool LiveDTK consists of multiple OLE Control Extensions (OCXs) that will support Microsoft Visual Basic V4.0/5.0 and Microsoft Visual C++ V4.0/5.0. These OCXs provide access to all major functions within the PictureTel system software. The OCXs that are included in the LiveDTK are: Call Interface, Audio, Video, LiveShare Plus and Address Book.
  Versions 2.0 on Windows95 and 2.1 on Windows NT (with quite numerous limitations!)
  Call Interface OCX includes:
  - Three controls for call management functions: Call control for Outgoing Calls, Incoming Call control, Call Progress Control.
  - Event status for information: Call Dialling, Call Proceeding, Call Offering, Call Accepted, Call Idle, and Call Disconnected.
  - Methods for call operations: Connect, Disconnect, Show Dial Setting, and Show Config Dialog.
  Audio OCX includes:
  - Audio Algorithm selection (combo box), Audio On for audio mute (button), Audio Quality selection (combo box), and Volume for audio volume adjustment (slider).
  - Events and Methods: Algorithm and quality selection, audio on/off, volume setting and show or hide display of control.

Video OCX includes:

- Eleven controls for video selections and adjustments: AV Mute for audio/video on or off (button), Brightness/Contrast /Saturation (sliders), Local On and Remote On (buttons), Local Window and Remote Window (video windows), Video Algorithm and Video Quality (combo boxes).
- Events and Methods: Algorithm and quality selection, video on/off and display adjustment setting, show or hide display of control.

LiveShare Plus OCX includes:

- Eight controls for access to full LiveShare Plus functionality and related status information: share for application selection and sharing, UnShare for application selection and "unsharing", Attach-Detach for applications, Remote Control, Whiteboard for launching whiteboard application, Message for launching message application, File Transfer for launching file transfer application, Share Clipboard for sharing and unsharing local Windows clipboard.

Address Book OCX

- Three controls for address book data management: data control (supports "data aware" controls) List Control (tree view), Entry Control (tabbed dialog boxes)
- Methods for standard database operations: create/open/close address book database files, displays views for entry selection, displays dialogs for entry modification, add/edit/delete person entries, add/edit/delete location entries, search by name or sequentially, retrieve data from records.

Maintainability
Warranty: Hardware: 1 year, Software: 90 days.

Platform
Windows 95/98 (no H.323 !) Windows NT Workstation 4.0.
PictureTel is one of the leaders in videoconferencing systems.

Price
About 1510 Euros (LiveDTK not included).

7.5.4.8 Sony Trinicom 500 Plus
General Description
This videoconference Kit is provided as a codec card with a camera and audio set (headphones, microphone), conference software and data collaboration software:
    http://bpgprod.sel.sony.com/bpcnav/app/99999/1/4/17226.99902.product.BPC.htm
l?reload=1
Sony extends its desktop/office conferencing solution with the TriniCom Digital Meeting System (VMU1100SG), a compact peripheral device that easily attaches to a desktop notebook PC enabling simultaneous video and conferencing. This functionality is very similar to the PCB 500 Plus but limited to H.320 videoconferencing.

Available Functionality
This kit includes the Databeam FarSite software a T.120 client system with application sharing, white board, file transfer functionality, telephone directory, picture-in-picture… Support of Microsoft NetMeeting is also ensured.

Two video inputs. H.261 video compression is provided. For audio, G.711, G.722, G.728 are available. Most video and audio features such as contrast, hue, brightness, video quality adjustments, echo suppression, etc. are software controlled.

Possibility if adjusting audio/video quality balance.

An optional software development tool is available. No detailed information could be collected on it.

Reliability, Maintainability
Benefits from traditional Sony quality. Simple set of Drivers, limited help-desk are accessible on Sony's Web site.

Learnability
Plug&play solution with an easy user interface.

Platform
Windows96/98/NT 4.0

Price
PCB-500P Kit for PC: about 1400 Euros, SDK Software Development Kit about 2720 Euros

7.5.4.9 VCON Desktop Systems
General Description
Set of solutions for H.320 and H.323 conferencing: Escort 25 (H.323 only), Cruiser 75 (H.323 and H.320 at 128 kbps, 1 Basic Rate Interface (BRI)), Cruiser 150 (H.323 and H.320 at 128 kbps, 1 BRI), Cruiser 384 (H.323 and H.320 at 384 kbps, 3 BRI):
     http://www.vcon.com

Available Functionality
H.320 and H.323-v2 compatible. NetMeeting is used for the T.120 compatibility level.

Video compression based on H.261 and H.263 compatible achieving a transmission of CIF and QCIF of up to 30 fps, 2 video inputs.

Audio compression G.711, G.722, G.728.

Provides also a H.281 compatible Far End Camera Control compatibility.

All of desktop systems have the PacketAssist Architecture. This feature prevents loss of packets and addresses problems such as lip sync of audio data systems and video data systems, the reordering of incoming streams of packets and jitters, all of which can affect the quality of a videoconference over a packet network. This is a quite unique feature of VCON solutions enabling the introduction of QoS functionality and possibilities for reaching up to 1,5 Mbps conferences. On the other hand, this technology "plus" can induce some inter-operability problems with heterogeneous solutions.

Said to provide good video quality sometimes to the detriment of the audio quality when automatic adjustment is enabled. It is not possible to change audio algorithm during conference.

- About VCON's SDK

The VCON Development Kit (VDK) Software Development Kit that allows customized videoconferencing on both group and desktop systems in one package. It is a complete set of 32 bit OLE Control Extension (OCX) custom for integrating all of VCON's visual communication capabilities into new or existing applications. VDK is a software package designed for use by developers for customizing applications to the specific needs of the customer. It enables the developer to create custom-built videoconferencing applications on top of VCON's hardware systems in various types of communication environments such as ISDN or IP in a LAN/WAN.

Desktop and Group applications use the same development package, available for Microsoft Visual Basic, Microsoft Visual C++ and Delphi editors. It includes a complete set of controls for video, audio and data functions. No royalty fee for VDK-developed applications are mandatory.

VCON proposes as well some add-on software compatible with their products:

- TopSecret IP encryption, which provides security against unauthorised participation and eavesdropping during videoconferences over IP networks. TopSecret IP consists of a choice of three real-time encryption/decryption algorithms, each of which is effective in securing video, audio and data broadband streams. They are all based on the private/public key mechanism considered by security experts to be ultra-effective against penetration.
- Interactive Multicast technology allows users to actively participate in streaming. It enables the multicasting of audio and video to participants using VCON endpoints or Cisco IP/ viewers, while allowing any participant using an endpoint for fully interact during the conference. In addition, it allows Cisco IP/TV viewers to participate in "receive mode" during VCON multicasts. VCON's Interactive Multicast uses standard IP multicast technology running on a standard VCON H.323 client to add an interactive component to a formerly one-way only video technology.

Reliability, Maintainability
Support, maintenance, upgrades and factory maintenance is usually proposed for about 150 Euros in average. VCON offers a direct support and maintenance contract for its VDK customer. Price from 1100 Euros for 10 hours.

Platform
Windows 95/98/NT 4.0

Price
Escort 25 around 1000 Euros, Cruiser 75 1100 Euros.
VDK (development kit) from 2000 Euros.

7.5.4.10 VTel Smartstation

General Description
This solution is based on a PCI single-slot card, fixed camera with included microphone and speakers. (Pan-Tilt-Zoom camera with separated on-table microphone is optional). AppsView software is provided on CD-ROM:

    http:// www.vtel.com

Available Functionality
H.323 (not on Windows NT) and H.320 conferencing with H.261 and H.263 video codecs. FCIF transmissions reach up to 15fps, 30 fps for QCIF (128 series). G.711, G.722 and G.728 are also available. Microsoft NetMeeting is bundled and thus provides T.120 compatibility.

Two video inputs, limited audio controls. ISDN and LAN products are separated products!

The system provides SNMP-based management, which can be coupled with Smart VideoNet Manager software proposed by VTEL for overall management and control of endpoints.

On the other hand, no openness seems to be available for, e.g. integration of user graphical interfaces in external applications.

Reliability, Maintainability
The Smartstation is provided with the release 5.0 of the AppsView 5.0. Basic support and FAQ are available on Web site.

Platform
Windows 95/98 (H.323), 95/98/NT 4.0 (H.320).

Price
The PC-kit is proposed at about 1500 Euros.

7.5.4.11 Aethra SDV 92000

General Description
Combined ISDN-video board, high-quality analogue colour camera with integrated microphone for speakerphone operation, comfortable headset. Transmission rate up to 768 kbps over IP networks, leased line or satellite connection:

    http://www.aethra.com

Available Functionality
ISDN connection Basic Rate Interface (S0 bus, I,430) and ISDN PBX systems with S0 interface, D-channel protocols DSS1 (Euro-ISDN), 1TR6 (German national ISDN), AT&T5ESS Custom, point-to-multipoint connection, point-to-point National ISDN-1, DGT1 (Taiwan)

Common ISDN API (CAPI) Version 2.0 software interface.

Two analogue video inputs (PAL or NTSC standard composite FBAS signal) or one S-Video-In and one Video-In.

H.320 support: H.261, H.242, H.221, G.711, G.722, and G.728

H.323 support: Videoconference in TCP/IP network, H.261, G.711 and T.120 data conference through NetMeeting.

Video resolution: up to 30 frames per sec., freely resizable window; high-resolution (704 x 576 pixels) still picture transfer compliant to H.261, annex D.

Audio connections: Headset (Audio-In and Out), Line-In, Line-Out (speakers)

Real-time or video-synchronised sound transmission, Camera control via serial interface.

Good possibilities of adjusting bandwidth, video coding and monitoring during communications. Snapshot of local or remote video window, Contrast/brightness/colour/hue control on camera control.

No information available about an eventual SDK.

Reliability, Maintainability
Support on-line using the Web or a dedicated hotline (with pricing). Installation Guide (languages: I, D, UK, F, E, NL). Online Manual (languages: I, D, UK, F).

Platform
Windows 95/98/NT 4.0.

Price
The PC-kit is proposed at about 650 Euros.

7.5.4.12 Zydacron OnWAN Solutions
General Description
The OnWAN 340 and 350 systems include hardware (Z340/Z350/Z360 PCI Codec board; can be purchased separately), application software, and a camera with built in microphone in an easy to install and use system. It offers a solution for IP (H.323) videoconferencing corporate environments. It can be installed into any PCI slot and connects to most VGA controllers.

The Z360 card enables integration PC hardware to deliver "plug and play" videoconferencing over ISDN, V35 or IP, including native ATM H.323.

Available Functionality
The main characteristics are:

H.323 version 2 standards compliant, H.320 compliant, up to 30 fps, single board, PCI-based codec, H.323 calls up to 384kbps, call size up to 384kbps with triple BRI add-in board, Native ATM support, Microsoft NetMeeting integration which runs dynamically in the background for T.120 support, MCU support, balanced microphone support.

The Z340/350 boards family offer H.323 and H.320 standards:

• Connectors:
    − 3.5mm headset

- Line Input
- S-Video and - S-Video to RCA
- Sound card connector
- ISDN

• Video codecs: H.261 and H.263 (H.323 only). No info about audio codecs obtained (seem to be nevertheless hardware supported).

As option, a development kit is provided (ZDK) allowing to build Custom Applications, internationalise Zydacron applications, DLL's and drivers, create camera control DLL's for any camera for use with FECC...

With Zydacron's ZDK, clear documentation and extensive sample code makes that possible. Whether you want to make small changes to the existing Zydacron Visual Basic application, develop a new idea in Visual Basic or Delphi, or develop a next-generation application in C++, the ZDK allows you to get results in a remarkably short period of time. The ZDK includes Custom Controls to provide easy access to videoconferencing functionality. Add videoconferencing to any application that supports ActiveX with the 32-bit ZDK and codec drivers.

Reliability, Maintainability

A quite complete set of support information is available on-line. The drivers for codec cards are presently in their 3.2 version. More info at:

http://www.zydacron.com/mainsite/support.htm

Zydacron presents a solid experience as videoconferencing provider (codec software and hardware) and collect some good business references.

Platform

Windows 95/98/NT.

Price

Around 1500 Euros.

7.5.4.13 Some Video Capture-Only Cards

The solutions listed below are well suited for video/audio authoring, video streaming, coupling with multimedia peripherals like DVD units. They do not support most of standards required for conferencing but can improve general video production and management operations.

• ATI All-In-Wonder 128

Based on ATI's Rage 128 technology, this card provides 3D graphics acceleration functions, DVD video playback, still and motion video capture, "intelligent TV-Tuner", instant replay, digital VCR with real-time video compression software, MPEG-2 video compression from any source, video output to TV and VCR:

http://www.ati.com

System Requirements:

Windows98, Windows95 (no NT, no Linux), PCI version: Pentium/Pro/II/III or compatible with 33 MHz PCI local bus 2.1; AGP version: Pentium II/III or compatible with AGP 2X bus (AGP 1.0 compliant)

Miscellaneous:

Video compression: "Full IBP compression". Neither H.261 nor H.263 video compression are supported; Same problem wrt. audio compression. Support for DirectX 6.0 and OpenGL.

Good technical support pages on the web with technical support centres phone numbers, FAQs, downloadable drivers and user manuals.

Price: from 75 Euros.

* Matrox Marvel G200-TV

Onboard chip from Zoran that provides real-time Motion JPEG compression/decompression. This takes the compression/decompression responsibility away from the CPU and hard drive--most of which are not capable of handling full-screen, 30-frame-per-second capture:

> http://www.matrox.com

Capture format: MPEG and JPEG (size 704x480). MPEG-2 decoding (hardware); 8 to 16 MB Video RAM.

Drivers available for Windows 95, Windows 98

Software included: Avid Cinema, Photo Express 2.0, Tonic Trouble, PC/VCR Remote

Direct3D, OpenGL, QuakeGL 3D standards supported.

Price: from 260 Euros.

7.5.5 Examples of Meeting Room Videoconferencing Systems

These group systems are designed for ease of use and for high quality pictures and sound. The more you pay the better the system you get. They also necessitate higher bandwidths because of the amount of movement, which occurs naturally in large groups of people. Most systems are designed to operate over high bandwidth pipes such as multiple ISDN lines. Installation is generally complex and requires specialised knowledge.

Larger groups present a problem to the simple desktop system. However, room or group systems have powered Pan, Tilt, and Zoom (PTZ) cameras that enable each subject to be framed properly as they speak. The camera can be operated from either the near or the far end by an infrared remote control. This remote can have pre-set positions stored in it so that you do not have to hunt around for the subject speaking each time they speak.

Some systems from most known vendors are shortly presented in the following sections.

7.5.5.1 VCON MediaConnect 8000 Series
General Description

The MediaConnect 8000 Series is VCON's flagship VGA-based system family supporting multiple network interfaces such as ISDN, IP (LAN), satellite communication and private lines. In addition, the MediaConnect 8000Pro and compact models range from single monitor configurations to dual/triple monitor configurations, making them flexible and expandable and giving users the investment protection they require:

http://www.vcon.com

The MediaConnect 8000 Series distinguishes itself in the market by providing true dual-mode support (H.320/H.323), with ISDN rates up to 384Kbps and LAN rates up to 1.5Mbps and optional communication via V.35/RS-449. An ISDN or V.35 call can be followed immediately by a LAN call with no need for configuration changes or system restart.

The MediaConnect 8000 Series is not just a videoconferencing system. It is built on a powerful multimedia PC that can also be used for training, project team meetings and classroom settings.

A Super VGA-based system will sometimes be used for video and data conferencing and at other times as a forum for presentations, to access the Internet or for other group activities.

Available Functionality
In Camera Control: H.281 Far End Camera Control (FECC)
- Video:
  Compression: H.261, H.263 (Px64) compatible; Transmitted CIF (352x288 pixels) up to 30 frames/sec; QCIF (176x144) up to 30 frames/sec.
  Input: 1x Y/C (S-Video), 2x Composite (RCA phono)
  Output: 1xSVGA (25 D-type), 1x Y/C (S-Video), 1x Composite (RCA phono)

- Audio:
  Compression: G.711 3.4 kHz at 56Kbps, G.728 3.4 kHz at 16Kbps, G.722 7.0 kHz at 48, 56 or 64Kbps, full duplex echo cancellation, bandwidth 50 - 7000 Hz...
- Rates Increments
  H.320 56/64 Kbps - 384 Kbps
  H.323 64 Kbps - 1.5 Mbps
  T.120 support through Microsoft NetMeeting. Supports VCON Development Kit (VDK).
  Compatible with Ezenia! (see section 7.5.6.2), RADvision, Accord and Cisco Multicast Unit (MCU) and Gateways.

Reliability, Maintainability
VCON is market share leader in the IP desktop videoconferencing arena. Extensive support and training services are available (see also section 7.5.4.9. for desktop systems).

Platform
Windows NT.

Price
Around 10000 Euros.

The 6000 Model a portable group system that supports both H.320 video conferencing at speeds from 64 Kbps to 384 Kbps via ISDN and H.323 conferencing from 64 Kbps to1.5 Mbps via LAN at around 8000 Euros is also available.

7.5.5.2 PictureTel SwiftSite II Series

General Description

The second-generation compact, simple, and portable systems from PictureTel. Available in two models, the 740 and 760. The SwiftSite 740 has a highly reliable electronic pan-tilt-zoom camera that is perfect for a smaller room environment like an office or small conference room. The SwiftSite 760 is the high-end compact with a mechanical pan-tilt-zoom camera, designed for small to medium-sized conference rooms. These systems enable users to launch calls and change settings without being in the same room and support the best quality audio and video using less bandwidth:

> http:// www.picturetel.com

It delivers high-quality, standards-based videoconferencing with PictureTel performance enhancements.

It comes as an integrated, all-in-one unit in a ship-and-carry box for "go anywhere" convenience.

It enables users to receive instant software updates and upgrades via a convenient dial-in server, features a built-in Superdirective Microphone high-quality audio with no cable connections.

Available Functionality

Mechanical PTZ Camera type: 1/4" Hi-res color CCD, automatic focus, Zoom range: 10x, auto or manual exposure and white balance.

Automatic camera positioning, Web-browser based remote management, headset jack, guided setup program ship and carry box

H.281 Far-end camera control, Picture-in-Picture windowing (PIP)

On-screen menus, context-sensitive help, Local and Central Speed dial directory 10 Near-end camera presets, H.320 bridge compatible, supports monitor sizes 20 – 35 inches, Stereo VCR pass-through with volume control

PC Card slot (Type I/II), Languages available for menus, QuickPad II and User Guide: English, French, German, Italian, Spanish, Portuguese, Japanese, Chinese

H.320 frame rate (max.): 15 fps standard at 128 kbps, 30 fps at 384 kbps with Tri-BRI option.

Video coding: H.261/H.263

Network Interface Supported:

ISDN BRI (S-interface) (2B+D) standard; 10 Base-T Ethernet standard; Tri-BRI (S-interface) optional

Reliability, Maintainability

Diagnostic, Power-on and Call-in-Progress LEDs.

Platform

Windows NT.

Price

Around 10000 Euros.

7.5.6 Gatekeepers, Gateways, and MultiCast Units (MCUs)

A presentation, definition and roles of these network elements in H.32x conferences can be found in section 7.4.4.5.

7.5.6.1 Return on Investment

As is true in many types of business situations, once a company crosses a certain volume threshold, the economics justify taking a different path. Once a company has crossed some "multipoint minutes per month" level, it is economically feasible to have its own MCU.

Companies that make extensive use of videoconferencing, specifically multipoint calls, should use their own MCUs because they allow the company to move traffic onto its private network, which provides significant savings. However, replacing the valuable functions provided by outside multipoint services vendors in favour of managing videoconferencing bridging internally is a decision that must be made with caution.

See for example a typical study case:

http://www.teleconferencemagazine.com/issues/1999/novdec/casestudy.htm

7.5.6.2 Ezenia! Encounter Family Products

General Description

This is a set of IP conferencing products. Velocity and Series 2000 products from Ezenia! are also available for switched networks (ISDN based multimedia conferencing).

The Encounter range includes:

- Encounter NetServer - a multimedia communications server that enables users on IP networks - corporate LANs or Intranets - to create and participate in multipoint, multimedia conferences, using any combination of voice, video and data.
- Encounter NetGate - a gateway that enables multimedia communication between ISDN and IP-based devices.
- Encounter Gatekeeper - a software application, which enables administrators to set network policies and control access and bandwidth utilization for a zone of endpoint terminals, gateways and multimedia conference servers on the network.
- Encounter NetServer ADX 1000 - voice and data conferencing server to accommodate both traditional phone (POTS) users and Voice over IP (VoIP) users for multiparty voice conferencing.

More about Encounter NetServer software:

http://www.ezenia.com

Available Functionality

A browser-based user interface provides convenient access to scheduling and managing your conferences. With a click on your browser, you can access the user interface to create, schedule, and control your meetings.

Ezenia!'s Encounter NetServer can be configured as any combination of voice conference server, voice-data conference server, and videoconference server. It supports the H.261 and H.263 video standards, G.711 and G.723.1 audio standards and T.120 data standards. The Encounter NetServer even performs audio transcoding so that conferences can contain a mix of audio participants, enabling PSTN audio participants using a standard telephone to join the same conference as H.323 LAN-based conference endpoints.

The Encounter NetServer uses specialised hardware to provide more varied and better-quality audio performance than its competitors.

● System Capacity

Maximum of 48 simultaneous conference users: up to 32 H.323 audio-video endpoints; up to 23 Plain Old Telephone Services (POTS) audio endpoints (US) (24 in Europe); up to 48 T.120 endpoints

Types of Endpoints: H.323 audio/video/data, T.120 data over IP, H.323 Internet Telephony, POTS (phone).

● Software provided:

Encounter NetServer, version 1.2, Microsoft Windows NT, version 4.0, Microsoft Internet Information Web Server S/W, Microsoft Access database.

● System Modules:

Ethernet Interface - 10/100Base T Ethernet, ISDN Interface - Dual T1/PRI and Dual E1/PRI, MPU (Media Streams Processor Unit)

Transfer Rates up to 1.5 Mbps.

Monitoring and Status are available through an SNMP agent with Ethernet MIB support

● Administrator Interface:

Browser access via Microsoft Internet Explorer, version 3.02 or higher with Authenticode, Administration Services, Administrator Log-in, system, conference, and User Event Log, System resource status and availability, FTP/Telnet, Call tracking for billing, diagnostics, gatekeeper Registration/Re-registration.

Reliability, Maintainability
Well-documented support is available with different offers for service agreements, training etc. No particular concern about reliability of the systems has been identified. Awarded by "Network magazine" in 1999.

Platform
Windows NT server.

Price
Around 3000 Euros for Encounter NetServer SW.
Hardware: From 27000 Euros for an eight-port version to 75000 Euros for a 48-port version.

7.5.6.3   elemedia H.323 Gatekeeper Platform
General Description
The elemedia H.323 Gatekeeper Platform is a software package that enables rapid development of high-performance H.323 Gatekeeper applications. This modular

software provides the components necessary to build H.323 version 2 compliant gatekeeper applications. Designed to interface easily to existing systems, it also provides stand-alone services for the H.323 environment:

> http://www.elemedia.com/Main/h323center/centerhome.htm

Available Functionality

- Core Module

The core module contains the gatekeeper call control and registration functions, shielding the developer from the nuances and complexity of H.323 protocols. This core module interfaces with the other modules via an easy-to-use and well-documented C++ API.

- Policy and Management Modules:

The platform also contains policy and management modules which functionality beyond the scope of the H.323 standard. These modules can be easily customised or replaced. The elemedia H.323 Gatekeeper Software Platform is shipped with default policy and management modules that allow the application developer to build a "vanilla" gatekeeper out-of-the-box. This "ease of usability" gives customers the advantage of simple gatekeeper testing and provides a baseline development environment as unique gatekeeper applications are developed.

The latest release of the elemedia GK2000S Gatekeeper, built on the elemedia H.323 Protocol Stack, includes support for the following new features:

- Party Number Alias Address Type
- User-to User Information Elements (UUIE's)
- H.245 Tunneling
- Dual Tone Multi-Frequency (DTMF) Signaling via H.245
- Tokens/Cryptotokens and supporting Security Fields
- Q.931 Messages: Progress Messages; Setup/Acknowledgment Messages.

The elemedia H.323 Gatekeeper Platform provides many basic services as well as optional add-on modules.

- Basic Services

The basic services provided by the elemedia H.323 Gatekeeper Platform include:

- Ability to support gatekeeper routed call model, direct call model, and non Registration/Admission/Status (RAS) clients
- Address resolution and routing module
- All H.323 call control and protocol handling
- Auditing of endpoints and conferences
- Authentication service module
- Bandwidth management service module
- Conference management
  1. Endpoint management
  2. Exception loggers including security log, error log, system log, and conference log
  3. Full event recording for network engineering
  4. Full suite of test tools including, an H.323 simulator
  5. Generation of conference (call) detail records
  6. Graphical User Interface (GUI)
  7. H.323 version 2 compliance

- Add-on Modules

In addition to the basic services, the following are also available as add-on modules: Lightweight Directory Access Protocol (LDAP)-based authenticator and LDAP-based router

The elemedia LDAP-based authenticator uses an LDAP directory to authenticate and authorize endpoints and callers. The LDAP-based router uses an LDAP-directory to provide provision mappings for E.164 numbers and gateway(s) that support them.

Both modules are built on a sophisticated LDAP Session Manager that reliably handles interactions with multiple LDAP database servers.

Reliability, Maintainability
The elemedia software venture is wholly owned by Lucent and was launched in September 1996.

Different types of pricing models (evaluation free of charge), developers, commercial license are available. Software maintenance agreements include consultation, support, and software upgrades. But also they provide upgrades that include the changes that occur to the H.323 standard.

Platforms
NT, Solaris, and HP–UX versions.

Elemedia provides as well H.323 protocol stacks: its next release of its Classic Protocol Stack will be newly-rearchitected to take advantage of a lower-level C core while utilising a higher-level C++ Application Programming Interface (API). This combination, engineered by Bell Labs, provides developers with a unique platform on which to design and support a variety of applications – from general-purpose processors and desktop applications to carrier class solutions.

Price
No publicly available price.

7.5.6.4   Radvision L2W-323Gateway
General Description
The L2W-323 is a fully self-contained "standalone" gateway that translates between H-323 and H.320 protocols, and converts multimedia information from circuit switch to H.323 IP packets. On the PSTN side it supports voice-only calls, as well as H.320 videoconferencing sessions. The L2W-323P uses a highly reliable, RISC architecture and is SNMP (Simple Network Management Protocol) configurable.

RADVision also offers a simplified version, the VIU-323, a self-contained "terminal adapter" that connects H.320 systems to IP networks (LANs/intranets/Internet) without affecting current H.320 ISDN capabilities. The VIU translates between the H.323 and H.320 compliant video and audio streams and communications protocols, providing complete end-to-end interoperability:

     http://www.radvision.com

Available Functionality
Depending on the network provisioning on the wide area, the L2W-323 enables users to exchange audio, video and data in real time at 64kbps, 128kbps, 256kbps or 384kbps. "Voice Over IP" gateway features include Interactive Voice Response (IVR), echo cancellation and Dual Tone Multi-Frequency (DTMF) support.

The L2W-323 supports up to eight concurrent voice calls or four concurrent video calls between users on different networks. Users of an L2W-323-enabled network also benefit from full end-to-end support for T.120 sessions, provided all terminals support the standard in their collaborative applications.

The built-in GateKeeper Provides Virtual PBX Call Control: the L2W-323 Gateway, working in conjunction with an embedded RADVision H.323 GateKeeper, provides the functionality of a multimedia Private Branch Exchange (PBX) allowing inter-network calls, Direct Inward Dialling (DID), call forward and transfer, and custom call control via IVR and DTMF signalling. Real time routing (by-pass routing) between network segments is provided. Optional hardware modules perform real-time audio transcoding between G.723 to G.711, and G.728 to G.711.

Switched Connections: Expandable two or four WAN ports - ISDN (BRI), V.35/RS366 or V.25bis.

Modularity: each L2W-323 can be configured with up to four switched ports. Multiple gateways may be cascaded to support more WAN connections. Gatekeeper may be disabled in multiple Gateway configurations.

Reliability, Maintainability
Diagnostics: Built-in test – CPU, peripherals and memories are tested when turned on (at "power on"), front panel LED indications, remote diagnostics configurable via modem.

Easy Installation, configuration and management using a Windows SNMP-based application utility, a TS232 serial/modem port for remote configuration and diagnostics.

Support and training services are available on request.

Platforms
Software tools: Windows 95, NT

Price
On request. Somehow identical to concurrence.

7.5.6.5 Cisco IP/VC Systems Family
General Description
The Cisco videoconferencing solution is the Cisco IP/VC product family. This product family is primarily comprised of the Cisco IP/VC 3500 Series which consists of the Cisco IP/VC 3510 Multipoint Control Unit (MCU), the Cisco IP/VC 3520 and IP/VC 3525 Videoconferencing Gateways, and the Cisco IP/VC 3530 Video Terminal Adapter (VTA):

http://www.cisco.com/warp/public/cc/pd/mxsv/ipvc3500/index.shtml

Available Functionality

* Cisco IP/VC 3510 Videoconferencing Multipoint Control Unit

The IP/VC 3510 MCU is designed to allow users to spontaneously initiate full multimedia, multipoint conferences, including data conferencing. It runs unattended; there is no need to schedule conferences in advance. With the IP/VC 3510, a user simply dials the conference number and the MCU automatically sets up the session. Others who wish to join dial that same number and are immediately connected to the conference.

Alternatively, the person who initiates the conference can add users to the conference.

Each IP/VC 3510 can support up to 15 simultaneous users. Its compact design also provides a way to cascade multiple MCUs together to support larger conferences. For small videoconferencing networks, the MCU features built-in gatekeeper functions. It is based upon a highly reliable Reduced Instruction Set Computer (RISC) architecture and is simple to install.

The Cisco IP/VC 3510 provides built-in gatekeeper functions, enabling H.323 management and control services (registration, address resolution, and bandwidth control) for remote offices or small videoconferencing networks. For larger networks, the Cisco Multimedia Conference Manager (MCM) provides gatekeeper and proxy functionality, including provisions for quality of service (QoS) over wide-area network links.

Each unit contains a multipoint controller (MC) and a multipoint processor (MP). Each MC can manage up to three MPs.

Video Coding: only H.261, QCIF/CIF
Audio Coding: only G.711, A/µ Law

* Cisco IP/VC 3520 and IP/VC 3525 Videoconferencing Gateways

These gateways let users connect IP-based H.323 videoconference endpoints to legacy circuit-switched H.320 systems.

The IP/VC 3520 Gateway offers two or four Basic Rate Interface (BRI) or V.35 WAN ports or a combination of both BRI and V.35 ports. It supports up to four calls at 128 kbps (BRI interfaces) or 384 kbps (V.35 interfaces). All ports include audio transcoders for optimal video/audio quality and bandwidth utilisation. The BRI ports come standard with echo cancellation. The V.35 ports support EIA/TIA-366 (RS-366) signalling for call set-up.

The Cisco IP/VC 3525 Gateway offers a single Primary Rate Interface (PRI) to the Public Switched Telephone Network (PSTN). It supports T1 and E1 connections. The IP/VC 3525 Gateway supports three calls at 384 kbps on a T1 connection, four calls on an E1, or up to eight calls at 128 kbps. Audio transcoding is also supported as a standard feature for optimal audio quality.

Like the IP/VC 3510 MCU, the IP/VC Gateways offer built-in gatekeeper functions for small videoconferencing networks, a compact design, and reliable RISC architecture.

Supports ITU audio transcoding (G.711/G.723 and G.711/G.728)

* Cisco IP/VC 3530 Video Terminal Adapter

The IP/VC 3530 Video Terminal Adapter (VTA) is a self-contained video interface that connects one H.320 system to an IP network communications. The IP/VC 3530

VTA connects an H.320 room-based system or small-group system to a LAN. It offers two V.35 WAN interfaces, EIA/TIA-366 signalling, a low-profile compact design, and RISC architecture to ensure reliability and easy installation.

- Cisco Multimedia Conference Manager

The Multimedia Conference Manager (MCM) software is part of Cisco IOS software. It functions as a high-performance H.323 gatekeeper and proxy, enabling network managers to control bandwidth and priority settings for H.323 videoconferencing services based on individual network configurations and capacities. The MCM is available across a wide range of Cisco router platforms, including the Cisco 2500, 2600 and 3600, 7200 and the MC3810 multiservice access concentrator.

The MCM H.323 gatekeeper subsystem functions as a point of control for various H.323 components attached to an IP network: videoconferencing endpoints, MCUs, H.320-to-H.323 gateways, IP telephony devices, and PSTN-IP telephony gateways.

The MCM proxy subsystem ensures high-quality H.323 conferencing calls over LAN and WAN infrastructures, and supports H.323 call establishment through firewalls. To ensure quality, the proxy provides two types of IP quality-of-service (QoS) functions: IP Precedence packet classification and Resource Reservation Protocol (RSVP) bandwidth reservation for videoconferencing packet flows. The MCM proxy also works in conjunction with Cisco IOS and PIX Firewalls to enable secure H.323 connections.

The MCM differentiates itself from other gatekeepers by offering critical proxy services, by providing gatekeeper and routing capabilities on a single hardware platform, and by offering excellent scalability and price/performance for small to very large H.323 deployments.

Reliability, Maintainability
Power on self-test for CPU, interfaces, and memory when unit is turned on, Front panel LED indicators, Telnet monitoring capabilities, Serial console.

Good FAQs and online documentation on Cisco's Web site.

Maintenance eased by: Windows SNMP-based configuration utility; Telnet, Local configuration via serial port or network, Remote configuration via modem (PPP), remote software upgrades via the network.

Price
List price for the Cisco IP/VC Multipoint Control Unit is U.S. $19,950. The Cisco IP/VC 3520 Gateway ranges from U.S. $9,890 to $10,640, and the Cisco IP/VC 3525 lists for U.S. $29,450. The Cisco IP/VC 3530 VTA is priced at U.S. $4,350. The Cisco MCM is a Cisco IOS® image that can be purchased as an upgrade, starting at U.S. $2,300, or as a standard software feature, starting at U.S. $3,100.

7.5.6.6 Accord MGC-100

General Description

The MGC-100 is basically a MCU hardware, which accommodates both ISDN-based and IP-based (H.320/H.323) conference and gateway connections into a single platform. It seems to be the only one that can do all in one.

MGC stands for Multiple Gateway and Control network types are managed through a common management and reservation system, making conferencing easier, faster and more reliable than the first generation of multipoint control units. It includes RADVision's H.323 protocol stack.

Available Functionality

Fully customisable conference welcome screens and audio messages,

Operator can guide users through every part of the conference: by, for example, dragging and dropping participants between conferences, creating sub-conferences on the fly.

Under the umbrella of the MGC Manager, a Windows 95/NT based management system, users can quickly and easily connect to and manage multiple MGC-100s via the Internet, LAN, dial-up modem, or RS-232. Regardless of the network you are using to collaborate, you can manage any number of MCUs located anywhere in the world. From reservations and diagnostics to conference management and call records with conference analysis, one management system does it all.

Other features include:

• Enhanced Continuous Presence

Provides you with 6 different layouts to select the video layout that best meets the needs of your conference - and be able to change it on-the-fly. Select the sites you want fixed on the screen and those you would like to appear via voice activation.

• Multi-way Transcoding

Assures that sites always connect at their optimal capabilities. Conference quality does not have to be sacrificed in order to match the common capabilities of all sites. Conferences also begin on time due to enhanced connection reliability.

• Integrated Gateway Functionality

Transparently connect IP, ISDN and ATM sites into the same conference on a single platform- there's no need to deal with the complexity and cost of external gateway boxes.

• Conference Management

Allows you to take full control of your conference and simultaneously manage multiple MCUs and conferences (Table 5). Optional web browser and touch-tone telephone interfaces empower users to manage their own conferences

• Conference Scheduling

Initiate ad-hoc conferences, or configure and reserve conferences for a future date and time.

• Billing Support

Generate billing records or call statistics from the MGC's stored Call Data Records (CDRs).

Table 5. MGC-100 capacities

System Capacity	ISDN	ATM	IP
Max No. Sites	96	80	96
Max No. Simultaneous Conferences	24	20	24
Max No. Continuous Presence conferences	16	16	16

Videoconferencing H.320, H.323, H.321, T.120; Telephony H.320; Multi-way H.231, H.243 Cascading and Chair Control; H.281 FECC (Far End Camera Control)

Video H.261, H.263; Audio G.711, G.722, G.728

Data H.243 LSD, T.122/T.125 (MCS), T.123, T.124 (GCC); Communications H.221, H.242

External Communications: data rates 56 Kbps - 2 Mbps

Clock synchronisation: Synchronises to external network

Network Interfaces: 25 Mbps ATM (FVC) PRI-T1 (ISDN signalling) V.35/RS-449/EIA-530 155 Mbps ATM (FVC) E1/T1 Leased Line RS-366 dialling 100/10 Mbps Ethernet PRI-E1 (ISDN signalling) Key Generator (KG) Support.

Reliability, Maintainability

On-line diagnostics continually monitor every component of the system, not only to identify problems, but also to anticipate them. If a failure or potential failure is flagged, repairs are quick and easy. The fully modular construction allows faulty modules to be hot-swapped, and new modules are self-configuring, making change-outs if required, almost painless.

Remotely access the MCU, via the Internet/IP connection, to monitor system performance, for every module. With front-accessible, hot-swappable, self-configuring modules and universal slot architecture, engineers are not required to reconfigure or replace modules. Remote software upgrades allow for fast and easy implementation of newly released features without ever visiting the MCU site.

A comprehensive helpdesk and different services on-line are available from the Web site. Three different levels of support can be purchased. Several training for operators and/or administrators are available.

It has been chosen by VCON as official partner for multi-point conference solutions. It is a well-rated product and products in several study cases. Additional info is available at URL:

http://www.teleconferencemagazine.com/issues/1999/novdec/casestudy.htm.

Platforms

MGC Webcommander, MGC Manager and other Software tools: Windows 95, NT

Price

Average price per port 1500 to 2000 Euros.

7.5.6.7   Radvision MCU-323

General Description

The MCU-323 represents a price/performance breakthrough for MCU. The RADVision "cascadable" and stackable MCU architecture provides an affordable, entry-level configuration that can be expanded in either large or small increments. A unique distributed topology using an MC (Multipoint Controller) and one or more MPs (Multipoint Processors) optimises system and network resources. MCU-323 capabilities include audio mixing plus video switching or locking and built-in gatekeeper functionality. The network is not required to support multicast in order to allow MCU-323 conferences. It uses a highly reliable, RISC architecture and is SNMP (Simple Network Management Protocol) configurable:

> http:// www.radvision.com

Available Functionality

Each unit supports up to 15 simultaneous multimedia calls or up to 24 voice-only calls. Multiple MCUs may be used to transparently increase the number of concurrent conferences. MCUs may be centralised or distributed.

Cascading of units provides a solution for very large conferences, conference panels with many remote viewers, and joining remote groups of participants to a conference through narrow communication channels. MCUs may be centralised or distributed.

- Bandwidth Support
  A wide range of call bandwidths starting from 64Kbps (for voice-only calls), 128Kbps and up to 1.5Mbps (for multimedia calls).
- Web Interface
  Enables easy conference monitoring, chair control including disconnecting parties and locking video streams, spontaneous invitation of new participants during ongoing conferences, data collaboration initiation.
- Security
  Optional password protection for conference to ensure privacy; each unit is password protected.
- Optional Gatekeeper
  RADVision's Windows NT-based NGK-100 H.323 Version 2-compliant Gatekeeper application supports 300 registrations and 60 concurrent calls.
- LAN Interface: 10BaseT - IEEE 802-3 Ethernet port
- Terminal Port: RS232, 9-pin D-type, DCE
- Protocols: H.323, H.225, H.245, RTP/RTCP
- Video coding: H.261, QCIF/CIF.
- Audio Coding: G.711, A/µ Law
- Panel LEDs: Power, Test, Link, Session, CPU Load

Reliability, Maintainability

Robust design based on RISC architecture to ensure high reliability; easy Installation, Configuration, and Management through SNMP-based administration and configuration utility.

Remote configuration via the LAN port

Diagnostics with built-in Test CPU, peripherals and memories are tested at "Power On", front panel LED indications.

Support and training services are available on request.

Platforms

Manager software available on Windows NT.

RADVision proposes as well award winning industry standard toolkits related to the H.323 standard. The RADVision H.323 protocol toolkit is available for numerous operating systems including various Unix versions, real time OSs for embedded systems, as well as Windows, including Windows NT and Win CE. It can also be easily ported to other operating systems.

7.5.6.8   White Pine's MeetingPoint

General Description

MeetingPoint is White Pine's H.323 standards based Videoconferencing Server software (H.323 MCU) allowing you to create a virtual conference room on your existing IP network. MeetingPoint allows users of, for instance, Microsoft NetMeeting, CU-SeeMe, Intel ProShare and any of VCON's H.323 products to participate in a simultaneous group conference:

http://www.cuseeme.com/products/index.htm

Available Functionality

Allows to simply choose from MeetingPoint's simple conference list to find a meeting, use the MeetingPlanner tool to schedule meetings and notify participants of time and location via automatic e-mail invitation.

You can control who you want to see and hear with VideoSwitcher, a Java applet that allows H.323 end-users to choose which participant to watch and hear in addition to the traditional voice-activated conference mode.

MeetingPoint lets the Information Technology (IT) Manager control how much video audio traffic is allowed on the network, by conference, and user. MeetingPoint has several advanced features for managing bandwidth and security.

A built-in gatekeeper allows you to set bandwidth limits per conference and per user. The gatekeeper also controls who can access the conference by providing authentication services.

MeetingPoint can send audio and video data in multicast format so that one stream of data is sent over the network and shared by multiple users. MeetingPoint Servers can be linked together so that conferences can shared and the conference manager can load-balance the traffic on the network.

- MeetingPoint Standards

  Communications: H.323, CU-SeeMe

  Audio: G.711, G.723

  Video: H.261, H.263

  Data: T.120

- H.323 Management

MeetingPoint includes an internal Gatekeeper for H.323 call management. Alternatively, MeetingPoint supports third-party Gatekeepers.

- Transmission Method
  IP Multicast or IP Unicast
- Administration
  Conference Administration Web Pages provide a browser-based interface for conference administration and user access to conferences. A conference Administration Database maintains user authentication information

  As HTTP server, you have the option of using Internet Information Server (IIS) on Windows NT® or Apache on UNIX.

  Dynamic Monitoring of conference and network statistics is provided.
- Billing and Tracking
  MeetingPoint is compatible with RADIUS authentication, billing and tracking systems.

Reliability, Maintainability

The software is now in its 4.0.2 version. It is widely used in H.323 based conferences and received several technological awards from the field.

It has an extensive set of diagnostic tools and logging functions for monitoring bandwidth consumption and testing the connections between the MCU and specific conference participants.

A good support interface with FAQ, release notes etc is available online.

A lack of audio-mixing capabilities is reported to seriously hinder audio performance.

Platform

MeetingPoint v4.0 is supported under Windows NT Server 4.0 and requires a 333 MHz or faster processor and a Java compliant web browser such as Internet Explorer v5 or Netscape Navigator v4.6.1

For SUN platforms, MeetingPoint v4.0 is supported under Solaris 2.6 running on a 300 MHz or faster UltraSPARC-II processor.

A Linux version is also available.

Price

MeetingPoint H.323 Multipoint Conferencing Server:
10 User License: about 9000 Euros, 25 users license about 16500 Euros.

7.5.6.9 PictureTel 330

General Description

The PictureTel 330 H.323 MCU is available in 8- or 24-port configurations as a software-only product leveraging existing Intel Pentium II processor-based, industry-standard PC server platforms. All configurations include PictureTel's multipoint conferencing software and scheduling and conference management software:

      http:// www.picturetel.com

Available Functionality
- Administration utilities

NetConference Administrator Java-Applet, NetConference Management and Administration, defines number of rooms and seats in each, defines which algorithms (Gxxx & Hxxx) may be used by each room, continuous presence, Add/Drop users

PictureTel Web Center Java-Applet for Meeting Management Control allows users to:
- Display a roster of virtual conference rooms and the attendees in each room
- Invite additional attendees to join a meeting
- Lock/unlock the virtual conference room to prevent unauthorised access and facilitate private discussions
- Disconnect a user from a meeting
- Clear the virtual conference room of all users
- Join/interrupt a meeting in progress
- Display the operating mode of the room, Continuous Presence, or switch-on-voice
- View a single participant regardless of current speaker , Broadcaster Select
- Choose a virtual conference room by clicking the Connect-Me Button
- Standards

Video: H.261, H.263
Audio: G.723, G.711, and G.722
Document/application sharing: T.120, Communications: H.323
- Conference Set-up

Meet-me (dial in), Add a Participant (dial out), Connect-me (dial in)
- Conference control

Voice-activated, continuous presence, cascading

Reliability, Maintainability
PictureTel 330 NetConference Multipoint Server Software ships with a 90-day warranty for software. Warranty also includes one year of telephone support. In addition to the product warranty, PictureTel also provides other cost-effective support options at preferred rates including: Help Desk telephone support; software updates; technical training; and network integration and consulting services.

NetConference reported to have a weak support for H.323 clients of the three products tested and is suitable only for organisations that have standardised on a single H.323 client.

Platform
Windows NT

Price
Ranges from 15000 Euros for eight-port model to 28000 Euros for 24-port model

Appendix A1. Product Classification Summary

A1.1   Product Classification Table

The results of analysis of the technologies and products mentioned in this book and their applicability to fulfil the Distributed System Engineering (DSE) User Requirements are summarized in Table 1.

Table 1. Technologies and products analysis

Product	DSE Architecture Layer	DSE associated Standards & Technologies	CMN (Co-Ver & Co-Des)	Co-Des PDR	Co-Des CSD	Co-Des ASD	Co-Ver SPC
Existing DSE practices: Collaborative Systems Design and Analysis							
DOORS	A(PDM,GW)		F	F		F	
MATLAB	A(Sim)		F			F	
Simulink	A(Sim)			F	F		
ACTS MULTICUBE	NI,A(GW)	TCP/IP, ATM	C			C	O
Existing DSE practices: Collaborative Systems Verification							
VIS/Mockup and VIS/View	A(AIV,CAX)		F,O	F		F	O
NCRDB	A(PDM,AIV, WF)	Web	F,O,C	F		F	DSA ,O
AIVDB	A(AIV,PDM)	SGML	F,C	F		F	DSA ,O,P
CATIA	A(PDM,CAX)	CORBA, STEP, COM+, CAD	F	F,C		F	DSA
DynaWorks	A(AIV)		F				O,P
Middleware							
DMSO RTI 1.3	A(Sim)	HLA	F		F,P	F,O	
DMSO RTI 1.3 NG	A(Sim)	HLA	F		F,P	F,O	
Osim Framework	A(Sim)	HLA	F		F,P	F,O	
IONA iPortal Suite	MW	CORBA, XML, EJB, COM+	F,O,P,C	F	O	F,O	

K. Drira, A. Martelli, T. Villemur (Eds.): Cooperative Environments, LNCS 2236, pp. 263-269, 2001.
© Springer-Verlag Berlin Heidelberg 2001

Product	DSE Architecture Layer	DSE associated Standards & Technologies	DSE User Requirements				
			CMN (Co-Ver & Co-Des)	Co-Des			Co-Ver
				PDR	CSD	ASD	SPC
Component Broker	MW	CORBA, EJB, Web, XML	F,O,P,C	F	O	F,O	
VisiBroker 4.0	MW	CORBA, RMI	F,O,P,C	F	O	F,O	
TAO	MW	CORBA, CCM	F,O,P,C	F	O	F,O	
LiveContent BROKER 3.2	MW	CORBA, COM	F,O,P,C	F	O	F,O	
BEA WebLogic Enterprise™	MW	CORBA, EJB, Web	F,O,P,C	F	O	F,O	
ObjecTime Developer	MW	UML				O	
Exceed WEB	MW	CORBA, Web, Java	F,C	C		F	DSA
BizTalk Server	MW	Web, SOAP, XML	C	F		O	
Product Data Management, exchange and interoperability							
ENOVIAPM	A(PDM,WF)	Web, CAD	O,C	C,P		+	
ENOVIAVPM	A(PDM,WF)	Web, CAD	O,C	C,P		+	
Windchill	A(PDM,WF)	Web, XML	O,C	C,P		+	
Metaphase Technology	A(PDM,WF)	Web, CAD, CORBA, STEP	O,C	C,P		+	
MatrixOne	A(PDM)	Web, CORBA	O,C	C,P		+	
e-Vis.com	A(PDM,GW)	Web, CAD, HTTPS	F,O	F		F,O	DSA
Workflow Management							
Oracle Workflow	A(WF)	SQL, Web	+	F,P		O	
C4 Software – Process Director	A(WF)	CORBA, EJB, ActiveX, Web	+	F			
COSA Workflow	A(WF)	Web	+	F			
IBM – EDM Suite	A(WF)	Web	+	F			
JetForm	A(WF)	Web		F			
TeamWARE Flow	A(WF)	Web	+	F			
W4	A(WF)	Web	+	F			
Session Management							
TANGO	P&SM	Web, Java	F	+	F,P	+	

Product	DSE Architecture Layer	DSE associated Standards & Technologies	DSE User Requirements				
			CMN (Co-Ver & Co-Des)	Co-Des			Co-Ver
				PDR	CSD	ASD	SPC
Habanero	P&SM	Web, Java	F	+	F,P	+	
The Java Collaborative Toolset	P&SM	Java, Web	F	+	F,P	+	
CALTECH Infospheres system	P&SM	Web, Java	F	+	F,P	+	
InVerse	P&SM	Web, Java	F	+	F,P	+	
DOE2000 Real-Time Collaboration Management Project	P&SM	Web, Java, CORBA	F	+	F,P	+	
Multicast Network Tools							
Multicast Configuration Debug Tools	NI		F,C			O	O
Performance Measurement Tools	NI		F,C			O	O
Multicast Libraries: MCL, MDPv2, OmniCast, PGM for FreeBSD, WhiteBarn's PGM, RMDP, RMF, RMTP-II, JRMS, Swarmcast	NI		F,C		P	F,P ,O	O
Application Sharing							
VNC	A(GW)	TCP/IP, UDP	F,O	F	F,O ,P	F,O	DSA ,RC
Real Presenter	A(GW)	Web	F,O	F	F,O ,P	F,O	DSA ,RC
XTVision / XMX	A(GW)	X11	F,O	F	F,O ,P	F,O	DSA ,RC
Magics Communicator	A(GW)	CAD	F,O	F	F,O ,P	F,O	DSA ,RC
CATIA Conferencning Groupware	A(GW)	CAD	F,O	F	F,O ,P	F,O	DSA ,RC
Timbuktu	A(GW)	LDAP, TCP/IP, UDP	F,O	F	F,O ,P	F,O	DSA ,RC
PcAnywhere	A(GW)	TCP/IP, UDP	F,O	F	F,O ,P	F,O	DSA ,RC

Product	DSE Architecture Layer	DSE associated Standards & Technologies	DSE User Requirements				
			CMN (Co-Ver & Co-Des)	Co-Des			Co-Ver
				PDR	CSD	ASD	SPC
Web Conferencing							
Mirabilis ICQ	A(GW)	Web, ODBC 2.0	F				
Imeet	A(GW)	Web	F	F			DSA
WebEx	A(GW)	Web	F	F			DSA
PlaceWare	A(GW)	Web	F	F			DSA
H.323 Terminals. T.120 Clients							
Mbone Tools	A(GW)	H.323, T120, RTP	F,O	F			VC
Mash project	A(GW)	H.323, T120	F,O	F			VC
SunForum	A(GW)	H.323, T.120	F,O	F			VC, RC
Lotus Sametime	A(GW)	T.120, IMPP	F,O	F			VC, RC
Cu-SeeMe	A(GW)	H.323	F,O	F			VC, RC
NetMeeting	A(GW)	H.323, T.120, LDAP	F,O	F			VC, RC
VDOPhone	A(GW)	H.323, H.324	F,O	F			VC, RC
Internet CommSuite	A(GW)	H.323	F,O	F			VC, RC
Vocaltec Internet Phone	A(GW)	H.323	F,O	F			VC, RC
EasyAxess	A(GW)	H.323, H.324	F,O	F			VC, RC
WebPhone	A(GW)	H.323	F,O	F			VC
Bull Jingle	A(GW)	H.323, LDAP	F,O	F			VC, RC
Desktop Videoconf Systems							
SunVideoPlus	A(GW)	H.323	F,O,P,C	F,C	P	P	VC, RC
Osprey Cards	A(GW)	H.323	F,O,P,C	F,C	P	P	VC, RC
Winnov Videum	A(GW)	H320, H.323, H.324	F,O,P,C	F,C	P	P	VC, RC
MAX.i.c. Live	A(GW)	H.323, H.324	F,O,P,C	F,C	P	P	VC, RC
ELSA Vision II	A(GW)	H.320, H.323	F,O,P,C	F,C	P	P	VC, RC

Product	DSE Architecture Layer	DSE associated Standards & Technologies	DSE User Requirements				
			CMN (Co-Ver & Co-Des)	Co-Des			Co-Ver
				PDR	CSD	ASD	SPC
Intel Proshare 500	A(GW)	H.320, H.323	F,O,P,C	F,C	P	P	VC, RC
PictureTel 550	A(GW)	H.320, H.323	F,O,P,C	F,C	P	P	VC, RC
Sony Trinicom 500 Plus	A(GW)	H.320, H.323	F,O,P,C	F,C	P	P	VC, RC
VCON Desktop Systems	A(GW)	H.320, H.323	F,O,P,C	F,C	P	P	VC, RC
Vtel Smartstation	A(GW)	H.320, H.323	F,O,P,C	F,C	P	P	VC, RC
Zydacron OnWan	A(GW)	H.320, H.323	F,O,P,C	F,C	P	P	VC, RC
Meeting Rooms Videoconferencing Systems							
VCON MediaConnect 8000	A(GW)	H.320, H.323	F,O,P,C	F,C	P	P	VC, RC
PictureTel SwiftSite II	A(GW)	H.320, H.323	F,O,P,C	F,C	P	P	VC, RC
Conference Gatekeepers, MCUs							
Ezenia! Encounter	NI	H.320, H.323	F,C	F	P	O,P	VC
Elemedia H.323 Gatekeeper	NI	H.323, LDAP	F,C	F	P	O,P	VC
RadVision L2W-323 Gateway	NI	H.320, H.323	F,C	F	P	O,P	VC
Cisco IP/VC Systems Family	NI	H.320, H.323	F,C	F	P	O,P	VC
Accord MGC-100	NI	H.320, H.321, H.323	F,C	F	P	O,P	VC
Radvision MCU-323	NI	H.323	F,C	F	P	O,P	VC
WhitePine's MeetingPoint	NI	H.323	F,C	F	P	O,P	VC
PictureTel 330	NI	H.323	F,C	F	P	O,P	VC

A1.2 Acronyms and Abbreviations Used in the Product Classification Table

Architecture Layer:
- A –Applications;
- MW – Middleware;
- NI – Network Infrastructure;
- P&SM – Process and Session Management.

Application Functionality:
- PDM – Product Data Management;
- WF – Workflow Management;
- GW - GroupWare;
- Sim – Simulation;
- AIV – Assembly, Integration and Verification processes/
- CAX – Computer-Aided Design, Engineering and Software Engineering.

DSE associated Standards and Technologies:
- CORBA – Common Object Broker Architecture;
- UML – Unified Modeling Language;
- HLA – Hi-Level Architecture;
- XML – eXtensible Markup Language;
- Web – based on HTTP and other hi-level Internet Protocols
- STEP – Standard for the Exchange of Product Model Data
- Others – according to partners opinion.

DSE User Requirements:
- CMN – Common (these User Requirements coincide in both Co-Des and Co-Ver contexts);
- Co-Des – (Collaborative Design):
    PDR –Preliminary Design Review scenario;
    CSD –Spacecraft Control System Design scenario;
    ASD –Aerospace System Design Process scenario;
- Co-Ver – (Collaborative Verification):
    SPC – Specific.

User Requirements Classification Identifiers:
- C – Constrained;
- F - Functional;
- O - Operational;
- P – Performance;
- I – Implementation (Co-Ver only);
- DSA – Document Server Access (Co-Ver only);
- RC – Remote Control (Co-Ver only);
- VC – Video Conferencing (Co-Ver only).

A1.3   Product Classification Table Syntax

The Product Classification Table uses the following syntax:
- DSE Architecture Layer column: any one or few of the abbreviations A; MW; NI; P&SM delimited by comma. Optionally A is followed by any one or few comma delimited Application Functionalities enclosed in ( );

- DSE associated Standards & Technologies column: any one or few of abbreviations CORBA, UML, HLA, XML, Web, STEP or Others (according to partners opinion) delimited by comma;
- DSE User Requirements columns: any one or few of User Requirements Classification identifiers or "+" if there is no detailed information or empty.

Appendix A2. Acronyms and Abbreviations

AIT	Assembly, Integration and Testing
ALSP	Aggregate Level Simulation Protocol
AP	Application Protocol
API	Application Programming Interface
ARPA	Advanced Research Project Agency
ASCII	American Standard Code for Information Interchange
ASP	Active Server Pages
ATM	Asynchronous Transmission Mode
ATV	Automated Transfer Vehicle
BRI	Basic Rate Interface
CAD	Computer Aided Design
CAE	Computer Aided Engineering
CAPI	COMMON-ISDN-API
CASE	Computer-Aided Software Engineering
CAX	Computer-Aided Design, Engineering and Software Engineering
CGI	Common Gateway Interface
CIF/FCIF	Common Intermediate Format/Full Common Intermediate Format
CMG	Control Moment Gyro
CMMS	Conceptual Models of Mission Space
CODEC	COder/DECoder (telecommunication terminology) or Compressor/DECompressor (computing terminology)
CORBA	Common Object Request Broker Architecture
[C]OTS	[Commercial] Off-The-Shelf
CSCW	Computer Supported Collaborative Work
CSS	Cascading Style Sheets
DB	Data Base
DBA	Data Base Administrator
DMSO	Defence Modelling and Simulation Office
DIF	Data Interchange Format
DIS	Distributed Interactive Simulation
DISF	Distributed Interactive Simulation Facilities
DNA	Distributed interNet Applications
DOM	Document Object Model
DS	Data Standardization
DTVC	DeskTop Video Conferencing
DVMRP	Distance Vector Multicast Routing Protocol
ECMA	European Computer Manufacturers Association
EJB	Enterprise Java Beans
ERA	European Robotic Arm
ERLE	Echo Return Loss Enhancement
ESA	European Space Agency
ETSI	European Telecommunications Standards Institute
FDDI	Fibber Distributed Data Interface
FECC	Far End Camera Control
FEDEP	Federation Development and Execution Process

K. Drira, A. Martelli, T. Villemur (Eds.): Cooperative Environments, LNCS 2236, pp. 271-273, 2001.
© Springer-Verlag Berlin Heidelberg 2001

FedExec	Federation Executive process
FOM	Federation Object Model
GAT	Generic Application Template
GCC	Generic Conference Control
GUI	Graphical User Interface
G.711	common audio codec for H.32x series standards (except H.324
HLA	High Level Architecture
HTTPS	Secure HTTP
H.261	Video encoding format for the H.32x series video conferencing standards
H.245	mandatory part of H.323 standard
H.320	standard for multimedia conferences over ISDN
H.325	ITU security standard for multimedia conferencing
H.323	standard for conferencing over networks that does not guarantee QoS
IDL	Interface Definition Language
IEEE	Institute of Electrical and Electronics Engineers
IETF	Internet Engineering Task Force
IGMP	Internet Group Management Protocol
IIOP	Internet Inter-ORB Protocol
IIS	Internet Information Server
ILS	Internet Locator Server
IP	Internet Protocol
ISDN	Integrated Service Digital Network
ISS	International Space Station
ITU	International Telecommunications Union
ITU-T	International Telecommunications Union - Telecommunication standardisation sector
JPEG	Joint Photographic Experts Group
JVM	Java Virtual Machine
JSP	Java Server Pages
J2EE	Java2 Enterprise Edition
LAN	Local Area Network
LBNL	Lawrence Berkeley National Laboratory
LDAP	Lightweight Directory Access Protocol
LRC	Local RTI Component
MBONE	Multicast BackBone
MCS	Multipoint Conferencing Server
MCU	Multipoint Control Unit
MJPEG	Motion JPEG
MOF	Meta Object Facility
MOM	Management Object Model
MOM	Message Oriented Middleware
MPEG	Motion Picture Experts Group
MPEG-1	standard for motion video compression at CD-ROM bitrates
MVM	Mission and Vehicle Management
N/A	Not Applicable
NCR	Non Conformance Report
NCSA	National Center for Supercomputing Applications

NIMI	National Internet Measurement Infrastructure
NIST	National Institute of Standards and Technology
OLE	Object Linking and Embedding
OMG	Object Management Group
ORB	Object Request Broker
PDM	Product Data Management
PDR	Preliminary Design review
PDU	Protocol Data Unit
PKI	Public Keys Infrastructure
PIP	Picture-in-Picture windowing
POTS	Plain Old Telephone Services
PSTN	Public Switched Telephone Networks
QoS	Quality of Service
RAS	Registration/Admission/Status protocol
RID	RTI Initialisation Data
RID	Review Item Discrepancy
RSVP	Resource reSerVation Protocol
RTI	Run-Time Infrastructure
RtiExec	RTI Executive process
RTP	Real-time Transport Protocol
RVD	Rendez-Vous and Docking
S/C, SC	Spacecraft
SGML	Standard Generalized Markup Language
SOAP	Simple Object Access Protocol
SOM	Simulation Object Model
SSL	Secure Socket Layer
SST	Spacecraft Simulation Test
STEP	Standard for the Exchange of Product Model Data
SUT	System Under Test
TAO	The ACE ORB
TBC	To Be Confirmed
TF	Test Facilities
TTL	Time To Live
TWAIN	a scanner interface specification/standard
T.120	ITU-T standard for data conferencing
UML	Unified Modelling Language
URD	User Requirements Document
UUT	Unit Under Test
WAN	Wide Area Network
WF	Work Flow
WFMC	Work Flow Management Coalition
W3C	World Wide Web Consortium
XMI	XML Metadata Interchange format
XML	Extensible Markup Language

References

1. H. Abdel-Wahab and M. Feit. Xtv: A framework for sharing x window clients in remote synchronous collaboration. In IEEE TriComm '91: Communications for Distributed Applications and Systems, April 1991.

2. H. Abdel-Wahab, B. Kvande, S. Nanjangud, O. Kim and J. P. Favreau. Using Java for Multimedia Collaborative Applications. Proceedings of the 3rd International Workshop on Protocols for Multimedia Systems (PROMS'96), Madrid, Spain, October 1996.

3. H. Abdel-Wahab, B. Kvande, O. Kim and J. P. Favreau. An Internet Collaborative Environment for Sharing Java Applications. Proceedings of the 5th IEEE Computer Society Workshop on Future Trends of Distributed Computing Systems (FTDCS'97), Tunis, Tunisia, pp. 112-117, October 29-31, 1997.

4. K. Almeroth. Managing IP Multicast Traffic: A First Look at the Issues, Tools, and Challenges, February 1999. IP Multicast Initiative White Paper.

5. K. Almeroth. The evolution of multicast: from the mbone to inter-domain multicast to internet2 deployment. IEEE Network, Special Issue on Multicasting, January 2000.

6. An Architecture for Differentiated Services (RFC 2475), Request for Comments 2475, http://www.ietf.org/rfc/rfc2475.txt, December 1998.

7. Ballardie, R. Perlman, C. Lee and J. Crowcroft. Simple scalable internet multicast. Technical report, University College London (UCL), April 1999.

8. T. Bates, R. Chandra, D. Katz and Y. Rekhter. Multiprotocol Extensions for BGP-4, February 1998. RFC 2283.

9. L. Beca, G. Cheng, G. C. Fox, T. Jurga, K. Olszewski, M. Podgorny, P. Sokolowski, T. Stachowiak and K. Walczak. Tango – a Collaborative Environment for the World-Wide Web. Northeast Parallel Architectures Center, Syracuse University, New York, http://trurl.npac.syr.edu/tango/papers/tangowp.html, 1997.

10. S. Bhattacharyya and C. Diot. Deployment of PIM-SO at Sprint, March 2000. Work in Progress: draft-bhattach-diot-pimso-00.txt.

11. S. Bhattacharyya, D. Towsley and J. Kurose. The loss path multiplicity problem in multicast. In IEEE INFOCOM'99, March 1999.

12. Bommaiah, A. McAuley, R. Talpade and M. Liu. AMRoute: Adhoc multicast routing protocol, August 1998. Work in progress; draft-manet-amroute-00.txt.

13. D. Burdick. SAP Enhances PDM Product Vision with new capabilities, Document P-09-2469, 2 November 1999.

14. W. Burkett. Product Data Markup Language A New Paradigm for Product Data Exchange and Integration, http://www.pdit.com/pdml/

15. A. Chanbert, E. Grossman, L. Jackson and S. Pietrovicz. NCSA Habanero- Synchronous collaborative framework and environment, Software Development Division at the National Center for Supercomputing Applications, white paper, 1998.

16. A. Clerget. A tag-based UDP multicast flow control protocol. Technical Report 3728 3728, INRIA, July 1999.

17. CORBA, XML and XMI Resource Page, http://www.omg.org/technology/xml/index.htm

18. Décision Micro & Réseaux, January 2000.

19. D. Deckmyn. Product Data Management Moves Toward Mainstream. Computer World. http://www.computerworld.com/home/print.nsf/all/991108CAEE, November 1999.

20. Differentiated Services (diffserv) working group of the IETF, http://www.ietf.org/html.charters/diffserv-charter.html.

21. DOE200, EMSL DOE2000, Real-time Collaboration Management Project Summary, Argonne National Laboratory (ANL), Pacific Northwest National Laboratory (PNNL), National Center for Supercomputing Applications (NCSA), http://www.emsl.pnl.gov:2080/docs/collab/research/CMResearch.html, 20th February 1999.

22. H. P. Dommel and J. J. Garcia Luna Aceves. Group Coordination Support for synchronous Internet collaboration, University of California, Santa Cruz, IEEE Internet Computing, pp. 74-80, March-April 1999.

23. D. Estrin, D. Farinacci, A. Helmy, V. Jacobson and L. Wei. Protocol Independent Multicast Version 2, Dense Mode Specification, May 1997. Work in Progress: draft-ietf-idmr-pim-dm-spec-05.txt.

24. D. Farinacci, Y. Rekhter, D. Meyer, P. Lothberg, H. Kilmer and J. Hall. Multicast Source Discovery Protocol (MSDP), February 2000. Internet-draft: draft-ietf-msdp-spec-05.txt.

25. S. Floyd and V. Jacobson. Random early detection gateways for congestion avoidance. IEEE/ACM Transactions on Networking, 1(4):397-413, August 1993.

26. S. Floyd, V. Jacobson, S. McCanne, C. Liu and L. Zhang. A reliable multicast framework for lightweight sessions and application level framing. In IEEE SIGCOMM'95, 1995.

27. P. Francis. Yoid: extending the multicast internet architecture. Unrefered Report; http://www.aciri.org/yoid/, September 1999.

28. D. S. Frankel. XMI: The OMG's XML Metadata Interchange Standard, http://www.sys-con.com/xml/archives/0104/Frankel/index.html

29. M. Handley, B. Whetten, R. Kermode, S. Floyd, L. Vicisano and M. Luby. The Reliable Multicast Design Space for Bulk Data Transfer, March 2000. Work in Progress, draft-ietf-rmt-design-space-01.txt.

30. M. Henning and S. Vinoski. Advanced CORBA Programming with C++. Addison-Vesley Professional Computing Series, 1999.

31. High Level Architecture Federation Development and Execution Process (FEDEP) Model. Version 1.0. 6, September 1996.

32. High Level Architecture Interface Specification, Version 1.3, US Department of Defense, April 1998.

33. High Level Architecture Run-Time Infrastructure Programmer's Guide 1.3 Version 7, US Department of Defense, March 1999.

34. High Level Architecture Run-Time Infrastructure RTI 1.3-Next Generation Programmer's Guide, US Department of Defense, September 1999.

35. H. Holbrook and B. Cain. Source-Specific Multicast for IP, March 2000. Work in Progress draft-holbrook-ssm-00.txt.

36. H. Holbrook and D.R. Cheriton. Ip multicast channels: Express support for large-scale single-source applications. In ACM SIGCOMM'99, September 1999.

37. C. Huitema. The case for packet level FEC. In Protocols for High Speed Networks (PfHSN'96), October 1996.

38. K. Hunt, J. Dahmann, R. Lutz and J. Sheehan. Planning For the Evolution Of Automated Tools In HLA.

39. T. Jurga. Session Management in Web Collaborator Systems, Master thesis Northeast Parallel architectures Center (NPAC), Syracuse University, New York, http://tango.npac.syr.edu/tomj/mt/thesis/, 1997.

40. B. Kvande. Java Collaborator Toolset, Master's Project Report, Department of Computer Science, Old Dominion University, http://www.cs.odu.edu/~kvande/Projects/Collaborator, August 1996.

41. S-J. Lee, W. Su, J. Hsu, M. Gerla and R. Bagrodia. A performance comparison study of ad hoc wireless multicast protocols. In IEEE INFOCOM'00, March 2000.

42. X. Li and M. Ammar. Bandwidth control for replicated-stream multicast video distribution. In HPDC-5, August 1996.

43. C.R. Lin and K-M. Wang. Mobile multicast support in Ip networks. In IEEE INFOCOM'00, March 2000.

44. M. Liu, R. Talpade and A. McAuley. Amroute: Adhoc multicast routing protocol. Technical Report TR 99-1, CSHCN, 1999.

45. M. Luby, J. Gemmell, L. Vicisano, L. Rizzo, J. Crowcroft and B. Lueckenhoff. Asynchronous Layered Coding (ALC): a scalable reliable multicast protocol, March 2000. Work in Progress: draft-ietf-rmt-pi-alc-00.txt.

46. M. Luby, J. Gemmell, L. Vicisano, L. Rizzo, J. Crowcroft and B. Lueckenhoff. Reliable multicast transport building block: Forward Error Correction codes, March 2000. Work in Progress: draft-ietf-rmt-bb-fec-00.txt.

47. M. Luby, L. Vicisano and T. Speakman. Heterogeneous multicast congestion control based on router packet filtering, June 1999. Work in Progress, presented at RMRG meeting, Pisa.

48. D. De Lucia and K. Obraczka. Congestion Control Mechanism for Reliable Multicast, September 1997. presentation during Reliable Multicast (RM) meeting.

49. K. Mani Chandy, A. Rifkin, P. A. G. Sivilotti, J. Mandelson, M. Richardson, W. Tanaka and L. Weisman. A World-Wide Distributed System Using Java and the Internet. Proceedings of the Workshop on Multimedia and Collaborative Environments, High Performance Distributed Computing (HPDC-5), Syracuse, August 1996.

50. A. Martelli and D. Cortese. Distributed System Engineering - DSE Concurrent and Distributed Engineering Environment for Design, Simulations and Verifications in Space Project. Proceedings of the 6th International Workshop on Simulation for European Space Programmes, Noordwijk, The Netherlands, 10-12 October 2000.

51 A. Mauthe, D. Hutchinson, G. Coulson and S. Namuye. From requirements to services : Group communication support for distributed multimedia systems. In Second International Workshop, IWACA'94, 1994.

52. A.J. McAuley. Reliable broadband communications using a burst erasure correcting code. In ACM SIGCOMM'90, September 1990.

53. S. McCanne and V. Jacobson. vic: A Flexible Framework for Packet Video, ACM Multimedia '95.

54. S. McCanne, V. Jacobson and M. Vetterli. Receiver-driven layered multicast. In ACM SIGCOMM'96, October 1996.

55. Meta Object Facility V1.3 RTF. http://www.omg.org/technology/cwm/index.htm

56. T. Montgomery. A loss tolerant rate controller for reliable multicast. Technical Report IVV-97-011, NASA, August 1997.

57. J. Moy. Multicast Extensions to OSPF, March 1994. RFC 1584.

58. J. Myers, N. Chonacky, T. Dunning and E. Leber. Collaborators: Bringing National Laboratory into the undergraduate classroom and Laboratory via the Internet, Council on Undergraduate research Quarterly vol. 17, number 3, March 1997.

59. C. Neil. Manufacturing Enterprise Integration, http://www.mel.nist.gov/projs/msid/manen.html

60. J. Nonnenmacher, E. Biersack and D. Towsley. Parity-based loss recovery for reliable multicast transmissions. In ACM SIGCOMM'97, September 1997. also in IEEE Transactions on Networking, 1998.

61. OMG consortium. Common Object Request Broker Architecture, July 1995.

62. OMG consortium. The Common Object Request Broker: Architecture and Specification Revision 2.4 (Section 24), http://www.omg.org, October 2000.

63. OMG consortium. CORBA 3.0 - http://www.omg.org/technology/corba/corba3releaseinfo.htm

64. OMG consortium. OMG Common Object Services Specifications -
    http://www.omg.org/technology/documents/formal/corba_services_available_electro.htm

65. OMG Unified Modeling Language Specification. Version 1.3. First Edition: March 2000;
    http://www.rational.com/uml/index.jsp

66. T. Ott, J. Kemperman and M. Mathis. The stationary behaviour of ideal TCP congestion
    avoidance. in preprint. http://popeye.snu.ac.kr/schoi/TcpPerf.html.

67. S. Paul. Multicasting on the Internet and its Applications. Kluwer Academic Publishers,
    1998.

68. PDES, Inc. Document MG001.04.00 pg

69. PDM Enablers, http://www.omg.org/homepages/mfg/mfgppepdm.htm

70. PDM Forum 2000. PDM Implementor Forum, Usage Guide for Step PDM Schema,
    http://WWW.PDM-IF.ORG/pdm_schema/usageguide/pdmug_release4_1.pdf,   February
    2000.

71. I. Pyarali. Real-Time CORBA, Washington University, St. Louis
    http://www.cs.wustl.edu/~schmidt/TAO/rtcorba4.ps.gz, April 2000.

72. L. Rizzo and L. Vicisano. Effective erasure codes for reliable computer communication
    protocols. ACM Computer Communication Review, 27(2), April 1997.

73. E. Rosen. Personal Videoconferencing, Softbound, ISBN 013268327X, 1996.

74. L. Sahasrabuddhe and B. Mukherjee. Multicast routing algorithms and protocols: a
    tutorial. IEEE Network, pages 90-102, January 2000.

75. H. Sandick and B. Cain. PIM-SM rules for support of Single-Source Multicast, March
    2000. Work in Progress draft-sandick-pimsm-ssmrules-00.txt.

76. T. Sano, N. Yamanouchi, T. Shiroshita and O. Takahashi. Flow and congestion control for
    bulk reliable multicast. In IEEE INFOCOM'98, February 1998.

77. S. K. Singhal, B. Q. Nguyen, J. Nguyen, R. Redpath and M. Fraenkel. InVerse: Designing
    an Interactive Universe Architecture for Scalability and Extensibility. Proceedings of the
    Sixth IEEE International Symposium on High Performance distributed computing Portland
    State University, Portland Oregon, August 5-8, 1997.

78. Schulzrinne, Casner, Frederick and Jacobson. RTP: A Transport Protocol for Real-Time
    Applications, June 1999. Work in Progress, draft-ietf-avt-rtp-new-04.txt.

79. J. Stark. Introduction to EDM/PDM Systems, http://www.johnstark.com, 1998.

80. Step Centers - http://isc.aticorp.org/

81. D. Thaler, D. Estrin and D. Meyer. Border Gateway Multicast Protocol, January 2000.
    Internet-draft: draft-ietf-bgmp-spec-00.txt.

82. D. Thaler, M. Handley and D. Estrin. The Internet Multicast Address Allocation
    Architecture, January 2000. Work in Progress, draft-ietf-malloc-arch-04.txt.

83. A. Thyagarajan B. Cain and S. Deering. Internet Group Management Protocol, Version 3,
    November 1999. Work in Progress: draft-ietf-idmr-igmp-v3-02.txt.

84. L. A. Toupin. The changing face of PDM, Design News,
    http://www.manufacturing.net/magazine/dn/archives/2000/dn0207.00/03f2026.htm,
    February 7 2000.

85. T. Turletti, S.F. Parisis and J. Bolot. Experiments with a layered transmission scheme over
    the internet. In IEEE INFOCOM'98, February 1998.

86. L. Vicisano, L. Rizzo and J. Crowcroft. TCP-like congestion control for layered multicast
    data transfer. In IEEE INFOCOM'98, February 1998.

87. S. Vinoski. CORBA: Integrating Diverse Applications Within Distributed Heterogeneous
    Environments, IEEE Communications Magazine, February 1997.

88. D. Waitzman, C. Partridge and S. Deering. Distance Vector Multicast Routing Protocol,
    November 1988. RFC 1075.

89. B. Wang and J. Hou. Multicast routing and its QoS extension: problems, algorithms, and protocols. IEEE Network, pages 22-36, January 2000.

90. H. Wang and M. Schwartz. Achieving bounded fairness for multicast and TCP traffic in the Internet. In ACM SIGCOMM'98, September 1998.

91. L. Wei, D. Estrin, D. Farinacci, A. Helmy, D. Thaler, S. Deering, M. Handley, V. Jacobson, C. Liu and P. Sharma. Protocol Independent Multicast-Sparse Mode (PIM-SM): Protocol Specification, November 1999. Work in Progress, draft-ietf-pim-v2-sm-01.txt.

92. West and Matte. Integration of Industrial Data for Exchanging Access and Sharing: Architecture Overview and Description,
http://www.mel.nist.gov/sc4/wg_qc/wg10/current/n254/wg10n254.htm, 1999.

93. B. Whetten, L. Vicisano, R. Kermode, M. Handley, S. Floyd and M.Luby. Work in Progress, draft-ietf-rmt-buildingblocks-02.txt, May 2001.

Author Index

Lecture Notes in Computer Science

For information about Vols. 1–2179
please contact your bookseller or Springer-Verlag